Pursuing Equality

Social and Economic Papers No. 20
Institute of Social and Economic Research
Memorial University of Newfoundland

Pursuing Equality

Historical Perspectives on Women in Newfoundland and Labrador

Linda Kealey, Editor

ISER

**Institute of Social and
Economic Research**

Published by the
Institute of Social and Economic Research
Memorial University of Newfoundland
St. John's, Newfoundland, Canada
ISBN 0-919666-77-9

Over 50% recycled paper
including 10% post
consumer fibre
Plus de 50 p. 100 de
papier recyclé dont 10 p.
100 de fibres post-
consommation.

M - Official mark of Environment Canada
M - Marque officielle d'Environnement Canada.

Canadian Cataloguing in Publication Data

Main entry under title:

Pursuing equality

(Social and economic papers ; no. 20)

Includes bibliographical references and index.
ISBN 0-919666-77-9

1. Women -- Newfoundland -- History. 2. Feminism --
Newfoundland -- History. I. Kealey, Linda, 1947-
II. Memorial University of Newfoundland. Institute of Social and
Economic Research. III. Series.

HQ1459.N5P87 1993   305.42'09718   C93-098556-7

Contents

Acknowledgements

This book was the brainchild of a group of women concerned with the lack of readily accessible material on the history of women in Newfoundland and Labrador. Membership in the Women and History Group has varied since the group began in 1987 as an ad-hoc gathering of interested individuals. Members have included the authors of the essays as well as Roberta Buchanan, Anne Hart, Linda Kealey, Lee-Ann Montgomery, Bernice Morgan, Martha Muzychka, and Pat O'Brien. The group has benefitted from the advice and contributions of Margot Duley, Carmelita McGrath and Susan Hart, as well as the support of Ann Bell and Wendy Williams of the Provincial Advisory Council on the Status of Women. In the early stages of this project the PACSW provided substantial support for meetings, grant applications and xeroxing.

Financial assistance for the research, writing and editing has come from many sources: Canada Employment and Immigration; the Federal Department of the Secretary of State and the Dean of Arts at Memorial University of Newfoundland.

In particular, the Women and History Group wishes to acknowledge the financial assistance of the Law Foundation of Newfoundland. The Law Foundation, established in February, 1980, provides grants to advance public understanding of the law and access to legal services.

As editor, special thanks go to Joan Butler at Memorial University for her efficient keyboarding of the manuscript and her patience with the many editorial changes. Anne Hart, Sharon Pope and Linda Cullum generously assisted in the final stages of preparing the manuscript for publication. Thanks are also due to the staff of the Centre for Newfoundland Studies and its archives, the Provincial Archives of Newfoundland and Labrador and Photographic Services at Memorial University. To all those groups and individuals who aided us in our search for information, photographs and financial assistance, we gratefully acknowledge your support. Finally, the authors and the editor wish to thank the staff of ISER Books at the Institute of Social and Economic Research at Memorial for the production of this volume.

Linda Kealey, Editor

Acronyms/Abbreviations

BDWSU	British Dominions Woman Suffrage Union
CARAL	Canadian Abortion Rights Action League (formerly Canadian Association for the Repeal of the Abortion Law)
CEIC	Canadian Employment and Immigration Commission
CFUW	Canadian Federation of University Women
CR	Consciousness-raising
LCW	Legal Council of Women
LEAF	Legal Education Action Fund
MACOWIE	Ministerial Advisory Committee on Women's Issues in Education
MHA	Member of the House of Assembly
MUN	Memorial University of Newfoundland
NAC	National Action Committee on the Status of Women
NAPE	Newfoundland Association of Public Employees
NCO	Non-commissioned Officer
NDP	New Democratic Party
NFFAWU	Newfoundland Fishermen, Food and Allied Workers' Union
NONIA	Newfoundland Outport Nursing and Industrial Association

NSWC	Newfoundland Status of Women Council
NTA	Newfoundland Teachers' Association
PACSW	Provincial Advisory Council on the Status of Women
RC	Roman Catholic
UIC	Unemployment Insurance Commission
VAD	Voluntary Aid Detachment
WCTU	Woman's Christian Temperance Union
WHEP	Women's Health and Education Project
WI	Women's Institute
WIN	Women's Involvement Committee
WISE	Women Interested in Successful Employment
WPA	Women's Patriotic Association
YWCA	Young Women's Christian Association

Introduction 1

Linda Kealey

Reading the history of Newfoundland and Labrador, one is struck by the "silences" on women's experiences. This volume "breaks the silence," so to speak, by highlighting the political and legal history of women in the province in the nineteenth and twentieth centuries as a starting point for understanding how women's lives have been shaped by the social structures of the past. While women had little input or influence over these political and legal structures, this is not to say that they did not feel the constraints, nor does such a statement deny that women challenged the limits placed on them by institutions such as the law or the political system. Indeed, the essays in this volume amply document women's active engagement in campaigns which sought to provide a voice for their gender in public life. In addition, the material gathered here underlines the close relationship between their public and private experiences. While early work on women's history distinguished between women's private or domestic world and the male public domain of business and politics, this distinction has often hidden the important relationship between the private and the public in women's lives, as well as men's.

The essays in this collection draw on both private research and reflection and public collaboration. The idea for such a book was born in 1987 when an ad-hoc group of women writers, researchers and academics began to meet to discuss a project which encompassed several potential volumes on women's history in the province. With the assistance of summer employment grants and through contact with historian Margot Duley, the group was able to put together the present volume of essays on the suffrage movement, the legal history of women and the recent women's movement. Although the essays use academic footnoting style, the volume is intended for the general reader as well as the academic interested in women's history. By providing the sources for the research and short documents from the period studied, this volume will enable others to pursue further research in the area.

Both general readers and academics will find it useful to place this volume in the context of previous writing on women and on the province. What follows is a discussion of women's history in general, women's history in the Canadian setting and comments on how women have been written about in the regional context, not only historically but also in the social sciences more broadly defined. Suggestions for further research are contained in the concluding section.

I. HISTORY AND GENDER

Women's history begins with the assumption that previous written history has insufficiently explained the experiences of women. One has only to consult standard texts to find that most writers presume that their accounts include explanations which cover both sexes, that their selection of events and their explanations of the reasons for historical change apply universally. With the development of interest in social history, particularly in the 1960s and '70s, and with the simultaneous revival of interest in social movements, such as the women's movement, questions were asked about the adequacy of a history that ignored the experiences of many groups in society: women, ethnic groups, workers and others. From this beginning we have seen the tremendous growth of interest among historians in documenting the lives of people who were not counted among the elite: those who were not the political and economic movers and shakers written about in more traditional historical accounts. Historians became interested in exploring the lives of the less well-known in order to better understand the dynamics of the family, social mobility, the formation of social classes, ethnic conflict and many other questions. These interests also opened up the potential for historical research in Canada which questioned the dominance of a central-Canadian focus and stimulated the development of regional perspectives.

While historians began by filling in the gaps in our knowledge about women, those of us engaged in the difficult task of uncovering women's history (often from sources that, at least initially, did not appear to yield much information, since they were collected for other purposes) found ourselves not satisfied with the fill-in-the-gaps approach. Such an approach seemed to result in a valuable, but limited, cache of information that isolated women's experiences in a category unrelated to the rest of society—a confirmation of the old idea that women lived in a "separate sphere" that revolved around family and domestic life, or at least that women's experiences remained, in Simone de Beauvoir's words, "other." Rather than viewing women as "other," or as victim, historians of women began to ask questions about the historical construction of gender divisions in the workplace, in the home, in the professions, in education and in politics. How could we explain the pattern of women's work and the seeming constancy of job segregation and low pay, the roles of women in the family, the reluctance to accept women into higher education and the professions, and the rarity of women in positions of political authority? What was needed, many concluded, was a systematic examination of gender as a category of historical analysis. By "gender" I mean the social and cultural definition of what it means to be a woman (or a man) in a given society. While there are similarities among western societies historically in the outlines of gender roles and expectations, there are also variations within those societies and over time. For example, historians have suggested that the evidence from medieval Europe seems to indicate that women in Northwestern Europe learned the skills of horsemanship, took up arms and were often responsible for running vast estates. These roles were gradually lost in the late medieval and renaissance period as women were defined more closely with domestic and family affairs and were more subject to patriarchal authority. Other examples could be cited, but the point is that gender roles for women have not always been the same and are subject to change and thus analysis. Women's history, then, is not just about filling in the gaps in our knowledge; it is also a way of seeing, which involves a sensitivity to how gender is constructed both for women and for men.

II. BEYOND CENTRAL CANADA

Closer to home, when we examine Canadian women's history, what do we find? Initially, much of what was written focused on the middle-class women who left behind evidence of their lives and

activities. As with most recent women's history, one of the first areas
to receive attention in Canada was the late nineteenth century social
reform movement and the campaign for the vote.[1] Women's work in
the past also received some attention, thus opening the way for
research on working-class women in addition to the mainly middle-
and upper-middle-class women who belonged to the suffrage, temperance and other reform organizations of the period. Much of this
was a necessary filling-in-the-gaps process which led to a recognition that women's history varied according to social class, ethnicity
and region. Despite this recognition of regional difference, Atlantic
Canada in general, and Newfoundland in particular, remain largely
absent from recent, more ambitious accounts of women's history in
Canada. As Gail Campbell points out in a recent review essay,
attempts to move beyond a central Canadian focus "have generally
been hampered by a continuing lack of published secondary sources
upon which to draw."[2] Campbell cites several major studies, including Ruth Pierson's *"They're Still Women After All": The Second World
War and Canadian Womanhood* (1986), Veronica Strong-Boag's *The
New Day Recalled: Lives of Girls and Women in English Canada,
1919–1939* (1988) and *Canadian Women: A History* (1988), written
by a team of six women, as examples of the problem of lack of
information on Atlantic Canadian women.[3] Of Pierson and Strong-
Boag, Campbell notes:

> Both these monographs focus on the general, rather than the
> unique or different. Thus, while Pierson notes that women war
> workers from the east and west were encouraged to relocate in
> central Canada, she does not consider the implications for the
> hinterland regions. Nor does she consider differential rates of
> participation in various wartime activities across regional, class,
> religious or ethnic groups. Strong-Boag, in contrast, does draw
> important distinctions between the experiences of rural and urban,
> rich and poor, immigrant and native-born women. The implications
> of differences within and among regions are not overlooked in her
> book, but discussion of such differences is peripheral to the main
> theme.[4]

Campbell is more positive overall about *Canadian Women: A
History* which she praises for succeeding in achieving a regional
balance despite the limitations in the published literature. However,
even here she is critical of the final section of the book dealing with
the period since 1960 for its omissions of material on some aspects
of Atlantic Canadian women's experiences. One might add, as well,
that their account of Newfoundland suffrage fails to recognize that
women won the vote in 1925. How do we explain this? Quite simply,

Campbell is right—the lack of published material which documents women's history in Newfoundland and Labrador means that the rest of Canada knows little about the topic.

III. NEWFOUNDLAND AND LABRADOR

It is striking that much of the published material on women in the province has come from two sources: folklore and anthropology/ sociology. Most of this work focuses on women's work and family life. Hilda Chaulk Murray's *More than Fifty Percent* (1979) and Dona Lee Davis' *Blood and Nerves* (1983), have become standard texts. Murray's book describes women's work in an outport community in the half century before 1950. As such, it provides a detailed account of women's work in Elliston, Trinity Bay, describing the types of work according to the seasons and the stages of women's life cycles. Davis also studies one community, "Grey Rock Harbour," in order to explore women's roles, changing family structures and women's issues such as menopause. She argues that outport women have managed to combine the best of traditional and modern lifestyles and disputes previous work that emphasized the negative aspects of twentieth century changes in family structures.[5] Wider in scope, sociologist Marilyn Porter's work has addressed a variety of prob-lems related to outport women: the sexual division of labour, household economic strategies, labour force participation, the changing values among women compared to men, and lifestyle changes for women within the same families. In studying several communities, Porter has come to realize the immense variety in what constitutes women's work. She emphasized, however, that a com-mon expectation existed for outport women—"that they would contribute economically in whatever way was available."[6]

Most of the published work on women centres around outport women and much of it focuses on women's contributions to the fishery in particular. One of the more recent collections by Dona Lee Davis and Jane Nadel-Klein continues this theme but attempts to make comparative statements by bringing together a number of articles on women in different types of fishing economies.[7]

In addition to the material on women's work and family life just described, students of Newfoundland women can turn to a number of autobiographical accounts, most of them by Labrador women. The best known, an account by Elizabeth Goudie, recalls her childhood memories, her experiences as a trapper's wife and later, the family's changed life at Happy Valley, site of the United States Air Force base where her husband found employment. Spanning the entire twentieth century, her life is a study of cultural and socio-economic change in Labrador.[8]

Nursing and midwifery have also provided the raw material for several autobiographical accounts and studies. Margaret Giovannini's brief reminiscence in *Outport Nurse* recalls her experiences between 1939–41 in several outport communities where she was often doctor, dentist, nurse and midwife rolled into one.[9] Even after marriage in 1942 and a move to the fluorspar mining community of St. Lawrence, Giovannini was frequently called upon for medical assistance before the hospital was built. The relative scarcity of medical assistance in outport Newfoundland is a recurring theme in this province's history.

Midwifery has also been the subject of two recent studies by folklorist Janet McNaughton and sociologist Cecilia Benoit.[10] While McNaughton explores the role of the traditional community midwife and suggests that midwifery provided a valuable role for women in rural communities in this century, Benoit emphasizes the limits of this role for the homebirth attendant who had "little control over the remunerative value of her work."[11] None of Benoit's informants favoured a return to homebirths, and her own analysis suggests that midwives working in cottage hospitals were better able to establish themselves as autonomous specialists with a secure income than were the traditional grannies, or midwives working in larger clinics or hospitals. Benoit's viewpoint differs from most feminist writers who have highlighted the traditional midwife's independent and valued position which was undermined by the medical profession.

While some aspects of women's experiences have received attention in the published literature, others have not. Politics is a good example of an area which lacks research on women. An exception in the social science literature is Marilyn Porter's paper, "'The Tangly Bunch,'" which suggests that outport women have constructed "their politics within their culture while men have separated the two and elevated politics over culture."[12] Based on research among women from the Southern Avalon peninsula and their voluntary organizations and communication networks, Porter's assertion that these women have turned away from "traditional" politics has been received with some degree of controversy. As one recent critic notes, there is a need for more research on women's political activities and opinions and perhaps a reassessment of what constitutes politics before conclusions can be drawn. Recent historical literature on women's political activism, however, also argues for a much broader definition of politics, noting the importance of women's grass roots political activism.

When we turn to examine Newfoundland history, per se, the shelves are relatively much barer. Standard accounts of our history have little to say about women, or perhaps at best, mention that they played a role in the fishery or note the passage of women's suffrage in 1925.[13] Fortunately, this is beginning to change, but very slowly. The noticeable interest in women's roles in health care so prominent in folklore and anthropology/sociology has until recently been lacking in history, with some exceptions, particularly Joyce Nevitt's popular history *White Caps and Black Bands: Nursing in Newfoundland to 1934* (1978). Nevitt's early work will be considerably strengthened by Linda White's (1992) study of "The General Hospital School of Nursing, 1903–30."[14] The other important profession for women in the late nineteenth and twentieth centuries is, of course, teaching. While historical studies of women's roles as teachers have mushroomed elsewhere in Canada in this period, as in the recently published *Women Who Taught: Perspectives on the History of Women and Teaching* (1991), edited by Alison Prentice and Marjorie Theobald, there is a puzzling lack of attention to the feminization of teaching in this province.[15] With the exception of several histories of Catholic orders of nuns (Sister M. J. Dinn on the Presentation Sisters and, more recently, Sister Hogan's work on the Mercy Convent), little else is available to us.[16] One exception is an article recently published by educational historian Phillip McCann, entitled "Class, Gender and Religion in Newfoundland Education, 1836–1901," which contains some preliminary information and comparisons with historical findings on women teachers elsewhere in Canada at the time. Not surprisingly, McCann found the same arguments for employing more women as teachers, such as that women were better adapted to teaching children and that women could be paid less than men.[17]

Aside from professional work, women's work more generally has not been well-researched. An exception to this appears in Nancy Forestell's 1987 Master's thesis and a recently published article drawn from the thesis.[18] Forestell examined women's work in St. John's between World War I and II, using the 1921 and 1935 manuscript census, an option unavailable to historians in other jurisdictions where the federal manuscript census remains closed to researchers after 1901. Most women in the labour force came from working-class backgrounds and found employment as domestic servants, factory operatives, tailoresses or sales clerks. The majority were young (under twenty-five) and single and their paid labour was usually relinquished upon marriage, although Forestell did find that hard economic times in the 1930s resulted in a shift in age, with more older women in the labour force. While Forestell's study focused on St. John's, her thesis contains an interesting chapter on young women who moved from "around the bay" into the city, drawn to jobs as domestics in St. John's. Much research remains to be done on women's work, particularly in the rest of the province, outside St. John's.

Recent work in Newfoundland history, including the essays in this volume, has demonstrated the wealth of information available to historians about women and the social construction of gender roles. If we return to the example of women's suffrage, considerable research has been done, although it has been, until now, relatively inaccessible. Margot Duley's essay in this volume begins the task of remedying the gaps in our knowledge of Newfoundland's suffrage movement. Perhaps the most striking feature of her research is the discovery of the vast international network that Newfoundland women suffragists participated in, in the early part of this century, a network that materially assisted the fledgling Newfoundland movement. Duley has identified an inner core of older, mostly married women, wives of prominent businessmen and professionals, with ties to the International Alliance of Women, a broad umbrella group of women's organizations based in London and founded in 1904. She also notes the cross-denominational ties of the Newfoundland movement, noting the involvement of Catholic women as well as Protestants, and has found evidence of the involvement of outport women in gathering petitions supporting the franchise for women. In short, Duley's work provides the first comprehensive account of women's suffrage in the province and is a very necessary addition to our understanding of women's history.

Duley's research, however, opens up more than just the women's suffrage movement. It also reminds us that we know little about women's political activities and legal status in the broader sense. Linda Cullum and Maeve Baird's essay in this volume provides the first account of women's legal history in the province. Statutes, case records, government documents and newspapers provide a wealth of rich detail on women's history, as this essay demonstrates. Concentrating on the period from the late nineteenth century through to the recent past, the authors examine laws affecting women using a life cycle approach from childhood to widowhood and old age. While noting the restrictions on citizenship for women barring them not only from the franchise but also from juries, from the legal profession and from other professions such as medicine, some of the most interesting research examines cases of young women accused of crimes particular to women, such as infanticide or concealment of birth, a less serious charge. Discussion of trials for sexual assault remind us that women then, as now, had to contend with judicial assumptions that victims were responsible for the crimes committed against them. In addition, the authors have documented women's property rights, restricted access to separation or divorce and the legal ramifications of marriage for women, among other issues.

Court records have also been an important source for Sean Cadigan's doctoral research on the Northeast Coast fishery in the nineteenth century.[19] Cadigan's research pays attention to the gender division of labour in household production and its role in the development of the Northeast Coast fishery. Acknowledging the importance of the migration of women to late eighteenth and early nineteenth century Newfoundland, his study also examines the evidence for the establishment of patriarchal family structures based on West Country English society. Disputes over property and inheritance reveal the legal and social presumption that property belonged to male heirs, whether sons or sons-in-law, the latter assuming ownership of their wives' inherited property, in an era which presumed that men usually governed the process of intergenerational household formation. While the courts usually specified that mothers or mothers-in-law be provided for out of estates, it was also usually the case that a widow inherited property for use only during her lifetime; property was not to be alienated from the family line of a deceased husband. Occasionally, women asserted their inheritance rights to the fishing equipment of deceased husbands. Although women's work in "making" the fish was essential, Cadigan notes that women's work patterns in the fishery were dictated by the rhythms of men's work in the catching of fish and that women were not recognized as formal partners in their households' dealings with merchants. Despite lack of official recognition, women did appear in court to defend their households' interests, and occasionally resorted to profanity, blows and weapons in doing so. In addition to their roles within the fishery, Cadigan also explores women's particular roles in caring for livestock and gardens through court cases in which disputes over straying animals or theft of topsoil were the issues, thus underlining the meagre resources at stake. Thus, Cadigan suggests that women's labour in household subsistence production was tied almost completely to the production of the staple, fish, leaving them little opportunity to engage in the production of other subsistence goods which elsewhere in Canada contributed to the development of a capitalist market.[20]

In addition to Cadigan's work on the Northeast Coast, Peter Pope's recent doctoral study provides some much needed commentary on early women settlers in the seventeenth century.[21] Based on colonial office records, contemporary commentaries, censuses, petitions and archaeological evidence, Pope suggests that, while men certainly outnumbered women on the Southern Avalon peninsula, previous writers have underestimated the female population by relying too heavily on seventeenth century censuses which did not report the names of wives, children and servants. Only women heads of households, that is widows, were named in the censuses of 1675 and 1677. Planters' wives and daughters were significant participants in the fishery as well as central figures within their households, baking, brewing, dairying and caring for poultry and pigs. According to Pope, several widows ran substantial plantations employing a larger number of servants than the average plantation. In a patriarchal society, it was not uncommon for wives or widows to assume male roles in attending to family interests, when their husbands were absent or deceased. Furthermore, as Pope notes, some widows did not remarry and thus retained control of their family's holdings, giving them a higher social status than would have been possible as an economically dependent wife in a new household. While Pope has provided valuable information on women in the planter category, the evidence is much scarcer in the records for women servants whose lives must have been more precarious.

These examples of recent work have opened up new areas of research and debate within Newfoundland history, particularly with regard to the political and legal history of women, but also in terms of understanding women's work, both in household production and in wage labour. Beyond this recent work, we are also able to examine the evidence of contemporary political activism among the province's women. Sharon Gray Pope's and Jane Burnham's essay in this volume provides a survey of the recent history of the women's movement which concentrates on the "second wave" of feminism in the last two decades. Noting some of the important organizations that pre-dated the second wave, including the Jubilee Guilds, Women's Institutes, Newfoundland Outport Nursing and Industrial Association (NONIA), the Canadian Federation of University Women and the short-lived Local Council of Women, the authors suggest that later women's groups differed in many respects from these earlier groups.

Inspired by the development of women's groups across Canada which espoused that "the personal is political," often through consciousness-raising groups, women in St. John's and later elsewhere in the province began to form new women's organizations. Unlike the earlier women's groups, these new organizations more directly concerned themselves with social and political action which challenged women's roles in contemporary society. Initially galvanized by women's conferences, visiting speakers and the Royal Commission on the Status of Women, women in the province gradually began to build a women's movement in the early 1970s which eventually created alliances with more traditional women's groups. As this essay indicates, divisions between women's groups, especially between St. John's and groups located elsewhere in the province, have been significant, yet there is also ample evidence of concerted cooperation, particularly in the last decade, on issues of mutual concern. In the course of two decades of feminist activism, women in the contemporary movement have begun to recognize and deal with differences and to work together despite these differences.

IV. FUTURE RESEARCH

This volume has begun the process of breaking the silence in Newfoundland women's history. There remain, however, many unanswered research questions which need our attention. By way of conclusion, this section will outline some of the important areas for further research.

In terms of a gender-sensitive political and legal history of the province, we need to examine several key areas of women's experiences. First, our increased knowledge of the women's suffrage movement and the recent women's movement suggests that other women's organizations deserve more intensive research. Groups such as the Woman's Christian Temperance Union (WCTU), NONIA and the Jubilee Guilds (which later merged into the Women's Institutes) involved women in locally-based organizations which responded to social and economic problems in the province. While the aims of the WCTU in North America have been extensively researched, such is not the case here. In the rest of North America, this women's organization came to play a political role in agitating for temperance through legislation aimed at restricting or eliminating the consumption of alcohol; these concerns led WCTU activists to support the vote for women as a means of accomplishing their aims. While the Newfoundland organization also supported women's suffrage, little more is known about the women who belonged, their motivations, their class background or their methods of work. Similarly, little information is available on the specifics of the Jubilee Guilds and NONIA, both of which responded to economic crises in the outports in the twentieth century. Fortunately, in terms of the former organization, a study by Agnes Richard has been published; in addition, researcher Linda Cullum is currently working on a study of the guild which examines the interaction between class divisions and gender roles. Such a study should provide some answers to questions related to motivation, class background, and organizational strategies. As a result, it should be possible also to arrive at some conclusions regarding women's activism and to integrate that into the general history of the province.[22]

Organized politics and women's participation in political parties and elections have yet to be studied, apart from some recognition of the attempts of Julia Salter Earle and suffragists Fannie McNeil and May Kennedy to run for office in 1925 and the controversial election of Helena Squires in 1930. While few women were successful in attaining public office in this century, we have no systematic study of past elections and the women who ran for office in the province. In addition, major political campaigns, such as the confederation debates of the late 1940s, have not been analyzed from the perspective of women who were allegedly attracted to a pro-confederate stand by the promise of the "baby bonus" and other Canadian social benefits. The entire experience of women during World War II remains a subject for historical research.

While Cullum and Baird's essay has begun the task of outlining women's relationship to the law and legal structures, clearly much more might be done in this area. Court records themselves are extremely useful for tracing patterns of prosecution in both criminal and civil cases; these cases tell us about the points of tension in a society related to gender. In cases of sexual assault, for example, the records reveal expectations relating to gender roles and the consequences of straying from them. Court cases also tell us about the distribution of property and other economic resources, thus opening up investigation into the world of women's work and family lives in the past. In general, legal records can assist in answering a variety of questions related to women's lives.

Finally, these essays have mentioned the names of many women about whom we know very little. Tracing the lives of these women is part of the project of restoring women to history and of claiming a history for women. Not only do we need to know more about the "movers and shakers," the activist women who have tried to change women's position in Newfoundland and Labrador, but we also need to know much more about the daily lives of women in the outports, in mill and mining towns and in St. John's. Incorporating women's experience would not just fill in the gaps, but would lead to a reassessment of the contours of our history. Indeed, such research could fundamentally reshape the history of Atlantic Canada. Perhaps future assessments of women's history in the Atlantic region would then strike a more positive note, with increased awareness of this rich history that includes the experiences of both women and men.

"The Radius of Her Influence for Good"   **2**

The Rise and Triumph of the Women's Suffrage Movement in Newfoundland, 1909–1925

Margot Iris Duley

The history of the women's suffrage movement in Newfoundland is a long and rich one. The suffrage victory in 1925 was the culmination of decades of growing political self-consciousness on the part of Newfoundland women. The 1920s women's suffrage campaign had been preceded by fiery debates in the 1890s, public and private discussions prior to World War I, and a growing conviction among many women during the Great War that in the peace to follow, women's voices must be heard. The Newfoundland Women's Franchise League, which led and orchestrated the final victory, had to overcome considerable resistance and public mockery, forging an alliance that crossed, albeit temporarily, barriers of class, religion and geography.

Yet, despite its long and dynamic history, the women's suffrage movement in Newfoundland has received short shrift in published, traditional histories of the province, once a Dominion. Two examples will suffice. S.J.R. Noel's *Politics in Newfoundland* devotes one clause of one sentence to the subject, with a further suggestion that the issue, though important, was "largely irrelevant" to the central problems facing the country at the time. A decade later, Frederick W. Rowe provides coverage in another sentence fragment.[1] In both instances the issue is depicted as an achievement of Prime Minister

Walter Monroe without reference to the struggles of women themselves and the cultural context. Like the goddess Athene springing
fully formed from the head of Zeus in Roman mythology, the Newfoundland women's suffrage movement is appropriated from its
feminist mothers and sired instead by a powerful male leader.

Why this treatment of the women's suffrage movement? In part,
the neglect of women's history in Newfoundland, as elsewhere, is a
product of generations of historiography which regarded political,
military and economic events and not culture as the real substance
of history. It should be noted, however, that the suffrage movement
was as much a political as it was a cultural phenomenon, so the
omission is curious even in traditional historical terms. Since the
1960s, cultural historians have made considerable headway in
arguing that gender, class, race, ethnicity and the lives of common
people must be considered for a holistic view of the past. Though
Newfoundland historiography has gained enormously in the past
two decades from treatments of topics such as emigration, immigration, industrial and fisheries unionization, and outport life (all of
which present a richer sense of the Newfoundland past) the use of
gender as a category of analysis has only just begun. Several short,
unpublished, though admirable, undergraduate papers have been
written on the women's suffrage movement, but to date no professional historian has undertaken a sustained examination of the first
wave of feminism in Newfoundland.[2]

This article utilizes sources hitherto used, though in greater
depth, including newspapers, records of the Women's Patriotic
Association, legislative records, and correspondence of Prime Minister Squires. However, I also found many new sources in
Newfoundland archives as well as in England and the United States,
for, as I discovered, the Newfoundland movement had international
connections both personal and organizational. Interviews with
younger friends and descendents of the suffrage generation have
also been invaluable. With enough historical detective work, the
sources can be and have been and continue to be unearthed. That
being the case, it is tempting to believe that the neglect of the early
women's movement reflects something more than documentary
difficulties.

In analyzing this lag, the legend of Athene is suggestive in yet
another respect: Zeus is said to have taken Athene from his pregnant
wife, Metis, and given birth to his daughter himself because he
feared her potential power. The women's suffrage movement raises
issues about male and female roles and the distribution of power
and rewards in society in both the public and domestic spheres that

are still disquieting. Arguments about the right of women to vote were about far more than the diffused power of the female citizen to impact upon public policy by marching to the ballot box. At issue were complex and deeply rooted notions of appropriate male and female roles, proper spheres of influence, the value of women's work to society, and female and male equality. Though the suffrage movement was led by upper-middle-class women in St. John's, they articulated aspirations, goals and grievances that other women supported at least in part in substantial numbers. The issues raised have contemporary analogues. Because this is so, it seems especially important that the modern Newfoundland women's movement be seen in historical context, and have its past restored.

The first campaign for women's suffrage occurred in the early 1890s led by the Woman's Christian Temperance Union (WCTU). The WCTU leaders and supporters were drawn from Methodist, Presbyterian and Congregational women's groups. The demand for the vote was restricted to "local option" or local prohibition, and the ideological justification was modestly framed in terms of protecting the home from poverty and domestic violence. However, in raising the issue of women voting in any form, the WCTU called forth a chorus of condemnation. The *Evening Telegram* accused the suffragists of "voluntarily unsex[ing] themselves," and Liberal Prime Minister William Whiteway invoked Pauline biblical verses that "woman shall be subject to the man" to justify his opposition. He painted a frightening picture of family disintegration if the franchise were conferred. If husband and wife entertained different political views, the peace and happiness of the home would be destroyed. The true role of woman was to be a "ministering angel" to her family. Politics was the realm of man. Female suffrage, in the words of T.J. Murphy (Liberal, St. John's East), was the equivalent of "unsexing woman."[3] The measure was debated twice in the legislature, defeated by votes of thirteen to ten in 1892, and seventeen to fourteen in 1893. In the face of disheartening and vitriolic opposition, the suffrage pioneers of the WCTU subsided into conventional channels of good works, such as a poor house and penitentiary mission and a coffee house for working men, run as an alternative to the tavern.

Even in the quiescent decade and a half which followed the WCTU's suffrage defeat, the issue of votes for women never entirely disappeared from public and private discourse. Newspapers reported periodically on the advance or defeat of the issue in the United States and throughout the British Empire, and impending votes in the British House of Commons sometimes stimulated male debating and fraternal societies in St. John's to tackle the question. These societies were important parts of the structure of political power, providing both a power base and proving ground for emerging politicians. The Methodist College Literary Institute, the Church of England Institute, and the Benevolent Irish Society all held debates. Generally a fear that "we lose the mother in the female politician" prevailed, and the notion of separate spheres remained strong.[4] What was missing were the voices of women themselves.

Yet, even in this era there was a circle of St. John's women, all of them close friends, who questioned the status quo. Many were well travelled, all were well read, though they generally lacked the formal education of their brothers. A few were foreign born, married to Newfoundlanders. Armine Gosling was the intellectual and organizational linchpin of this group which included Anna Mitchell, a WCTU activist; Lady Julia Horwood, wife of the Chief Justice; Adelaide Browning, whose husband owned Browning and Company, a major bakery; and Mary Miller, sister of Donald Morison who had sponsored the WCTU suffrage bill in the legislature. Most were prominent, married women whose lives were already filled with church and civic projects. Religiously, they were more diverse than the WCTU for several were Anglicans, and as their programme took definite shape they drew prominent Catholic women into the group. Initially, they discussed suffrage among themselves.

It was at first hard for this circle to see their way ahead politically. The WCTU suffrage ideology had proven denominationally divisive for prohibition was unpopular in Irish Catholic districts. In addition, some members of their own set were moderate drinkers and disagreed with prohibition and the WCTU evangelical outlook. Yet the content of a new appeal was by no means obvious. Should women claim their voting rights as mothers to preserve their homes and extend their nurturing abilities to society, as social or maternal feminists elsewhere argued; or, was that too limiting? Alternatively, should they claim the vote forthrightly as equal human beings possessed of equal rights with men, as did some of the more radical suffragists abroad; or, was that too frightening and alienating? How could they frame a message tailored to Newfoundland circumstances?

In 1909 their private discussions entered a more public forum. The Newfoundland press was filled with unsympathetic accounts of the militant "suffragettes" who had burst upon the British scene. Frustrated by many decades of political betrayal and the ineffectiveness of the moderate suffragists' petitioning and lobbying, the suffragettes led by Mrs. Emmeline Pankhurst had launched a campaign of civil disobedience which eventually escalated into destruction of property. Newfoundland papers painted a lurid picture of wanton, hysterical females without ever explaining the background of the unrest. The activities of the suffragettes prompted another debate at a male club.

Intellectually-oriented women had long been accustomed to attending lectures at the club, but in 1909 they were banned from future attendance. In the words of Myra Campbell, because "we had dared to voice our opinion or stand up for Woman's Cause, then, if you please, we were debarred for our 'caustic' remarks . . . . Some one said we were voted out because the members were shy to discuss or debate matters in the presence of ladies. Poor dears! We are sorry for them, and wonder how they ever did or ever will propose. But we understand. It's just the old prerogative asserting itself, which has been in them from centuries—namely, that of the subjugation of woman." "Why," she concluded, "that kind of opposition is the very way to make suffragettes . . . ."[5] Instead, in December 1909 they gathered at Mrs. Gosling's house at 77 LeMarchant Road and channelled their energies into forming a Ladies' Reading Room with an associated Current Events Club in which all manner of topics could be freely aired and debated. Mrs. Miller, who had gathered materials on the formation of women's clubs on a trip to Colorado, supplied helpful information.[6]

The Ladies' Reading Room was crucial to the development of the women's suffrage movement in Newfoundland for within its walls a generation of influential St. John's women were politicized. It was located in "a large and airy room" in the Lyon's Building, 158 Water Street. Situated on an upper floor it had a panoramic view of the Narrows, and its location on a busy shopping thoroughfare was inviting. It was open all day from ten until six, and the terms of membership, namely three dollars and the introduction of one member, made it accessible to at least the middle class. Within a few weeks, one hundred and twenty-five women joined. The Ladies' Reading Room provided social space, a selection of "the best English and American papers and magazines," and lectures and debates sponsored by the Current Events Club which met on Saturdays.

In its early years, the Current Events Club functioned virtually as a self-taught university in which members gave lengthy papers, developed debating and analytical skills, and gained confidence as public speakers. The range of topics was free thinking, including papers on socialism and Bahaism, a Persian religion that espouses a universal faith. With a room of their own, they also discussed women's status on many occasions. A sizeable and influential cohort of middle- and upper-middle-class women were converted to the suffrage cause in this questioning sanctuary, where they could also obtain a good strong cup of tea, beautifully served by volunteer hostesses, for the ladies maintained an impeccable, surface social convention. Here two women, Armine Gosling and Myra Campbell, emerged as divergent feminist theoreticians, though they were united in a belief that women's work was devalued. Each woman's thought was shaped not only by theoretical study but by the hard school of experience.

Armine Nutting Gosling (1864–1942) was forty-eight years old when she delivered an historic speech on women's suffrage on January 15th, 1912. The speech was considered so important it was delivered twice and reprinted in pamphlet form, selling for ten cents through the Ladies Reading Room.[7] It was compelling, well-researched and eloquently delivered as might have been expected of a former school principal, who was also a frequent dramatic reader and actress in performances staged for charities.

To all outward appearances, Armine Nutting Gosling was the epitome of upper-middle-class success and comfort. She was married to Gilbert Gosling, a director of Harvey and Company, who was soon to be mayor of St. John's. Her earlier life had not been so fortunate, and she had not forgotten it. Miss Nutting had been born into genteel poverty in the town of Waterloo, Quebec. Her mother Harriet, whom she adored and admired, struggled as a seamstress to provide for her family when her alcoholic husband, Vespasian, could not. Mrs. Gosling had a great deal of sympathy for the WCTU, but she was doubtless restrained politically by the fact that Harvey and Company were liquor importers. To the end of her life Armine never forgot her mother's hard work, courage, and thwarted ambitions as a writer, and this sense of the value of women's labour was central to her feminism.

After graduating from the local Shefford Academy, a leading high school in Quebec, Armine studied briefly in Ottawa, and then heard of an opening as principal of the Church of England Girl's School (later renamed Bishop Spencer College) in St. John's, at the promising salary of $600. A financial crisis at home compelled her to apply for and then accept the position in a country "quite out of the beaten path" as she put it.[8] She ventured alone at age twenty-one to assume the position. It says much about limited educational opportunities for girls in Newfoundland that one so inexperienced was appointed head of a leading school. Nevertheless, Armine was up to the challenge. A willingness to explore new avenues, intellectual venturesomeness, and strength of character marked her entire life. Her sister Adelaide, an equally remarkable woman, embarked on a nursing career, after teaching music briefly in St. John's, becoming the first professor of nursing in the United States.[9] Adelaide and Armine remained close friends and confidantes, and through her sister, who taught at Columbia University in New York, Mrs. Gosling and her husband were in touch with many currents of American progressive thought.

Armine married a young fellow immigrant to Newfoundland, Gilbert Gosling, a native of Bermuda. In many respects the marriage was a happy one. Gilbert was a man of advanced views who supported his wife's political beliefs, incorporating women's suffrage in the new St. John's municipal charter, enacted in 1921. As her children grew older, Armine Gosling became active in many organizations including the Cowan Mission, that ran a home for elderly gentlewomen, and the Church of England Orphanage, as well as golf and curling.[10] Consciousness and pride in women's abilities, born from her mother's example and further developed by her own civic involvements, gradually grew into explicit questioning of the limitations placed on women, and exasperation at the devaluation of women's work by many men. Things came to a head in 1904.

Gilbert was the secretary of the Anglican Cathedral Restoration Committee which was faced with the monumental task of raising funds and contracting architects and builders to rebuild the Victorian Gothic masterpiece burnt in the fire of 1892. For a series of years, in Armine's own words, "women of the various parishes gave hearty and generous help." The annual Cathedral Ladies Bazaar was one of the biggest fundraising events, and Mrs. Gosling served as treasurer. Though she detested bazaars, she threw herself into the work out of a sense of obligation to Gilbert.

Mrs. Gosling's ingenuity was taxed to the limit when she was asked to design a stall on the lines of a Chinese pagoda. "The work and responsibility and the expense of this thing are fast reducing me to a skeleton!" she wrote to her sister. "I am anxious to get thin, too, but not by such methods." Women, such as herself, put in weeks of work—organizing, baking, sewing, constructing and serving. They raised $5,600 in the 1904 bazaar alone. Indeed, roughly half of the total funds needed for the restoration were raised by Anglican women.[11] Yet they received only token recognition for their efforts, leading Armine to unburden herself with these thoughts:

> I find myself philosophizing over the position of women in connection with these matters, and reflecting on the willingness with which we women support so loyally an institution that encourages us to work and takes with eagerness all the money we can earn, but denies us any voice in its expenditure, and relegates us to outer

Armine Gosling, the "intellectual and organizational linchpin" of the women's suffrage movement in Newfoundland.

Credit: Centre for Newfoundland Studies, Memorial University of Newfoundland.

darkness as far as having any share in formulating its policies is concerned . . . But isn't that always the way of the Powers that be, both mundane and ecclesiastical, where women are concerned?[12]

Travel in England deepened her developing convictions. In the winter of 1904–5 she visited England for the first time taking her daughter Armine to public school, as was the custom with many of the children of the St. John's elite.[13] Here she met her sister's close friend, Lavinia Dock (1858–1956), a leader in the American nursing profession and the women's suffrage and labour movements. For twenty years, Dock worked on public health issues in the slums of New York at the Henry Street Settlement and she was also an ardent socialist. As Adelaide forewarned Armine "you will find her views most refreshing on all the nice, correct, conventional, stereotyped, hide-bound, English ways of doing things."[14] In the wake of this and subsequent trips, Armine began to subscribe to British suffrage newspapers and to attend suffrage meetings when she was in London.[15]

Mrs. Gosling's speech in 1912 reflected both personal experience and wide reading. Part of it was devoted to defending the British suffrage movement, including the suffragettes, because newspapers, as she put it, "exaggerate the bad, and suppress the good, and the truth is not in them."[16] The other portion of the speech enumerated the concrete improvements in law, education, child welfare, and poverty she hoped the women's vote would bring. Her suffrage ideology drew freely from both the maternal and equal rights traditions. In the former vein she argued: "It is just because men *are* men, and totally different from women, that they cannot satisfactorily legislate for both."[17] Women needed the vote to protect their own interests; equally it would advance society as a whole if women's nurturing capabilities were brought directly into the political process so that societal conditions could be improved. However, she also expressed admiration for the liberal philosopher John Stuart Mill, an intellectual father of the equal rights tradition. The emotional core of Armine Gosling's feminism, however, was the conviction that men have been "unappreciative of and ungrateful for the public work done by women. It has never been acknowledged at its full value, either in the industrial, social, political or religious world."[18]

A year later, in 1913, Myra Campbell delivered another feminist address at the Club. Entitled "Woman's Wrongs," it provided a radical critique not only of the imbalance of public power in society but of the structure of many marriages of her acquaintance. Like Mrs. Gosling, however, Mrs. Campbell shared an acute sense that women's work was not valued. There were other similarities. In an age which extolled female deference to male authority, especially in the middle class, Myra Campbell had the inspiration of strong female forebears to draw upon. Her paternal grandmother, Elizabeth Geddes Fisher, claimed to be a descendent of Jenny Geddes, who in a famous incident in the High Church of Edinburgh in 1637, hurled her stool at the dean during his sermon, outraged by what she saw as theological lapses. Myra also took pride in the fact that Grandmother Fisher herself "could run a furrow as straight as a man," while her maternal grandmother was, she claimed, "a most womanly woman [who] took prizes from a number of men in a carving and sawing contest."[19] Myra's own childhood dream, growing up in Bay of Islands, where her parents had emigrated from Nova Scotia in 1872, was to become a sea captain. Her parents, Christopher and Janet Fisher, were pioneers in opening up the Humber region to commercial logging; they prospered and established a sawmill.

Myra Fisher had confidence in herself and her opinions from a young age. She had an active, inquiring mind and she was a voracious reader, which made the Ladies' Reading Room an attractive venue. At sixteen she was engaged to a Presbyterian minister, but she broke it off because of his jealousy. In 1891 her mother died suddenly in childbirth and Myra was left in charge of the large household of seven siblings, three of whom were under ten, and her grandmother and her father. She objected vehemently to a woman her father was inclined to take as his second wife, and left home for Boston where she got a job in a factory sewing fine lingerie. She also worked briefly in Philadelphia. She thus had direct knowledge of life for single working women and of conditions in the United States. As it turned out her father actually married another woman, Janet Greenleaf, whom she liked very much, and she eventually returned to Corner Brook to teach. In 1899 she married John Campbell (1855–1936), a native of Scotland, who was a construction supervisor with the Reid Newfoundland Railway. They moved to St. John's, where they had five children. She believed passionately in the value of education for women and men, and all of her children had professions.[20] John Campbell was a quiet, retiring man and conservative in his views. Yet seemingly he did not object to his wife's activities and outspokenness. Mrs. Campbell was active in the Presbyterian Women's Missionary Society, and the newly formed Imperial Order of the Daughters of the Empire as well as the Ladies' Reading Room. She also corresponded to various newspapers under the pen name "Bay Isles."[21] In December 1913 she delivered an address to the Current Events Club that was considered so incendiary, its publication was suppressed.

Entitled "Woman's Wrongs" this address is the only radical feminist critique to have survived from this era. It was a lengthy, discursive, yet passionately-felt indictment of the "slavery of the home." A large number of members were in attendance. Drawing on incidents from the lives of women she knew—"these are not exaggerated reports of extreme cases but incidents of everyday life"—she condemned the existing structure of marriage, and linked it to the rise of the suffrage movement.[22]

She defended women who, contrary to the force of custom, wanted to remain single. She could not understand "why marriage should be the only ideal ambition for women." She also drew public attention to abusive situations within marriage that were rarely talked about. She told of a hardworking, devoted wife who had to beg for money from her spouse, yet "her husband had a salary of about $2000." He could go to his club, "wine and dine his friends," and "with a smile hand his mistress a cheque occasionally, but for his wife, the mother of his children, his housekeeper or home-keeper, which you will, his valet, chef, nurse and general lackey he couldn't afford the wages of a servant." Mrs. Campbell had dared to name the unnameable, "the mistress," and she shared with Armine Gosling an acute sense that women's work, even within the home, was devalued and underpaid. "Her servant, if she is able to keep one, gets her monthly wage and it is considered earns it, but the average housewife isn't considered as earning hers."[23] Wives, she further pointed out, had no rights over their husband's spending habits, and could live lives of self-denial while their husbands were profligate or made unwise business decisions, wrecking them both.

Women could no longer tolerate such conditions. They laid claim to the vote, symbol of equal citizenship, as well as the right to work outside the home. "We've listened to all your flattery," she declared, "married you, obeyed you, taken your cash and tried to make ends meet, wished your purse strings as elastic as your heart strings, borne your children in torture and anguish, made home for you, trained your servants, cooked your thankless meals (your mother always did better), so much for the compensations of life for mothers . . ." [who were] ". . . generally the most underpaid member of the family." "We have not the slightest intention of starting any Suffragette movement," she asserted; "we hold no brief for these extremists who use such drastic measures as blue vitriol, hatchets and shrieks, yet every revolt against oppression produces such and we find some of the incidents of daily life sufficient to turn one over to their ranks."[24]

The speech concluded, the officers of the Current Events Club faced a political crisis. Normally, major addresses were distributed to the press, and a reporter had requested a copy of this one. According to the *Daily News*, the Current Events Club "deprecated" its publication, fearful of the public response.[25] Yet there is evidence that at least some of her colleagues understood and privately sympathised with her beliefs. When suffrage was won, and Myra Campbell had moved to Ontario, she was toasted as an "absent friend" at the Victory Banquet. Nevertheless, Mrs. Campbell acquiesced in the suppression of her speech for, in her words, she "was not brave enough to endure all the unkind criticisms and opposition which publication of this would bring about."[26] Seven years later when the Newfoundland Women's Franchise League began the second formal suffrage campaign, the address was published at Myra Campbell's request, though the *Daily News* still felt it necessary to issue a disclaimer, and condemn it as "subversive of the sanctity of the home."[27]

It is not surprising that the feminists in the Ladies' Reading Room felt beleaguered in the face of public opinion. Even Mrs. Gosling's relatively moderate views, coupled with her qualified defence of the suffragettes, had been met with hostility from the *Daily News*, the leading daily paper, and from the pulpit. Columnist P.J. Kinsella, long antagonistic to votes for women, mounted the first attack. Several years before Gosling's speech he had written a lampoon, entitled the "Ladies Hit 'em Mission," which depicted an irrational and hysterical group of suffrage workers in the fictitious English village of Linstown.[28] Mrs. Gosling presented a tempting local target, part of the "evil" that had "now sprung up in our midst," as he put it. Suffragette tactics simply confirmed Kinsella in his belief that "politics is a matter of reason, woman does not reason, politics demand manly consideration—woman cannot give that." A country, he concluded, "at the mercy of woman's fickle sway, would quickly decay and totter." He longed for a return to the quiet, "calm and holy" woman of yesteryear.[29] Kinsella was not alone. Shortly thereafter Reverend Father O'Callaghan denounced the suffragettes and their "dastardly conduct" from the pulpit at the Roman Catholic Cathedral, linking them with callous, selfish, pleasure-seeking mothers. In contrast "his description of the true home presided over by the ideal mother was very beautiful," so the *Daily News* reported.[30]

On the eve of World War I, the re-emerging Newfoundland women's movement, centred on the Ladies' Reading Room, had not found a way to frame its message to evoke support beyond a narrow circle. There was a feeling that women's work, whether in the home or outside of it, was unrecognized at its true monetary and social value, but how to translate this understanding into a political campaign for the vote in Newfoundland's circumstances remained unclear. The events of World War I, coupled with organizing strategies suggested by the British Dominions Woman Suffrage Union (BDWSU) and later the International Alliance of Women, presented Newfoundland feminists with a partial solution.

The idea of uniting women suffragists in the British Dominions arose in New Zealand in February, 1913. Suffrage had already been won in New Zealand and in Australia, but women in Britain, South Africa, Newfoundland, Canada and India remained without a vote. Much could be learnt from the successful campaigns. Accordingly, an organizing conference was held in London in July 1914. The BDWSU contacted Newfoundland feminists during World War I, and by 1920 Newfoundland had a delegate on the BDWSU Committee in London. In 1921 the BDWSU merged with the International Women's Suffrage Alliance, an international network of suffrage societies which at its height in the late 1920s contained forty-six affiliates in countries as diverse as Finland, India, Italy, Syria, Ecuador, Great Britain, and the United States of America. Newfoundland joined this flourishing organization of suffrage activists and received, as we shall see, both moral and material support. The president of the International Alliance of Women, as it was renamed, was Carrie Chapman Catt, leader of the moderate suffragists in the U.S.A.

During World War I the international suffrage organizers urged women in Newfoundland and elsewhere to think ahead to "the coming period of social reconstruction and to work and pray that in the peace which will follow this war, the woman's voice may be heard."[31] The BDWSU urged suffragists to link together patriotic work and suffrage propaganda. It sent copies of London suffrage papers including the International Alliance of Women's paper, *Jus Suffragi*, to all the women's societies it knew of in the Dominions, and to influential individual women. It stressed that women's war work was a potent argument for the vote in war's aftermath. Armine Gosling wrote a lengthy article with echoes of this theme in 1916.[32] It appeared in *The Distaff*. Officially the organ of the Red Cross Branch of the Women's Patriotic Association headed by Adeline Browning, it had feminist undertones.

Edited by Mabel W. LeMessurier (1874–1954),[33] part of the Ladies' Reading Room circle, *The Distaff* was, as she said, "truly a woman's paper, devoting our space to an account of the work done in various spheres by wives and daughters of Newfoundland."[34] The front page of the first edition carried a picture of a Mrs. Hawco of Chapel Cove, "one of the many Women of Newfoundland who spin wool and knit it into socks for our soldiers." The same edition carried a melodramatic poem by P. Florence Miller, Topsail postmistress, entitled "the Knitting Marianna."

> With blackest omen hung the clouds
> The war-clouds o'er a darkling world;
> Men mustered to the call in crowds,
> The battle-flags were all unfurled
> The homes they left were gloomed with care,
> Where fields lay ripe before the door,
> But all the homely tasks were o'er
> And duty called them otherwhere.
>
> She only said—"O heart so weary,
> The lonely years ahead!
> But living men are cold and dreary,
> And one must knit," she said.[35]

The Distaff chronicled more than the knitting woman. It printed poetry, including that of the undeservedly neglected Rose M. Greene of Bell Island; it contained short stories and articles by women writers and photographs by Miss Elsie Holloway. It chronicled the achievements of amateur actresses and singers who raised money for the patriotic cause; it reported breakthroughs in Newfoundland women's sports; and it carried an anonymous first-person account by one of five St. John's ladies, who, in August 1916, decided to walk from St. John's to Victoria, Conception Bay, despite "much opposition on the part of our respective families and ridicule from many we had hitherto treated as our friends."[36] All in all, *The Distaff* was permeated with pride in female achievements.

Then there was coverage of the nurses. At least forty-three Newfoundland nurses, both graduates and "VADs" (Voluntary Aid Detachment workers with shortened training), served overseas with distinction during World War I, many in hospitals in England, others near the front lines.[37] A few, such as Elsie Crowdy, Mary Rendell, and Harriet Armine Gosling, Mrs. Gosling's daughter, drove ambulances risking their lives in the war zone. Great pride was taken in their heroism, for they provided feminists with telling arguments for women's claims to public recognition. At home in Newfoundland, graduate and VAD nurses provided additional examples of public service. They staffed six military hospitals, including Waterford Hall for convalescing soldiers, and the Jensen Camp founded by Adeline Browning for tubercular soldiers and sailors. These women proved their mettle during the catastrophic Spanish flu epidemic of 1918 which closed down business on the island for nearly a month, claiming a number of lives. The Seaman's Institute on Water Street was taken over as an emergency hospital. An exhausted Ethel G. Dickinson, a VAD nurse who had just returned from service in Ascot and Wandsworth Hospitals in Great Britain, fell victim to the flu at age thirty-nine. A monument was erected to her memory by public subscription in Cavendish Square.[38] Newfoundland feminists took this loss very personally. Ethel Dickinson was one of their own.[39] A graduate of the Methodist College, she subsequently became principal of the interdenominational Domestic Science School in St. John's. Placing housekeeping on a "scientific" basis was a characteristic cause of middle-class maternal feminists, and Dickinson contributed an article on the school to *The Distaff*. She stressed that the school appealed to women and girls of all religions and all classes.[40]

Military nursing aside, most women's work in Newfoundland during the war was of a traditional kind. Unlike the situation in the United States, Canada and Great Britain, women in Newfoundland did not enter the industrial workforce in large numbers, though some women did work in the Angel munitions factory in St. John's and in the small factory sector of light industries such as textiles, boots, cordage and bakeries.[41] Nevertheless, while feminists elsewhere pointed to women in munitions work, land armies, and heavy industry to prove their case that women deserved the vote because they had performed male jobs, in Newfoundland feminists idealized traditional distaff work particularly under the aegis of the Women's Patriotic Association (WPA) to prove their point.

The work of the Women's Patriotic Association deserves chronicling in its own right. The WPA was island-wide in scope. In September 1914, a circular letter was sent under the signature of the governor's wife, Lady Margaret Davidson, to all magistrates and justices of the peace throughout the island asking them to "call a meeting in conjunction with prominent ladies of the district" including "the wife of the Magistrate, the wife of the incumbent of the Church of England, the wife of the Methodist minister, the wife of the doctor and the school teachers."[42] Two hundred and eight branches were established, and by war's end at least fifteen thousand women from major settlements to remote outports had been drawn into WPA work.[43] Armine Gosling was the honorary secretary charged with corresponding with them. These contacts and others were subsequently used in an island-wide petition drive on behalf of women's suffrage.

Ethel Dickinson, former principal of the interdenominational Domestic Science School in St. John's. She served as a VAD World War I nurse. A monument stands in her memory in Cavendish Square, St. John's, Newfoundland.

Credit: Centre for Newfoundland Studies, Memorial University of Newfoundland.

Newfoundland women could take great pride in what distaff work accomplished during the Great War. The WPA was a complex organization. Talents that had hitherto run local charities or ladies' auxiliaries now coordinated thousands of volunteers in multiple branches and committees. A General Committee gave oversight. The basement of Government House functioned as a supply depot securing wool and flannel, dispatching it to areas in short supply, and receiving finished products. In any given weekday, two hundred and fifty workers sewed in afternoon shifts in the ballroom and drawing room. An Examining Committee scrutinized the quality of clothes produced at Government House, city and outport branches and dispatched defective ones to the Alterations Committee. A Cutting Committee cut cotton and flannel to pattern for subsequent assembly by sewing parties that sprang up all over St. John's including large groups at the Presbyterian Hall, St. Mary's and St. Thomas's Churches and at St. Bonaventure's College. A Packing Committee dispatched finished products to England. There were also two Red Cross branches in St. John's (Vigornia, headed by Adeline Browning, and at the Methodist College, headed by Miss Mary Mackay), as well as Red Cross branches in Grand Falls, Heart's Content, Fogo and Carbonear. They produced bandages and surgical dressings. Other outport branches produced "comforts," and collected sphagnum moss from local bogs for use in dressings for wounds.

The WPA comforts and especially the grey military sock assumed the status of icons during the Great War. Never before had women's work been so publicly visible and praised. Directions for WPA work groups, some under the authorship of Queen Mary, appeared as prominent articles in the press.[44] An exhibition of comforts was mounted in the shop window of a leading Water Street firm.[45] It was claimed by Lady Davidson after a trip to the Queen Mary's Needlecraft Guild in London that the Newfoundland sock was considered so good it had become "the recognized standard" in England.[46] There was soldierly collaboration of this claim in the letters of Frank "Mayo" Lind who sent reports back from the Front to the *Daily News*. On April 22, 1916 he wrote this from "Somewhere in France": "A Newfoundland sock is the best in the world and it is prized by every soldier. How many times at the Peninsula and before we ever saw Egypt have we been asked by soldiers of different regiments if we had a pair of Newfoundland socks to give them or sell them."[47] Sixty-nine days later Private Lind would walk and write no more.

Women's production of "comforts" was the subject of prose, poetry and art during the war, some of it intended as WPA fund raisers and morale builders. A WPA fine arts calendar featured "a young lady sewing bandages for the wounded heroes at the front." A short story by Tryphena Duley entitled "A Pair of Grey Socks" was distributed in pamphlet form "lovingly dedicated to the boys of the Newfoundland Regiment, and to every woman who has knitted a pair of grey socks." The grey sock became a proud symbol of distaff work in the public service. In Tryphena Duley's words:

> They were found on table or work basket in every house, both in parlour and kitchen. They were found at bridge tables; dummy knitted while her partner played the hand. They accompanied the worker to committee meetings and social calls. Knitting parties became the fashion, and they have even been seen in the theatre, and now some knit them even on Sundays. A pair of grey socks is a never-failing source of conversation. The different qualities of the wool, the various shapes of the heels, the many ways of narrowing the toes, the numbers of pairs accomplished, and above everything the excellences and discrepancies of our neighbour's knitting. They are a bond of unity between rich and poor, high and low, between all mothers who have sons at the war, between all women who knit. The grey sock has become the tie that binds.[48]

WPA work did not end there. A Visiting Committee made over four hundred visits per month to the families of men abroad.[49] Embarking and returning troops also had to be entertained; in cooperation with the Men's Patriotic Association the WPA ran a "soldier's and sailor's club" and a "Caribou Hut."[50] Ad hoc committees launched special appeals on behalf of Belgian refugees, the Nurse Edith Cavell Rest Houses in Kent, the victims of the Halifax explosion in 1917, the civilian blind, long neglected by the government, and for the Blue Cross League and the Royal Society for Prevention of Cruelty to Animals.[51] The latter two societies treated sick and wounded dogs and horses at the front—"a vast voiceless army, forced into battle and utterly helpless," as Armine Gosling put it.[52]

The WPA was also used by the Newfoundland government for propaganda purposes in the initial mobilization ("stirring up the men to action," as Governor Davidson expressed it), and later in 1918 in favour of an unpopular conscription.[53] By 1917 the Newfoundland government appointed a Food Control Board because adequate supplies of flour, sugar and molasses could no longer be imported. The WPA tried to interest people in "war bread" which involved flour substitutes, but Governor Harris, who replaced Davidson in 1917, complained that these efforts "had no great result among the humbler people."[54]

The Hospital Committee of the Women's Patriotic Association founded in 1914.

Credit: *Book of Newfoundland*, Vol. 1, p. 428.

Vast amounts of money were needed to support all of this work. St. John's and the larger outports had tag days, dinners, concerts and bazaars. The WPA placed money boxes in schools, issued a patriotic Christmas stamp, sold badges with a caribou's head, and sponsored a hockey match at the Prince's Rink in St. John's, among many other things. The outport women were not to be outdone. At White Rock, Trinity Bay, they sold potatoes; at Sommerville they raffled a watch; Topsail held a "grand bazaar," and Cow Head, a "sociable."[55] The ingenuity that had funded numerous local churches and charities was turned to a broader public purpose. By 1916 alone, Newfoundland women had raised the enormous sum of $205,614 in supplies and cash.[56] The total by the end of hostilities was closer to $500,000 in cash and goods. In terms of today's purchasing power in the clothing market this amount would be equivalent to $6.5 million, at a conservative estimate. Or, to place this fundraising achievement in another context, in 1915 a fine cashmere wool man's sock cost 30 cents and a six by seven foot quilt, $1.42.[57] All this was done in addition to the fundraising and work that continued in support of local charities and churches.[58]

At war's end, the work of the WPA received widespread public recognition. Some three dozen women received imperial honors including the WPA leaders in St. John's as well as Harbour Grace, Catalina, Bell Island, Grand Falls, Carbonear, Placentia, Bonne Bay, and Smith's Sound, Trinity Bay.[59] Even the *Daily News* acknowledged the sea change that was to lead inexorably to a demand for full citizenship. "[The vote] has come elsewhere; it is coming to

Newfoundland," the paper editorialized, "and the sooner it comes the better. One thing the war has conclusively proved, that the sphere of women is far wider than it was in the bygone years. What militant suffragism could never have won, the quiet service and unparalleled devotion of the women of the Empire has accomplished."[60] Tides of supportive public opinion and self-conception had been set in motion, yet it took five years of campaigning before a women's suffrage bill passed a reluctant Newfoundland legislature.

The campaign that the Newfoundland suffragists led from 1920, the year the Newfoundland Women's Franchise League was founded, until 1925 when victory was theirs, lacks the drama of mass demonstrations and civil disobedience staged by the militant branches of movements in the United States and Great Britain, yet Newfoundland leaders displayed their own particular brand of courage. They endured the mockery of opponents who refused to deal with the substance of their arguments, and dismissed them instead as grand dames, out of touch with the true feelings of homespun Newfoundland women. A number were educated abroad and a few were born there, leading to charges they were "faddists and imitators." Their education was turned against them with derisory comments that they had swallowed dictionaries. Above all they were charged, as were the WCTU pioneers before them, with threatening the bed-rock of civilization by neglecting their homes. One city clergyman used the opportunity of a Mother's Day sermon to condemn the suffragists and call for the return of "the good old days when the house was chockfull of children and mothers did all the cooking. When sometimes twelve, sometimes fourteen guests—all dear friends—would drop into dinner."[61] It took intellectual grit, emotional endurance and moral courage to withstand such bills of indictment.

The positions the leaders took were not uniformly accepted, even within their own social circles. Though most of the leaders' husbands were supportive, a few were not and in these cases the private stakes were even higher. In coming so visibly forward to champion the cause of women, all risked a loss of social respectability. They encountered anger in lobbying some powerful men of their class. Agnes Ayre recounted they were "surpris[ed] to find some otherwise delightful people fly into terrific rages and order us out of their offices, when they learnt what our mission was."[62]

The suffragists also needed a mixture of political savvy and patience. Scarcely has there been a less propitious time to launch a social movement. Newfoundland emerged from World War I with a sharply increased debt, compounded in 1920 by the financial drain of the uneconomic railway. To make matters worse, the fishery was in a serious slump with diminished catches as well as reduced markets because of economic dislocation in Europe and South America. Newfoundland's economy fell into a serious depression even before the great upheaval of the 1930s, and the unemployed marched in the streets. At times of stress people are as likely to cling to the old and familiar order, or even to embrace reaction, as they are to accept change. The message and methods of the suffragists were to prove critically important to the outcome.

The suffrage leaders also had to craft an alliance and a message that bridged religious differences. The WCTU had failed years before in part because it could only attract a narrow base of evangelical support. Aware of suffrage struggles elsewhere through their reading and their membership in the International Alliance of Women, the more discerning knew the potential dangers of clerical opposition. In France, Spain, Italy, Quebec, Latin America, and parts of the United States, Catholic clergy had proven a particularly powerful stumbling block. It was essential to attract church women of the main denominations, and especially Roman Catholic ones, to the cause. In 1921, the population was roughly thirty-three percent Roman Catholic, thirty-two percent Anglican, and twenty-eight percent Methodist, with the remainder from smaller Protestant groups, chiefly, Presbyterians, Congregationalists, Pentecostalists and members of the Salvation Army.

Finally, the suffragists had to frame an ideology and an organizing method that bridged class and geographical differences. It was undeniably true they were more affluent and more formally educated than the mass of women whose support they had to gain. There was the added difficulty that a few of their husbands were fish merchants and factory owners, the objects of mistrust and antagonism, especially in hard times. Though many were to the left of their menfolk, the question remained, would they be seen as independent human beings or ciphers? The way ahead was fraught with difficulty. Nevertheless, the sense among women of all classes that their work during the war mattered was a potentially important bridge.

Early in 1920 Armine Gosling and Anna Mitchell, long-time WCTU activist, decided the time had come to launch a movement for the parliamentary franchise. The initial organizing meeting, involving only a handful of women, was held at Mrs. Mitchell's home at One Devon Row within the shadow of Ethel Dickinson's monument. Subsequent meetings were held at the Ladies' Reading Room, until an anti-suffragist member (possibly Helena Squires) objected.[63] Eventually the Women's Franchise League, as it came to be named, secured a core group of one hundred financial subscribers by private solicitation. In the political context of the Newfoundland depression, suffragists felt that because sheer survival would "tax all the energies of the people . . . to attempt to look for money for any other cause than that of charity would at once make our movement unpopular."[64]

It is relatively easy to describe the officers and most active members of the Newfoundland Women's Franchise League in St. John's as a group. The inner circle were predominantly elite women, many in advanced middle age, who were either childless or whose children were grown. Most were married; about one quarter were single. It was they who had the time and money to organize, especially during a depression. Most of the suffragists had already achieved a certain stature and respect from their peers by reason of leadership in women's church and civic groups, and especially in the WPA. All were well aware of trends in the wider world. About one quarter of the leadership (Armine Gosling, Adelaide Browning, Antonia Hutton and Emilie Fraser) were born elsewhere, and the native-born Newfoundlanders (Fannie McNeil, May Goodridge, Margaret Burke, Agnes and Janet Ayre, and Mary Southcott, among others) characteristically had been educated abroad or had travelled outside the colony. This gave them a critical and comparative perspective on Newfoundland social norms. The Franchise League was not a testament to postwar youth—it was in the main the culmination of the demands of the well-established and married.[65] This predominance gave the movement's ideology a maternalist bent, though in emphasizing the value of traditional women's work during war and peace, and especially its economic value, they shaped it to Newfoundland circumstances.

The leadership, however, was not monolithic. There were some younger members, most of them daughters of suffragist mothers (Agnes and Janet Miller, Margaret Duley and Margaret Mitchell), and there were professional women, chiefly nurses (Mary Southcott) and school principals (Emilie Fraser and Violet Cherrington) who came to the fore in St. John's. Much less is known, as we shall see, about the leadership in outport communities. It was also a multidenominational group. Activists came from the Anglican (Armine Gosling, Adelaide Browning and Mary Southcott), Roman Catholic (May Kennedy Goodridge, Margaret Burke, and Antonia Hutton), Methodist (Maud Hutchings), Presbyterian (Helen Baird, Anna Mitchell) and Congregational (Margaret Duley) churches. This diversity was critical to their success given sectarian passions at the time.

The leaders were energetic and public spirited, and involved in a central way in a multiplicity of interrelated causes. For them suffrage was the centrepiece of a more generalized movement of women into civic prominence. The suffragists were also leaders in other organizations, including the Child Welfare Association, the Newfoundland Outport Nursing and Industrial Association (NONIA), and the Girl Guides. These three organizations were launched by essentially the same group of women and their sympathisers in the same era. A common ideological thread intertwines them all. Women, usually conceptualized as mothers, had something of value to do and say in postwar reconstruction. The Girl Guides stressed citizenship; NONIA continued the WPA tradition of women's craft work, developing and marketing it in peacetime; and the Child Welfare Association stressed both maternal and child health, in addition to municipal conditions especially sanitation. In each instance women asserted their needs and viewpoints as women. However, their passion to advance the world as they found it took them in other directions as well, including church groups, poor relief, animal welfare, and societies for arts and letters.

Armine Gosling, who had long been at the centre of the suffragist circle, was the president of the new League and for the first two years or so her intellectual fearlessness, drive, keen political sense, and writing ability remained crucial. Even while fighting the suffrage cause she was a founding member and secretary of the Girl Guide Association, and founding president of the Child Welfare Association. Unfortunately, by 1921 Gilbert Gosling was showing the first signs of the serious heart ailment which was to lead him to retire to Bermuda, his birthplace, by 1925. Armine's considerable energies were slowly sapped by mounting concern about her husband's health, and an impending move.

The weight of organizing gradually fell upon Fannie Knowling McNeil (1869–1928),[66] who served in the key position of secretary of the Franchise League. Calm, tactful, witty and persistent, she was a favourite with crowds as a public speaker. Agnes Ayre, who functioned as her young assistant, wrote: "Often when she was being heckled, she would answer thoughtfully and then add some witty remark that put everyone in a good humour, her lovely eyes lighting up with amusement: a great humanist if ever there was one."[67] Fannie's upbringing helped to mould her steadfastness and sense of certainty in espousing an unpopular position on women's rights, for both her father and mother were suffragists. Her father, George Knowling, a native of Silverton, Devon, had built up a very prosperous retail business with two branches on Water Street. A generous

Fannie McNeil, one of the most prominent suffrage leaders in the 1920s.

Credit: Centre for Newfoundland Studies Archives, Memorial University of New-foundland.

and strong-willed man, characteristics that Fannie shared, George Knowling supported women's suffrage in the 1890s when it was a wildly unpopular notion, arguing a case for it in a debate at the Church of England Institute.

Fannie Knowling was educated in part in England and she may have received formal art instruction there. Together with A.E. Harris she founded the Newfoundland Society of Art in 1925, and for four years she staged an annual Art Exhibition to benefit the Ladies' Reading Room (renamed the Old Colony Club in the late 1920s). She was successively honorary secretary (1918–25), then president of the club in the postwar period. She was also a published poet and had a love of literature. Her large collection of books went to Memorial College upon her death from cancer in 1928.

Though brought up in affluence and remembered for her high spirits and sense of fun, Fannie's early life was not without sadness. Two of her brothers died when they were very young. In 1902 Fannie experienced the tragedy of infant death more directly when her own son, John Ballard McNeil, died three days after his birth. As with Armine Gosling who also lost two infant children, Fannie McNeil's commitment to reducing the rate of infant mortality by better sanitation and health services was born of a mixture of personal experience and empathy. She ran unsuccessfully for the St. John's Municipal Council on this platform in 1925. Her other civic interests included the Playground Association and she was a fundraiser for United (i.e., Presbyterian, Congregational and Methodist) Schools. Though born an Anglican she followed her husband Hector McNeil into the Presbyterian Church and was active in women's groups of that denomination.

Hector is remembered as a quiet "typical accountant." Born in Scotland, he was paymaster for the Reid Newfoundland Railway. He backed his wife's suffrage activities. Along with other civil servants who were married to suffragists he was pressured by the Squires's government to muzzle his wife or go without a job. "What did you say?" he was asked by his wife's friends. "I told him he could jolly well go to the devil," he replied.[68] The McNeil home at 41 Queen's Road functioned as the office for the Newfoundland Women's Franchise League. Fannie McNeil played the leading role in the culminating two or three year's of the campaign.

May Kennedy Goodridge (1876–1974),[69] was honorary treasurer of the Newfoundland Franchise League and attended its founding meeting at Mrs. Mitchell's. She too played a major leadership role when Armine Gosling disengaged from activity. Like Fannie McNeil she was born in St. John's, though she was educated at a convent in Waterford, Ireland. Her father owned a prosperous tailor's establishment. She displayed great strength of character from an early age when she accompanied her tubercular brother to the Canary Islands, where unfortunately he died. She brought his body back to Newfoundland, showing it is said "the strength, and courage of ten men." Her only other sibling, a sister, died around 1910 and May Kennedy inherited a considerable amount of property. She married Thomas Goodridge late in life; they had no children. At the point she became active in the suffrage movement, she was single, independently wealthy, and voteless, a status she found unfair and incongruous. Though a wealthy woman, she had a progressive political vision that embraced "work and good wages for all," as she put it in a speech. She had also been active in the Ladies' Reading Room and the Women's Patriotic Association, working as a VAD in Waterford Hall. She became honorary treasurer of the Franchise League, and represented it at her own expense at Alliance Congresses in Rome and Paris, as well as at a Pan American Conference in Baltimore. In 1925, she unsuccessfully contested the St. John's Municipal election along with her close friend Fannie McNeil. Dedicated to relieving poverty in practical ways, Goodridge was also active in Catholic charities as were Margaret Burke and Antonia Hutton, other members of the inner circle.

Antonia D'Alberti Hutton (1875–1951)[70] married Sir Charles Hutton, K.C.S.G., founder of the music store, composer, teacher, choirmaster and Basilica organist, and for a time Liberal member for St. John's East (1894). His knighthood was received from the Pope.[71] Tony D'Alberti was one of three clever and talented sisters, all of whom had received operatic training. All three sisters were suffragists. Their Spanish mother and Italian father lived in London where their father represented a wine firm. Antonia's sisters Leonora and Amalia remained single, and worked for feminist causes in London. Leonora was editor of the *Catholic Times* as well as the *Catholic Suffragist*, the latter being the paper of the St. Joan's Social and Political Alliance. Articles from it were planted in the Newfoundland press to defuse clerical hostility,[72] and Leonora reported on the Newfoundland movement for *Jus Suffragi*, the International Alliance of Women's newspaper. (Together with Amalia she was commissioned by the Newfoundland government to translate and copy all documents contained in the Colonial Office for the period 1780 to 1925 related to the Labrador boundary dispute.)[73] As for Antonia, she met Charles Hutton in 1897–1898 when he was studying in England. He later proposed by letter, and they were married in St. John's in 1903.[74] Quite overshadowed by her husband in his

biography—aside from her wedding date, she is virtually invisible—
to the suffrage generation she was a vital participant. Her London
links were invaluable, as was her access to the St. John's music
world for fundraising.

She has been described as quiet and gentle but with flashes of
Spanish fire and temperament. Her demand for the vote was
prompted at least in part by her belief that "for every bad woman,
there are ten bad men." She had sympathy for underpaid women—
"No wonder they're out on the streets when they only earn $3 in the
stores." And she was capable of silencing hostile petty officials who
opposed women's franchise. An officious "tupenny ha'penny legislative clerk" refused to accept suffrage petitions brought by Mrs.
Hutton and other women in their own right until they had identified
their mothers and fathers. When Mrs. Hutton's turn came, she
grandly responded with lengthy hyphenated names in Spanish and
Italian which the official meekly recorded in an illegible scrawl,
rather than admit he was not her equal in foreign languages.[75]

Another important Catholic suffragist was Margaret Elizabeth
Mulcahy Burke (1868?–1963),[76] assistant treasurer of the Franchise League. Mrs. Burke was active in Catholic charities including
the Ladies' St. Vincent de Paul Society and the Knights of Columbus
Ladies Association. In 1908 she married Vincent Burke, superintendent of R.C. Schools and subsequently deputy minister of education.
Her sister, Sister Mary Pius, was superior at Littledale College, a
boarding school for Catholic girls run by the Mercy Order. Margaret
Burke had lived for a brief period in New York at the height of the
suffrage movement, when her husband attended Columbia University. She had thrown herself into the intellectual and political life of
the city and became convinced of the justice of the suffrage cause.
Back in St. John's, she joined the Ladies' Reading Room and headed
the St. Bonaventure's College branch of the WPA.

(Annie) Maud White Hutchings (1870?–1961)[77] brought quite a
different denominational perspective to the executive committee.
She provided an important connection with Methodist women's
groups, for she was St. John's district superintendent of the
Women's Missionary Society. The daughter of William and Annie
White of the Southside, St. John's, she was the eldest of twelve
children, two of whom died in infancy. Her sister, Edith White
Hunter, was president of the Woman's Christian Temperance Union
in the 1920s, and another suffrage supporter. Maud White was
educated at the Wesleyan Academy and married Charles Hutchings,
a lawyer, in 1893. He became provincial grand master of the Loyal
Orangeman's Association and entered politics. He was elected a

Liberal member of the House of Assembly for Bay de Verde in 1904 and subsequently served as deputy minister of justice under the Bond administration. Hutchings became inspector general of the Newfoundland Constabulary in 1917. Newfoundland suffragists could scarcely be accused of harboring thoughts of insurrection like their British and American sisters when the wife of the chief of police was a leader. It also says a great deal about the emergence of a sense of commonality based on gender among elite women in St. John's that wives of prominent Orangemen and Catholic laymen joined hands politically.

Anna Mitchell (1861–1946),[78] like the White sisters, provided an important bridge to the earlier tradition of evangelical, WCTU suffragism. A long-time member of the WCTU and its corresponding secretary, she was also president of the Presbyterian Women's Missionary Society. She was not easily intimidated. One day she was lobbying a "well-known gent." "Go home, madame, and learn to bake bread," he responded. "I bake excellent bread," she rejoined. Reform was a family tradition: Anna was a niece of Richard Barnes, founder of the Native Society, a 19th century expression of Newfoundland nationalism. Anna Barnes married J.B. Mitchell, a prosperous "commission agent" whose agencies included tea. She owned property in St. John's and her initial interest was in the municipal franchise. Mrs. Mitchell was involved in many causes, so many that a younger generation who did not share her commitments called her "Mrs. Committee Mitchell." She was a vegetarian for moral reasons and was active in the Society for the Protection of Animals. One who remembers her described her as "a very holy woman, driven by her conscience." Her son, Jack, a Rhodes Scholar, died in the Great War. Another, Harold, served at Gallipoli and survived to become president of the Great War Veteran's Association of Newfoundland. Mrs. Mitchell's mother's hand may be seen in the support that association was to lend in lobbying for women's suffrage. Mrs. Mitchell, and her daughter Marguerite, Kirk soloist, were also very active in the Child Welfare Association, another expression of this wave of feminism. Her daughter-in-law was the honorary secretary and a leading force in NONIA, another characteristic expression of the Newfoundland women's movement in this era.

Adeline Elizabeth Browning (1869–1950)[79] was another important participant. Adeline was originally from Jersey in the Channel Islands. Her father, John Hubert, was a master mariner and her mother, Elizabeth Jane Bichard, was born in Lower Canada, the daughter of a sailor. Adeline's father died when she was less than three, leaving a widow and three children, barely of school age. How the family surmounted these circumstances, how Adeline received her musical training, and how she met John Browning remain unsolved mysteries. She married the Honourable John Browning, a member of the Legislative Council of Newfoundland, and owner of G. Browning and Son, a partnership that included a large commercial bakery and later the Riverside Woolen Mills. Adeline entered into St. John's top social echelon. The Browning mansion at 21 King's Bridge Road, known in her day as "Vigornia," and later the United Family Court, but recently destroyed by fire, had six thousand square feet of space and featured a magnificent winding mahogany staircase. Invitations to Mrs. Browning's were much sought after by the socially aspiring. An acquaintance described her as "not just an act, she was the entire stage." Nevertheless, Adeline offered more than social eclat to the movement.

She had long had a deep, charitable interest. She arrived in St. John's shortly before the Newfoundland bank crash of 1894. Shocked by local conditions she was at once drawn into charity work and a room was set aside in her house for sewing parties for the needy. She had superb organizational skills, and remaining childless, she had more time than many of her contemporaries to exercise them. She was vice president of the Ladies' Reading Room, and president of the Alliance Française of Newfoundland, for which she received a French decoration. Around 1900 she formed a ladies' orchestra of about eight members, and for several decades they performed semi-classical music for charities. Antonia Hutton was among the original members of the ensemble.[80]

Adeline was part of a core group of feminists who were in key positions in the Women's Patriotic Association. She turned over her house to Red Cross work, chaired a reception committee for returned soldiers, and travelled throughout the United States and Canada at her own expense studying sanitorium organization, returning home to found the Jensen Camp for tubercular soldiers and sailors. She received the Order of the British Empire decoration in 1918 for her medical work with the WPA. Her intense interest in medical issues may suggest thwarted career ambitions. Adeline was a founding member of the Franchise League, and a few years after her husband's death in 1921 she took up residence in London where she acted as Newfoundland's liaison to the International Alliance of Women, declaring her intention to work in general for the women's movement.

Helen Marguerite Baird (1889–1965)[81] also served on the Executive Committees of the Franchise League and its successor, the League of Women Voters. She was active in Presbyterian women's groups. Her father was Alexander "Dick" Brown, a Scottish engineer who, like Hector McNeil, worked with the Reid Newfoundland Railway. Her mother was Margaret Angel. Helen was educated at the Methodist College, and then at a girl's public school, Penryth College, in Wales. In 1914 she married James Baird, a grandson of the Honourable James Baird, the founder of the Water Street merchant house of the same name. James, Junior at first went into business on his own as a wholesale provision dealer with premises on Water Street East, near the War Memorial. He prospered and in 1932, despite the Depression, built a new two story building. He eventually joined the family business as a director. James Baird is remembered as being "very conservative," so Helen Baird's involvement in suffrage activities was doubtless a step that required some daring. Her interests included painting, and among her prized possessions was a medal from the Royal Drawing Society. She was also active in the Society for the Blind. After the Great War she was awarded a medal from the Queen Mary's Needlecraft Guild, an honour which was given to only the most productive WPA knitters. At age thirty-two she was one of the two youngest members of a Franchise League executive dominated by the middle aged. The other young executive member was her close friend, Agnes Miller Ayre.

Agnes Miller Ayre (1890–1940)[82] and her younger sister Janet were both founding members of the Franchise League. Agnes was an executive member and served as Fannie McNeil's lieutenant accompanying her in lobbying. Janet held no formal office but performed a variety of tasks including writing letters to the newspapers. Like Fannie Knowling McNeil the sisters were born into a household where the justice of women's suffrage was a given for their mother was Mary Miller, a founder of the Ladies' Reading Room. Both girls were educated at Bishop Spencer College. Mrs. Miller believed in broadening travel as part of her children's upbringing, and she took them on trips to the United States, England and Scotland. Agnes Ayre described a trip to Great Britain:

> In Edinburgh, London and Glasgow I had attended Suffragette meetings and heard all the famous speakers for the Women's Cause, the Pankhursts, Mrs. Despard, Pethwick Lawrence and the others; sometimes went to the Anti's meetings out of curiosity to hear what they could find to say for themselves; later walked through London and saw the plateglass windows smashed by Suffragettes' hammers, cheered their processions, saw them chained to railings, annoying policemen, and sympathised with their hunger strikes and ways of annoying Mr. Asquith.[83]

Early in the history of the Ladies' Reading Room, Agnes Miller delivered a paper on 'Woman and the Franchise.'

In 1913 Agnes married Harold C. Ayre, a grandson of the founder of Ayre and Sons, and a director of the same firm, which operated extensive retail, wholesale and mail-order departments. In addition to the franchise movement Agnes Ayre's other civic and intellectual interests included NONIA, for which she designed a pattern, the Newfoundland Historical Society, and the Newfoundland Society of Art of which she was a founding member. Her most enduring intellectual contribution was as a distinguished amateur botanist, and as the author of "Wild Flowers of Newfoundland" (1935). She had three children, Lewis M. and Fred W. Ayre and Janet C. Murphy.

Janet Miller Ayre Murray (1892–1946)[84] was a pioneer in opening up the Newfoundland legal profession to women. After graduating from Spencer and placing second in the Jubilee Scholarship competition she read law, articling with her uncle Donald Morison's firm. To do this, she had to force the Law Society to accept her. After some debate, enabling legislation was passed in 1911. She had written her second year exams when the whirlwind of war altered her plans. Originally she was an active volunteer with the Belgian Relief Committee, a special WPA project run by younger women. When her fiancé Captain Eric Ayre was sent overseas, Janet went to Great Britain and the couple married in Scotland in June 1915. Janet worked as a VAD nurse in kitchens, and trained as an ambulance driver. Then her brother died of pneumonia while on leave from the front, and in the face of this tragedy Mrs. Miller and Janet's in-laws forbade her to go to the theatre of war. Further tragedy was to stalk the family: Eric Ayre, his brother Bernard, and two Ayre cousins were all killed on the fateful day of July 1st, 1916 at Beaumont Hamel on the Western Front. Upon returning to Newfoundland, Janet Ayre became honorary secretary of the Beaumont Hamel Memorial Fund.

Despite recent unhappiness, Janet Ayre found time to work for the Franchise League. Her other causes were the Child Welfare Association and NONIA. After suffrage was won she became second vice president of the League of Women Voters. In 1924 her personal life found a happier footing when she married Andrew H. Murray (1877–1965), an established and successful businessman who had founded a salt cod export business. They had one child, Gertrude (Mrs. A.H. Crosbie). It was one sign of changing times that Andrew Murray married a prominent suffragist. His father was James Murray, a member of the House of Assembly who had fervently opposed the notion of votes for women in the 1890s.

These women formed the inner circle of mostly older, married women. However, there were other activists who represented slightly different constituencies. Emilie G. Stirling Fraser (d. 1958) had been a principal of Bishop Spencer College from 1898 to 1920, when she married comparatively late in life. She had served on the executive of the Newfoundland Teacher's Association, usually as the only woman on the board, and equal pay was part of her suffrage motivation. Her successor at Spencer, Miss Violet M. Cherrington, was also a prominent supporter. Equal pay was also part of the suffrage ideology of Miss Margaret Duley, the novelist, who joined Mrs. Fraser, Agnes Ayre and others on a debating team which argued the case against a male team from the Methodist College Literary Institute. They lost. Their opponents included Raymond Gushue, later president of Memorial University of Newfoundland.[85] The low status and low pay of the nursing profession also drew Mary Southcott (1862–1943), former superintendent of nurses at the General Hospital into the fray, and she mobilized others including Emma Reid (1886–1989), matron of the Fever Hospital.[86]

The early 1920s was not an advantageous time to launch a new movement. Not only was the island in great financial distress but there was labour unrest, and the legislative sessions in 1921 and 1922 were among the stormiest in Newfoundland's history. Prime Minister Richard Squires headed a Liberal-Union Party pledged to progressive reforms. However, there were strong factional rivalries within his government revolving around William Coaker, president of the Fisherman's Protective Union, and George Warren, the minister of justice. Further, the Squires' government had to defend itself against a series of well-merited charges of corruption brought by a Conservative opposition whose base of strength included St. John's from which the suffrage movement emanated. Demands for women's suffrage soon got caught up in a vortex of political calculations by Members of the House of Assembly jockeying for position. Suffrage leaders had to contend with all of this in their lobbying in addition to prejudice about "woman's place."

The suffrage campaign began in May 1920 with a St. John's publicity blitz: articles to the daily papers, letters to the editor, and public canvassing as the suffragists went door to door and into the shops asking housewives and "working girls" for support. St. John's women were urged to sign petitions at the Ladies' Reading Room. Letters and telegrams were also sent to "leading ladies" in the outports asking for support, mirroring the earlier WPA organizing method. One of the more innovative publicity techniques was the projection of suffrage advertising displays onto the moving picture screens at the Nickel, Majestic, Star and Casino Theatres, the new media of mass entertainment. The giddy and trivializing flapper images of women projected by post-war Hollywood and English studios only further complicated the suffragists' task. The seriousness of their moral and political message contended with such film distractions as "The Loves of Mary Queen of Scots" ("A Queen But Only a Woman") or "Prowlers of the Sea" ("She Kissed Him, She Loved Him, She Betrayed Him") that played to packed audiences.

Print media of the era were only slightly more encouraging. While the editors of some leading newspapers including the *Daily News*, the *Evening Telegram*, and the *Evening Herald* were to write supportive editorials on votes for women, there were contending and ambivalent messages about women's place in advertising, other columns and wireservice copy, even in these same newspapers. Thus, even while the *Daily News* extolled the suffrage movement, it ran a feature story on Nobel Prize winning physicist Madame Curie, intended as a cautionary tale to those young girls who might aspire to follow her into a demanding profession. Next to a woebegone picture of Madame Curie ran the headline "The Woman who Found Radium but Lost Love." Allegedly hopelessly infatuated with a married man, the woman scientist "cries out from the depths of her suppressed nature for the one thing that every woman that was ever created wants above all other gifts—LOVE."[87]

If brilliance in women was of questionable use, then the emerging postwar freedom of "gadding about" was equally horrifying to traditionalists. Condemning the "simpering simpletons" as it called the young girls who were beginning to go out unchaperoned, the *Bay Roberts Guardian* predicted "ten to one, when married, she will develop into a slatternly gossip, if no greater misfortune befalls her." It was the "girl who loves home and helps her mother that wins the desirable man, and becomes an ornament to womanhood."[88] As in the 1890s when the WCTU first demanded the vote there was no end to the unsolicited advice directed at women and their behaviours in the 1920s. All of this was part of the cultural backdrop which the suffrage activists had to overcome if they were to be successful.

The carefully crafted wording of the petition which was the focus of suffragist organizing adroitly struck a balance between tradition and change, drawing on acceptable moral themes even while stretching the boundaries of woman's place. It read:

> Whereas we regard ourselves as Partners in the responsible business of home-keeping which is so vital to the best interests of the Dominion; and

> Whereas we are subject to all the laws and taxations which apply to men; and
>
> Whereas many of us are workers helping to produce the wealth of the Dominion; and
>
> Whereas in others parts of the British Empire women enjoy all the rights of the franchise, and assume its responsibilities; and
>
> Whereas the women of Newfoundland rose to every call made upon them during the Great War, and showed energy and executive ability in the organization of relief and other work, and that many of them served overseas as Nurses, VADs and Ambulance Drivers;
>
> Your petitioners therefore humbly pray that your Honourable House will, during the present Session, pass a law by which there will be given to the Women of the Dominion the rights of the franchise on conditions similar to those commonly required of men.[89]

The petition opens with a reaffirmation of woman's responsibilities as "homekeeper," but with the transforming notion that domestic life is a partnership, implying an equality of roles, themes that reflect the concerns of Gosling and Campbell earlier at the Current Events Club. Woman was not abandoning her home for politics, but taking on new responsibilities for which she had already shown herself capable. The case made in the petition and in associated writing in 1920 was framed not so much in terms of individual rights more familiar to the late twentieth century ear, but in terms of women's collective responsibility inside and outside of the home. In claiming a responsibility for the "best interests of the Dominion" the suffragists were broadening woman's sphere into politics in a way calculated to appeal to a highly patriotic era.

The suffrage writings and speeches that accompanied the petition campaign dwelt at length on the new and better Newfoundland women's political involvement would bring. In the midst of mounting despair about economic and social conditions, the suffragists held out hope of improvement, if not to the fishery, then at least to some conditions in village and towns. "A 'woman's sphere' extends to the farthest limits of the radius of her influence for good"; her vote would "render assistance in hastening on the dawn of progress," so Fannie McNeil argued.[90]

It is true that the case for suffrage was sometimes made in the unmistakable tones of the upper class. Armine Gosling, for example, was exasperated that illiterate male youths who had "no views worth considering on any subject" were able to vote while "women of culture and education" could not.[91] Nevertheless, the suffrage propaganda contained a number of "cross-over" issues that affected women of every class. Maternal and child health was one such issue. The infant mortality rate in Newfoundland was twice that of Canada; medical facilities were non-existent along lengthy stretches of the coastline, and midwives were mostly untrained. The suffragists argued that maternal health and child welfare were neglected by the existing political order, but that "in those countries where women have equal suffrage with men, infant mortality has decreased."[92] Many suffragists were simultaneously involved in founding the new Child Welfare Association and NONIA whose original aim was to support district nurses by the sale of outport women's crafts.

Education had also been badly neglected by successive governments, and the suffragists stood firmly for putting more money into the educational system. In Newfoundland's context of imperfectly trained teachers, one-room schools unevenly distributed among a dispersed population, and a high illiteracy rate, such a stance was broadly-speaking a populist one. It was the business of women as mothers to influence educational policy, so the suffragists argued. "Voteless the woman is powerless to prevent a Government from depriving schools of the money needed for teachers."[93]

In St. John's there were additional appeals that crossed class boundaries. Though their own circumstances were comfortable, the suffragists were very much aware that there were large sections of the town without running water or sewerage, and they were determined to do something about it. As was the case elsewhere, suffragists argued that women had a unique talent and interest in municipal government, which was homemaking writ large. St. John's, so they asserted, "magnificently situated—with ideal possibilities as far as sewerage is concerned—and swept by sea breezes —is a town of disease, sickness and filth! We have no women on our Municipal Council."[94]

Newfoundland arguments, especially as espoused by Fannie McNeil, often had a maternalist bias. A "Women's Mission," so Mrs. McNeil argued, extended outside the limits of her four walls. "Her womanly sympathies go out into the world. Wherever she sees wrong her instinct bids her put it right and the young, the aged, the deformed and all who suffer, come under her motherly care, for women are naturally all mothers."[95] McNeil's approach, while limiting, had the effect of undermining the arguments of traditionalists like Father O'Callaghan who eight years earlier had condemned suffrage activists as selfish women.

This sort of maternalist appeal was balanced, however, with a frequent recognition, both in the petition and in the accompanying propaganda, that many women actually worked outside the home "helping to produce the wealth of the Dominion," in factories, offices and especially in the fishery. Women in the waged labour force were not ignored: "Woman has been compelled to labor side by side with man equal in vigor and productiveness, but forced always to accept less compensation."[96] That the vote was needed to compel equal pay was a case that was often made by the suffragists, who it should be noted were for the most part not in the waged workforce themselves.

There were other grievances that received a good deal of publicity. "Suffragist," in this case probably Janet Miller Ayre, articulated a legal case. "The laws regarding marriage and the control of children, of intestacy, and the inheritance of property, and industrial conditions, are made for men and by men and needless to say are unjust, and in many cases, positively cruel to women."[97] What the writer was alluding to in part were the surviving remnants in the Newfoundland legal code of the old common law principle that a woman died a civil death upon marriage; hence, child custody in this era went to the father, and if a husband died intestate (without a will), the widow received only a one third share of his property for use in her lifetime, the rest passing automatically to the children. Other suffrage writers took up the issue of a legal sexual double standard, condemning a system of justice which punished the prostitute while "allowing the male to go comparatively free—and for the same offence."[98]

The petition which formed the focus of the campaign also put the Newfoundland demand in a broader British Imperial context. By 1920 the vote had been won in the sister Dominions of New Zealand (1893), Australia (1902) and Canada (1918) as well as Great Britain (1918) itself. What the petition did not mention, but which the Newfoundland leaders with their international connections were well aware of, was the upsurge of suffrage victories outside of the British Empire in the immediate postwar period. Virtually all of Northern Europe had conceded women the vote, namely, Finland, Denmark, Norway, Sweden and Iceland, as had fragile democracies in Eastern Europe, Austria and Germany. The United States had finally capitulated after a seventy-two year campaign in August 1920. Newfoundland was falling well behind the times.

The initial clarion calls to the public housekeepers of the island immediately netted seventeen hundred signatures in St. John's. Telegrams also came in from a number of outports "with lists of signatures of all the leading people of each district."[99] Though their opponents minimized the numbers, this was fair evidence of public support considering that the 1920 petition drive lasted only three weeks, and the leaders had little money at their disposal. Expanding the petition drive became the central organizing method in New-foundland.

Information about the specifics of the organizing drive outside of St. John's is sparse beyond the fact it existed and spread when the legislature put up resistance. Suffrage leaders certainly travelled to the accessible outports in Conception Bay. Indeed the one sur-viving photograph of their campaign was taken in Carbonear. An account of the initial organizing meeting in Grand Falls has come down to us, however, and the themes, while broadly similar to those in St. John's, were also shaped to local circumstances.

The speaker, Gwendolyn Cooper, had a skilful sense of her audience in the pulp and paper town.[100] In a company town where people had mixed feelings about the main employer, the Anglo-New-foundland Development Company, Mrs. Cooper spoke albeit in a muted way of improving industrial conditions, including the aboli-tion of child labour, which was unregulated in Newfoundland, and "equal recompense for equal labour." She also hoped female voters could impact upon "the high cost of living [which] is a domestic subject," and municipal problems like housing and sanitation. That she raised these issues at all is surprising for her husband was the town superintendent, appointed by the company. What also touched her listener's hearts, however, for she returned to the theme again and again, was a patriotic appeal that women "take more and more intelligent and thoughtful interest in the well-being of the country, and strive to raise it to a place of honour among nations of the world." In a time of economic distress it was a message of hope and improvement. To the timid, the Grand Falls suffragist made this point: "We here as individuals may not feel a desire to take an active part in the government but surely every Newfoundlander must love her country and would wish to do everything in her power for its betterment, and would be willing to sign this petition tonight so that other women . . . should have the opportunity given to them."[101] In effect, the patriotic service of the vote was an extension of the service of the WPA. The next day, following this public meeting, suffrage supporters canvassed the town. Three hundred and ninety-four women signed the petition and only two refused.

In outports dependent upon the fishing economy there was another theme woven into the overall suffrage message, the impor-tance of women's traditional work and yet its simultaneous devaluation. "Most of the working women in Newfoundland work just as hard as the men," proclaimed "Suffragist."

> In the fishing industry carried on in the outports, the women often
> have the hardest and most unpleasant part to do. Besides helping

strenuously with the fish, they have their houses and children to
look after, and help in the fields and gardens as well. As a general
thing they toil longer hours than their husbands, but if the latter—
or the children—are asked, 'What does your mother do?' in nine
out of ten they will reply 'She doesn't do anything; she stays at
home and minds the house.' This is the value placed on woman's
work — the honour and respect paid to it. It is all part and parcel
of the same injustice that classes women with lunatics and convicts
politically, and from the standpoint of citizenship treats them as
slaves.[102]

In raising the issue of the trivialization of women's traditional
distaff work the suffragists were returning with fresh vision to the
themes first outlined by Armine Gosling and Myra Campbell in
discussions at the Ladies' Reading Room before the war. This above
all was an issue that crossed class boundaries. The vote was in part
demanded as an affirmation of distaff roles; women's work was as
difficult and demanding in its own way as men's, and political
equality was a natural consequence. In the aftermath of World War
I in which women's work had proven to be of such demonstrable
value, this was surely a particularly potent appeal.

There were even hints of insurrection: "Were the women of
Newfoundland because they have no status in the eyes of the law,
to withhold all help from churches, schools and institutions, until
the Bill for equal rights were presented, the result can hardly be
realized," wrote a frustrated Agnes Ayre.[103] These moments of
irritation alternated with reassuring appeals that women did not
intend to abandon their roles as mothers and workers, merely
broaden their definitions into new channels of patriotic service and
improvement.

There were also special articles calculated to appeal to Catholic
voters. These appeared in the *Evening Herald*, owned by Sir Patrick
T. McGrath, president of the Legislative Council, and included pro
suffrage arguments from priests reprinted from the British *Catholic
Suffragist*.[104] The notion that the women's vote would raise standards of sexual purity and increase attention to the wants of the child
had particular appeal to the *Herald*, which also argued that by its
devotion to Mary, Catholicism "has placed womanhood on a pinna-
cle undreamt of by any other faith."[105] The vote was merely an
extension of this reverence for women. If there were any lingering
doubts among the religious that women deserved the vote, the
Evening Herald announced on June 10, 1920: "Eve fully Exonerated
from Responsibility." It went on to report that a new translation of
Babylonian tablets at the University of Pennsylvania Museum
showed Noah ate the apple, not Adam, and Eve was not even present

at the time. She thus could not be held responsible for the Fall of Mankind.[106] One suspects this particular argument was not convincing. Nevertheless, the revived Newfoundland women's suffrage movement was remarkable for the degree of support it elicited from Catholic politicians, including Sir Michael Cashin and W.J. Higgins, who in addition to representing St. John's East, was president of the Benevolent Irish Society. The pitfalls of the 1890s were avoided.

Occasionally suffrage appeals contained a disquieting note of class prejudice and racism, as in this letter from "Suffragist" who complained "that educated and intellectual women are classed with idiots and criminals, while the men in the poor-house and Chinese laundrymen in this place can exercise the franchise."[107] However, racist appeals were rare in comparison with suffrage campaigns in the United States and parts of the Canadian mainland for Newfoundland's non-British ethnic population, chiefly Chinese, Jews from Eastern Europe, Syrians, Lebanese, Micmac Indians and French on the west coast were less than one percent of the island's total inhabitants. Most writers assumed a loftier tack stressing such things as women's war work and the higher tone the women's vote would bring to Newfoundland politics.

From the outset of the campaign, suffrage leaders tried to get bipartisan backing for their measure.[108] They first asked the Liberal Prime Minister Richard Squires to present a franchise bill. Having received no reply from Squires, suffrage leaders secured the backing of two members who were known as the veterans' representatives. Sergeant Major F.P. LeGrow (Bay-de-Verde) and Lieutenant H. Small (Burgeo and LaPoile) were both "Blue Puttee Boys"; that is, members of the first contingent of volunteers. Most speakers in the subsequent debate stressed the services Newfoundland women rendered during the war, and hoped they would usher in cleaner politics.[109] As was true in the 1890 campaign, there was an ominous silence from the government side; not one member of the executive spoke in favour. Two weeks later, on a second reading, two Fishermen's Protective Union members, R. Jennings, minister of public works (Twillingate) and J. Guppy (Trinity) led the government attack saying they had not had time to consult their districts. With government Whips on, the measure was defeated by a straight party vote of thirteen Liberals to nine Conservatives.

While Richard Squires never publicly admitted to opposing women's suffrage, his private actions were at variance with his public protestations. More lay behind Jenning's and Guppy's apparently reasonable desires to consult their constituents than meets the eye. The 1920 session opened with charges of criminal misconduct brought against the Prime Minister by opposition leader Sir Michael Cashin. Squires sat for St. John's West, and he was likely very nervous about the direction the women's vote would take with its talk of political purity. Dependent upon Catholic support, he was also pledged to modify Prohibition, which was unpopular in Catholic districts. He may also have calculated that the women's vote would veer toward temperance. Finally, private antagonism toward suffrage underlay his attitude. Suffragists said he treated them contemptuously in private meetings. The Franchise League executive reported on one such meeting: "On being ushered into the Presence, we found the self-constituted arbiter of our destinies seated at the table with his back to us, smoking a cigar. He omitted to rise, or to greet us in any way, continuing to enjoy his cigar, as we seated ourselves at the table."[110] In the same interview Squires gave further offence by remarking that "wine, weeds and women are the three great factors in the world of men!"[111]

Lady Helena Squires (1879–1959)[112] also opposed votes for women. It was a supreme and galling irony to the suffragists that after their victory, Squires offered his wife a safe seat in a Lewisporte by-election, and she became the first female member of the House of Assembly in 1930. Lady Squires' education, speaking ability and intense interest in politics might seem at first glance to have better suited her to the role of suffragist leader than an "anti," but a painful childhood seems to have led this complex and able personality in the opposite direction.[113]

Helena Strong was born in Little Bay Islands, Green Bay, in 1879. One of a twin, from an early age she insisted on equal rights with her brother, Will, and this sense of determination and personal worth endured throughout her life and might well have formed the foundation for suffrage activism had it not been for other events. Helena's mother died shortly after the birth of the twins, and the young girl never got on well with her stepmother. Helena was sent to the Methodist College in St. John's as a boarding student. In her adult life, Lady Squires was unable to establish close relationships with women though she related easily with men.[114]

Helena Strong trained to be a teacher at Mount Allison University in New Brunswick, and married Richard Squires in 1905. She played a key role as his political hostess and confidant and reportedly arranged many deals for her husband. Paradoxically, Lady Squires was recognized as a presence and a charismatic personality by contemporaries even while espousing motherhood and housewifery as woman's proper role. Though she opposed the vote behind the scenes, she nevertheless shared the ideology of her bolder suffrage contemporaries about the importance of homemaking. Indeed, she was attracted to the "scientific housewifery" movement sweeping the United States, and studied Domestic Science at the Farmer Cooking School and Interior Decorating in New York. She lectured on the importance of both to young women in St. John's schools and clubs. When she belatedly converted to suffragism in 1930 it was with the explanation that "I am a mother to my constituents. My M.P. does not stand for Member of Parliament as much as it stands for Mother-Politician."[115] Meanwhile, the suffragists regarded her as an important private obstacle to their success.

Squires did his best through the columns of the *Daily Star*, which he owned, to turn women's suffrage into a class issue. The backers were referred to as "leading society ladies" or "gracious dames of varied types of beauty, some looking as old as they really were, others seemingly younger than their birth register testifies." C.J. Fox, the main legislative proponent, was described as an "ill-bred city snob" whose class considered it "their divine right . . . to be insolent to everybody who comes inside the narrows."[116] Squires, in contrast, was depicted as a stalwart bayman. The *Star* also devoted one half-page to a Bell Island correspondent who asked "how many true born Newfoundland women" wanted the vote? "It would be very valuable," the Bell Islander continued, "before such an important measure is railroaded through the assembly to have the opinion of some of those deep-breasted, red blooded women of Green Bay on the question, or the opinion of sun-tanned hospitable kind hearted women of Placentia Bay . . . . They can have opinions too, and good ones worth having, not given in an acquired accent, nor very drawling, but in good plain English."[117]

Another pro-Squires newspaper, the *Western Star* (Curling), was also hostile, reflecting the same anti-city biases. When petitions circulated in Bay of Islands, it pointed out they originated from St. John's and questioned "if the women of that city care any more for the women of the West Coast or their welfare than the men have shown in the past?"[118] Aside from a few hostile gibes, the *Western Star*, which was the leading West Coast newspaper, had virtually a news blackout on the women's suffrage movement at home and abroad. Even its "Official Synopsis" of House of Assembly debates on the issue was slanted. When women's suffrage eventually passed in 1925, it did not even report the outcome. There was thus ample opportunity for an organized opposition to the suffrage movement to arise as it had in the United States and Europe. However, this did not happen. During the suffrage campaign, Newfoundland women resisted the temptation to divide along class lines, though some hoped they would, including the Prime Minister.

Squires' public speeches on women's rights, however, were lofty enough. He could not afford an open confrontation when many St. John's suffragists had personal connections with members of the Liberal Party and when so many lived, with their voting husbands, in his district. There were also members in his own administration like Warren, Hutchings and Burke who were strong proponents, and married to suffragists. An evasive, tortuous ambiguity marked all of his actions.

If Squires were concerned about the women's vote in 1920, these fears surely increased in 1921. By May he was embroiled in mounting financial scandals. By this same month the suffrage petition drive had garnered ten thousand signatures.[119] Squires could not have been consoled by the words of Fannie McNeil, that "there is no doubt whatever that at least one reason for this movement on the part of our women was the political depravity in all our public affairs."[120]

Mounting evidence of public support for women's suffrage was not, however, enough to propel the measure through the 1921 session. Sir William Coaker, head of the FPU, was favorably disposed; and Jennings, having consulted Twillingate, now agreed to sponsor the bill. But Squires intervened to assert his own control. In a disingenuous manoeuver, he met with Franchise League leaders and offered to sponsor a government bill, allowing women to vote at age twenty-five but debarring them from membership in the House. The League was surprised at this offer but, lulled into a false hope that the conditions Squires had set indicated his seriousness and sincerity, they agreed to withdraw their own measure, which set the franchise at twenty-one and allowed women candidates. Squires subsequently betrayed this agreement and presented the measure as a private member's bill, not a government measure, and did little to shepherd it through the House. A member of his own party moved that women's suffrage be put up to a plebiscite, though this motion was subsequently withdrawn.[121] The referendum trial balloon infuriated suffrage leaders who pointed out that every widening of the number of male voters, including the complete adult male franchise in 1889, had passed by a simple parliamentary bill. The government also raised an important debate on the bill without notice, when its chief opposition supporter, Cyril J. Fox (St. John's East), was absent from the House.[122] Eventually the bill was referred to a hostile Select Committee upon adjournment.[123]

to table the Bill after having definitely pledged themselves to do so.

The women interested would infinitely prefer that the Bill should be made a Government measure during the present Session of the House; but they are determined that it shall be presented this year and if the Government does not see its way to meeting their views in the

To the Hon R. A. Squires K.C.
Prime Minister of Newfoundland.

Sir —

The promoters of the Woman's Suffrage movement beg to draw the attention of the Premier to the incomprehensible attitude of the Government towards the question of the enfranchisement of women, as evidenced in the failure of the two Government members

respect, the Woman's Party will see that it is presented by a member of the Opposition on Friday June 4th

A. M. Gosling
J. Macpherson
Janet Ayre
Mary Kennedy
Fannie McNeil
M. Rennie
Agnes M. Ayre
Helen M. Bard
Anna M. Mitchell
Adeline E. Browning

St Johns
June 2nd 1920

Letter to Sir Richard Squires, 2 June 1920, from women's suffrage supporters asking the Prime Minister to make the enfranchisement of women a government measure during the current session of the House.

Credit: Centre for Newfoundland Studies Archives, Memorial University of Newfoundland.

To the Hon. R.A. Squires K.C.
Prime Minister of Newfoundland

Sir-

The promoters of the Women's Suffrage movement beg to draw the attention of the Premier to the incomprehensible attitude of the Government towards the question of the enfranchisement of women, as evidenced in the failure of the two Government members to table the Bill after having definitely pledged themselves to do so.

The women interested would infinitely prefer that the Bill should be made a Government measure during the present session of the House; but they are determined that it should be presented this year and if the Government does not see its way to meeting their views in this respect, the Woman's Party will see that it is presented by a member of the Opposition on Friday June 4th.

St. John's
June 2nd 1920

A. N. Gosling
M. MacPherson
Janet Ayre
Mary Kennedy
Fannie MacNeil
M. Rennie
Agnes M. Ayre
Helen M. Baird
Anna M. Mitchell
Adeline E. Browning

The Franchise League was momentarily despondent, but outside aid in the form of an important International Alliance of Women speaker, Mrs. Kate Trounson, helped to sustain enthusiasm.[124] In March 1922, Kate Trounson, headquarter's secretary of the Alliance, arrived from London and addressed six meetings in five days in St. John's.[125] The largest and most important was at the Methodist College Hall, the largest auditorium in the city, which was filled to overflowing with a primarily female and enthusiastic audience.[126] Aside from needed publicity and a psychological boost, the Trounson visit also had several practical outcomes. Trounson subsequently arranged for Carrie Chapman Catt, Alliance president, to send the financially beleaguered Newfoundland activists $500 from the Leslie Commission Fund.[127] They had earlier obtained thousands of free pamphlets from Mrs. Catt which they distributed throughout the island. The *Western Star* was unappreciative, condemning them as "foreign importations" and insinuating dire things because they were written in the United States, "the land of easy divorce."[128]

In August 1922, the Alliance ensured that Squires received some negative publicity in London when he attended an imperial conference. An Alliance delegation pursued him to his suite in the Savoy Hotel to lobby him.[129] The *Daily News* also began to carry news items about the progress of the suffrage movement worldwide issued by the International Women's Suffrage Alliance News Service. The Squires' Liberal Reform Party seemed increasingly out of joint with the times.

The Trounson visit also cemented the relationship between the Franchise League and the Alliance. Newfoundland delegates began to attend international feminist conferences. May Kennedy, on a visit to New York, went on to Baltimore in 1922 to represent the island at the Pan-American Congress, sponsored by Catt and the League of Women Voters. In the following year, Kennedy represented Newfoundland at the Rome Congress of the Alliance where she delivered two speeches, one on the same platform as the illustrious British feminist, Chrystal Macmillan.[130] She and Adeline Browning also represented Newfoundland at the Paris Congress of the Alliance in 1926.[131] These international contacts left an ideological and organizational imprint on the Newfoundland movement. As the 1920s progressed, the case for women's suffrage began to be cast with frequent references to American events, history, and personalities. Whole newspaper columns of the Franchise League drew from scripted pieces written by the National American Women's Suffrage Association whose president was also Carrie Chapman Catt. Later suffrage arguments lacked the inventiveness and indigenous shaping of earlier letters and articles. On balance the relationship with the International Alliance of Women was a helpful one, though when its navigational charts were followed too closely, the Newfoundland ship risked losing its way.

As for the progress of the suffrage battle, the cause made no overt headway in 1923 and 1924, though organizing continued "discreetly in the background."[132] In March 1923 the Franchise League won a suffrage debate against the gentlemen of the Methodist College Literary Institute, who had mounted resistance once again.[133] Of more significance, the Honourable J.R. Bennett, leader of the opposition Liberal Progressive Party, made support of women's suffrage part of his election platform. In a further appeal to the women he also pledged assistance to the child welfare and outport nurses movement which this same wave of feminism shaped.[134]

However, Squires was returned to power despite the scandals, on the strength of his industrial development policies in the Humber River Valley. Arguably, the indirect influence of the women's movement was felt in St. John's West, where Squires retained his seat by only four votes, slipping from first to third in the polls in a three-member constituency. Ninety percent of the electorate had gone to the polls.[135] However, it is impossible to disentangle the suffrage factor from the general controversies that swirled about Squires. What is clear is that the Franchise League continued its petition campaign. By May 1923 they claimed to have eighteen thousand signatures,[136] and by 1925 this figure had risen to twenty thousand.[137] The vast majority of signators were women of legal age.

Patiently and methodically collecting this number of signatures was no mean achievement given the social and geographical circumstances. "We wrote to places all over the island. Wrote again, then once more, to ask if letters had been received. Wrote to ask what they were doing about it? . . . Often at Mrs. Goodridge's we licked stamps and envelopes for hours at a stretch," Agnes Ayre reported.[138] Newfoundland methods may have lacked drama but they did not lack effectiveness and involved their own difficulties. The population was highly decentralized, communications systems imperfect, and the illiteracy rate high. Nevertheless, around twenty thousand women were willing to come forward and express support. This represents about thirty percent of the adult female population, an accomplishment that ranks very favourably with the degree of female mobilization in other suffrage movements at the time.[139] It is also five thousand more signatures than the successful prohibition movement gathered in Newfoundland during World War I, and the same number of signatures that the repeal drive garnered in the early 1920s.

1920s women's suffrage supporters, most likely from Carbonear, Newfoundland. Standing, second from left, Fannie McNeil; seated left, Agnes Ayre; seated right, Janet Ayre.

Credit: Gertrude Crosbie.

For a woman, the act of signing a suffrage petition was in itself a culturally heretical act that should not be underestimated by those for whom the expression of political opinions in such a manner is routine. The archives of the Colonial Building contain petitions on a vast variety of subjects which have been sent to the House of Assembly over the years. What is noteworthy is that in the decades before women's suffrage was won, very few ever contained women's signatures or "X"s even when the subjects, such as education or health care, fell within woman's domain. In one rare exception, in 1913, when the "mothers, wives and sisters" of Port au Port petitioned the legislature, along with the men, for an extension of the railway, they felt compelled to apologize that in so doing "we are not suffragettes, and do not believe in the franchise for women."[140] Women were now prepared to sign a petition on their own behalf embracing what only a decade before had been disavowed.

Collecting signatures could expose women to the rude winds of contrary opinion. On one occasion the laborious collecting came to naught. Agnes Ayre recorded this tale: "A friend told me she had spent considerable time collecting the signatures of all the women in her scattered district. One evening in the study, her father, a clergyman, asked: 'What are you seeking, Jane?' 'Did Mrs. Smith leave a package for me to-day, father?' 'Do not trouble yourself to seek further,' he replied, 'I have put it in the fire.' 'You know,' she said, 'Woman Suffrage was like a red rag to a bull to poor pappa. I was so very annoyed I just could not bid him goodnight.'" Though the location of this incident is not identified, it likely was Fortune Bay for that was the only area the legislature had not heard from by 1921.[141]

Some analysts have expressed scepticism about the Franchise League's claims to even seven thousand, five hundred supporters.[142] While prudence is certainly warranted in accepting statistics generated by partisans, corroborating evidence supports the League's claim of twenty thousand signatures. First, the Franchise League had contacts in all the main outports thanks to the WPA branch lists and other connections. Second, the figures released to the public mount yearly, and it is clear from the League's reports to the Alliance that the petition drive continued to be central to their strategy. Finally, supporting evidence comes from the 1925 legislative session when suffrage finally passed.

In 1925 Newfoundland had a new government headed by Walter S. Monroe, leader of the merchant-dominated Liberal-Conservative Party. Squires was temporarily out of office, and indeed lost his seat in the wake of new revelations in the Hollis Walker Report of financial wrongdoing. In this session the franchise bill would almost certainly be passed. The new Prime Minister was a supporter, as were leading members of the Cabinet (Bennett, Higgins and Crosbie). The Franchise League secured official resolutions from the Great War Veterans Association urging the government to pass a bill. Deputations lobbied members before and after the election. They also mobilized the outports. Seven outport members representing five districts mentioned they had been lobbied at home. In Bonavista, Monroe's riding, votes for women had been raised in large meetings; in Ferryland, Peter Cashin reported being lobbied in his house-to-house visits; the Twillingate member G.W. Ashbourne, a veteran and a member of the Fisherman's Protective Union, said he had found the "greatest enthusiasm" for women's suffrage in his district; in Burin, the cautious H.B.C. Lake put the issue before several towns where it was publicly debated, and it was concluded that "the people of Burin are of the opinion that the ladies should have the vote"; two members, J.H. Scammell (St. Barbe) and W.J. Woodford, Minister of Posts and Telegraphs (Harbour Main), publicly recognized their reliance on women campaign workers, though the former reported apathy in the remote north. These speeches suggest that twenty thousand signatures on suffrage petitions is not an unreasonable claim.[143]

It was hard to resist women's demands by 1925. As the *Daily News* noted, Newfoundland and South Africa were the only British Dominions where women remained disenfranchised. Nevertheless, there continued to be moments of anxiety for the suffragists. The Speech from the Throne of the Monroe Government was a sore disappointment for it contained no reference to women's suffrage. A deputation of the Women's Franchise League followed, and Prime Minister Monroe agreed, in his own words, "to introduce the measure as a private Bill. Thus he would not demand the support of the members of his party, nor would it receive . . . the opposition of the other side of the House because a member of the Government side had introduced it."[144]

The terms of the subsequent franchise bill were marked by caution. There were two models of enfranchisement with which Monroe was familiar. In Britain the electoral reform bill of 1918 had enfranchised women at age thirty, while men could vote at age twenty-one. Women were in a demographic majority in Britain and the unequal franchise had been a method of preserving male political dominance. Members of Parliament had expressed fears about the sudden expansion of the franchise to an inexperienced and untrustworthy female electorate. The Canadian precedent, on the other hand, was one in which women received the franchise at the same age as men, namely twenty-one.

Prime Minister Monroe opted for what he considered to be the "happy medium" of age twenty-five. He considered thirty too advanced an age for "many young maidens just past the thirtieth mile post [would] be a little delicate about advertising the fact by their appearance in a public booth," and hence would not vote. However, he believed twenty-one was too young an age for either men or women. Twenty-five was his compromise. His bill also gave women the right to be elected to the House of Assembly.[145] The *Daily News* approved of the age disparity believing "a four year apprenticeship in politics is likely to prove beneficial."[146] The suffragists, though doubtlessly disappointed, apparently raised no public objections.

In the subsequent debate there was continuing nervousness on the part of some about the direction the women's vote would take. This uncertainty may help to explain why no member objected to the unequal terms of the new franchise. The women's vote was unpredictable, and less susceptible to one common form of bribery in Newfoundland elections: free rum at the polls. By some calculations, the merchant party of Walter Monroe might have expected to reap benefits. However, Franchise League leaders were often to the left of their class arguing for government intervention in prices, housing, sanitation, health services and child welfare, and some aligned themselves with the Liberals, despite Squires. Still, the Squires party had been pilloried for its "unparalleled duplicity," and if the rhetoric of the suffrage leaders was to be believed, they on balance had more to fear. Fear of retribution at the polls may have motivated A.E. Hickman (Harbour Grace), the opposition leader, to try to amend the act to permit male voters working seasonally in the Humber and on Bell Island to cast absentee ballots. Those votes, estimated at fifteen hundred, would likely go to the opposition and perhaps partially offset any angered women. Hickman demanded "whether it is right or not that men of this country who are compelled to leave their homes to earn a livelihood for their wives and their families should be disenfranchised."[147] However, the opposition did not want to risk delaying the bill further and withdrew the amendment. In April 1925, the bill finally passed unanimously through the House of Assembly and the Legislative Council (Upper House). Newfoundland women had finally won the franchise.

Resolutions of congratulations poured in from feminists all over the world. Pictures of Armine Gosling appeared on the front page of the next edition of *Jus Suffragi* to encourage disenfranchised women all over the globe to struggle on. In the fallow suffrage years of the mid 1920s a great deal was made of the Newfoundland victory, and in 1926 Newfoundland's delegates were the toasts of the Paris Congress.[148]

At home the suffragists celebrated with a victory banquet. It was a "woman-only" event held at Smithville on April 21st, 1925. The large banquet hall was "filled to the utmost." The Franchise League announced ambitious political plans to an enthusiastic audience seated at tables decorated with bouquets of sweet peas and spring chicks bearing yellow ribbons emblazoned with the words "Votes for Women." Between the many toasts to King, Country and "Absent Friends," and the entertainment provided by talented and sympathetic soloists, the Franchise League announced its transformation into a new League of Women Voters. The vote had been won, but suffragists were clear that now what mattered was how it was used. The League of Women Voters was to be non partisan, pledged only to work for progressive legislation. Representatives of many women's charitable and civic societies were added to the new executive committee. May Kennedy unveiled the forward-looking agenda:

> We stand for honest government, for compulsory education, for equal rights for rich and poor, for work and good wages for all. We shall make no political intrigue. We shall not disturb the peace of Newfoundland. Though we differ in many things—in religion, in race, in politics—we shall be a unit in our demand for a woman's share in all privileges, opportunities and responsibilities this country has to offer.[149]

This was a millennial vision. And even on the eve of the celebration, there was a disquieting note—no member of the press was present, signifying the powerful role of the media as gatekeepers in assisting or hindering a social movement. But at that hour in 1925 this generation of feminist activists could rejoice in what they had accomplished. They had won the vote in a petition campaign that had crossed, at least temporarily, religious, class and geographical lines to a remarkable degree. They had been accepted as peers by international feminist leaders of their day.

In subsequent years, though women did not vote as a block as the League had hoped, in their first island-wide election in 1928, the suffragists could nevertheless take satisfaction at the turnout: 52,343 women voted out of about 58,000 who were eligible, for roughly a ninety percent participation rate.[150] The vote was clearly not regarded as trivial by those who had just won it. Sadly, the tale of the League of Women Voters was to be a short one.

In 1933, faced with impending bankruptcy from the deepening Great Depression, the newly-elected government of Frederick Alderdice agreed to the suspension of Responsible Government. A "Commission of Government," consisting of three British and three Newfoundland Commissioners with the governor presiding, was appointed by Whitehall. This body assumed both executive and legislative functions. Voting was at an end, at least for a time.

Newfoundland's solvency was to return with the economic boom born of World War II, and in June 1946 Newfoundland's citizens elected a National Convention to discuss their future constitutional fate. In 1948 there were two hotly contested referenda on the issue and Confederation with Canada narrowly carried the day. In these elections, by action of the Commission, women voted on an equal footing with men. However, in the interim, the League of Women Voters had disappeared; its leaders were either too elderly or too absorbed in other causes to revive it. The disruption of democracy in Newfoundland and the devastating poverty of the thirties turned the attention of suffrage leaders to older, more familiar paths of women's activism: charities, civic groups, church organizations and the demands of family in difficult times. Women lost momentum as an organized political force.

Nevertheless, the WCTU pioneers and their Women's Franchise League successors had made the way easier for the generations of Newfoundland women that followed them. For the vote was a powerful symbol of altered power relations between women and men, a partial validation of women's roles and work, and a broadening of the female sphere. Both proponents and opponents realized these wider implications, which was why resistance had been so strong over so many years.

An anonymous Franchise League writer eloquently stated what the demand for the ballot had meant for her generation:

> It is no mad desire on the part of women to put a piece of paper in the ballot box. It is not the vote only that they seek, but what the ballot means—that freedom for which men have been fighting for all these many generations, the moral, mental, economic, and spiritual enfranchisement which political enfranchisement would help bring to pass.[151]

The beleaguered 1890s suffragists and their triumphant 1920s successors had challenged and modified a world view of what was appropriate female and male behaviour. Both generations had made a significant contribution to the slow and ongoing process of social justice. While suffragists' hopes and expectations for a dramatic transformation of society for the better were not met, and the suspension of democracy was a bitter though temporary blow, Newfoundland society would never be quite the same.

A Woman's Lot   3

Women and Law in Newfoundland from Early Settlement to the Twentieth Century*

Linda Cullum and Maeve Baird, with the assistance of Cynthia Penney

I. INTRODUCTION

The lives and experiences of women in the history of Newfoundland have remained hidden until relatively recently. Few research projects have focused on uncovering their role in the settlement, growth and development of Newfoundland. Rather, in much of the historical writing on Newfoundland, women appear as wives, daughters or "makers of fish," without stories of their own. Discovering individual lives by collecting oral history, compiling ethnographic accounts of women's lives, and researching the actual lived experiences of women remains to be done.

Primary research on the development of laws affecting women in Newfoundland and Labrador from its days as a colony of Britain, until its Confederation with Canada has not been tackled until now. This essay attempts to enrich our understanding of the ways in which laws influenced and shaped the lives of Newfoundland women.

The scope of the work is ambitious, covering the seventeenth to the twentieth centuries and a wide range of sources have been called upon: the legal history of Canada and England; case and statute law applicable to women in Newfoundland; government archival documents and court records; ethnographic studies of life in Newfoundland; newspapers from the 1800s to the 1980s; studies in the economic history of Newfoundland. Feminist analysis of both law and Canadian women's history have all provided valuable information in piecing this essay together.

Despite this array of sources, little primary research into women's legal history has occurred to date. Ethnographic accounts generally do not discuss events such as infanticide, sexual assault, separation or divorce and the struggles of women's lives have been omitted. Thus, locating women's own words on delicate issues such as these has been a difficult task. Fundamental to the absence of women's experiences is the continuing patriarchal structure of society and its institutions, including the newspapers and the law courts. Women were, and are, represented in narrow and limited ways, often with little input from themselves.

There are, however, some exceptions to the problem of locating information that describes and analyzes women's historical experiences. Statistical evidence, particularly regarding women's work in St. John's, is now available in Nancy Forestell's 1987 Master's thesis. Her data, based on a systematic sample of every third household containing a working woman, provides an invaluable "snapshot" of the lives and conditions of women's work in St. John's in the 1920s and 1930s.[1] Unfortunately, rich material such as this does not exist for other time periods or for much of rural Newfoundland.

Finally, most of the documented history of Newfoundland women describes the lives of English-speaking, white, upper-class and working-class women from St. John's or the lives and work of outport women. The few collections touching the lives of middle-class women or French-speaking women have been consulted in the hopes of including a broader perspective on women's lives. The lives and experiences of First Nations women in Newfoundland are not included in this essay due to the paucity of sources.

Laws affect women at every stage of their life cycle, often reflecting the dependent position in which most women have found themselves. In light of this, the structure of this essay acknowledges women's life cycle from childhood to old age and widowhood and explores the laws affecting women at each of these stages. Section II outlines the evolution of settlement in Newfoundland, views on women as settlers and the development of law in relation to settlement, the fishery and as a colony of Britain. Section III examines the experience of childhood for Newfoundland children, focusing on the experience of girls and young women. While laws were generally applicable to children regardless of sex, females played a distinct role in the Newfoundland home and community. In Section IV, the focus shifts from childhood to the adult world. The experiences of single and married women at home, at work and in relationships are considered. The laws created to protect women in the case of desertion or divorce and from violence are examined in Section V. Finally, in Section VI, the later years of a woman's life, especially following desertion, divorce or widowhood, are traced.

II. "SO LONGE AS THERE COMES NOE WOMEN": EARLY LAWMAKING

The development of early law in Newfoundland under British aegis was complex. This was due, in part, to the "informality and chaos of English government during the [seventeenth] century."[2] Early British settlers in Newfoundland, as elsewhere, were deemed to be bound by the criminal laws of England, including both common law and statute law in force at the time of settlement. In addition, letters of patent and Royal Charters established laws governing settlement in specific areas.[3] Over time, trade laws or Navigation Acts and various admiralty laws dealing with maritime issues were also enacted.

Economic and business concerns motivated the enactment of the earliest laws specifically pertaining to Newfoundland. Many of these laws were related to settlement and fishery issues, exclusively men's concerns; few were directed towards women. Matthews notes that "[L]aw was not some abstract means of regulating society, but a club with which private interests could be advanced."[4] Laws applicable to Newfoundland were passed in the English Parliament in response to pressure from private citizens or groups seeking to secure their own economic gain within the fishery. Generally the laws encouraged the migratory fishery and discouraged the expansion of settlement.[5] Royal Charters were granted to incorporated companies or individuals seeking to profit from the Newfoundland fishery by establishing limited, permanent settlements on the island.[6] Each of the charters stipulated the land area of the colony, as well as the government form and laws to be followed. A number of orders-in-council altering the Royal Charters were passed in England during the latter half of the seventeenth century. Successful enforcement of these orders or the laws established by Royal Charters seldom occurred due to the distance between England and Newfoundland and the lack of respect for laws which protected private interests. Left in the hands of merchant and fishing interests, the laws enacted had little positive impact on the settlement and development of Newfoundland during this period.[7]

The fishery received most attention in the development of law because of its economic importance to Britain. From its early days as a base for the British "floater fishery," Newfoundland was governed by the Fishing Admiral system of administering justice which developed by custom and tradition. The first captain to reach each harbour at the start of the spring fishing season became the "Fishing Admiral" charged with enforcing British law in the Island and Labrador fisheries.[8] The admirals could rule on most civil and criminal cases which arose between ships or between men, except for capital crimes of murder or theft up to forty shillings. These prosecutions were to be handled in England, with the understanding that two witnesses would travel overseas at their own expense to participate in the English trial.[9] Matthews notes that men convicted of other serious crimes could be executed in Newfoundland but most were sent back to England or Ireland to be hanged.[10] Although the Fishing Admirals were found to be partial in their judgements and more interested in catching fish than administering justice, the system remained in place for the next century.

King William's Act of 1699 determined the legal framework governing Newfoundland for the next one hundred years. Essentially, the act was concerned only with the fishery, but it confirmed and formalized the rules and regulations existing as the system of law.[11] The act did not include penalties for offences and only provided for a local judicial system during the seasonal migratory fishery.[12] While settlement was recognized in the act, the provisions were not designed to meet the needs of permanent settlers but those of merchants and businessmen with economic influence in England.

Permanent settlements slowly grew in Newfoundland. By 1677, female settlers consisted of ninety-four wives, one hundred and thirty daughters and thirteen female servants, some twelve percent of the inhabitants.[13] Initially, women came as wives or daughters of planters and boatkeepers[14] or arrived as passengers, marrying fishermen already established in the colony. The intermarriage of Newfoundland women and fishing servants from overseas was an important component in the creation of families in the early days of settlement.[15]

English merchants opposed to settlement employed the age-old argument of the inherent immorality of women and their potentially corrupting influence on men. Seeking to protect their investments in the Newfoundland-based fishery, merchants objected in 1670 to the arrival of women, claiming planters "[used] 'their womenfolk to debauch ignorant mariners.'"[16] Their concern about women settlers actually arose from the belief that without women, fishermen and

Palliser's Proclamation of 1764.

Credit: Provincial Archives of Newfoundland and Labrador.

Order for Masters of Merchtmen
not to Land any Women here, without
first giving Security for their good
behaviour etc.

By His Excellency Hugh Palliser
Governor Etc.

Whereas great Numbers of Poor Women are frequently
brought into this Country, and Particularly into this Port by
Vessels arriving from Ireland, who become distress'd and a
Charge to the Inhabitants and likewise Occasion much disorder
and Disturbance against the Peace of our Sovereign Lord the
King -

Notice is hereby given to all Masters of Vessels arriving
in this Country that from the First day of April next no Women
are to be Landed without Security being first given for their
good behaviour and that they shall not become Chargable to the
Inhabitants.

By Command of His Excellency

Jn Horsnaill
Given under my Hand at St. John's
2 July 1764 HP.

planters would not settle permanently in Newfoundland, securing for themselves the best fish processing locations around the coast. This practice of "wintering over" was perceived as an economic threat to the absentee British merchants. Addressing this concern, Captain Francis Wheler, master of H.M.S. Tiger reported back to England in 1684, "'so longe as there comes noe women they are not fixed.'"[17] Nevertheless, as an ongoing policy, discouraging female settlers was not very effective. By 1750, some 6,900 people lived on the island, 2,696 of them year-round residents. Of these, 931 were adult women.[18]

Women are seldom mentioned in official records or documents from this time. When issues related to women do appear in the record, they are in the form of prescriptive proclamations. Such proclamations appeared in both the 1760s and the early 1800s. In both instances, governors attempted to have women, whom they believed had become a charge on the inhabitants of the colony, returned to British Dominions by vessels leaving Newfoundland. The governors alleged great numbers of poor women were stranded in the colony, although official statistics for both time periods indicate little increase in female population. By 1805, there were only forty females for every one hundred men and by 1830, men still outnumbered women by more than two to one.[19] Records also show that while women may have been widowed or left alone on the island, most of those remarried. Some continued to gain a living from the fishery and others took whatever work was available to them as laundresses, cooks, boarding-house keepers, domestics or tavern-keepers. Daughters who had married and remained in Newfoundland also inherited property from their planter fathers who had retired to England.[20] As we can see from historical records, women played an important role in the permanent settlement and growth of early Newfoundland.

Newfoundland was governed by a plethora of laws and throughout the eighteenth century the legal system administering these laws also became more complex. Winter magistrates sat year round and heard every civil and criminal case brought before them. A Vice-Admiralty Court heard cases concerning smuggling, piracy and privateering and cases involving debt and landed property. Customs officers were appointed for outports and commissioners, naval governors and officers held legal appointments by the 1770s. As long as these courts did not challenge the jurisdiction of the fishing admirals under King William's Act of 1699, they were able to answer the legal needs of Newfoundland by adapting contemporary English norms to local circumstances.[21]

Both criminal and civil cases arose in Newfoundland. Criminal cases were generally dealt with under English law by jury trial. The sentences imposed by courts in Newfoundland tended to be fines rather than jail since the fines and penalties supported the officers, courts and jails in Newfoundland. Civil law, involving private disputes, was not specifically outlined for Newfoundland in legislation. As well, Fishing Admirals and magistrates often lacked clear understanding of the English common law they were to uphold. In this vacuum, civil law developed in Newfoundland on the basis of "common sense and judgement [of the magistrates and Fishing Admirals] as to what was fair and fitting to the fishery." Thus, Newfoundland common law practice differed from that of England.[22]

By 1788 the justice system in Newfoundland was complex, yet illegally administered because the various magistrates and courts made judgements in areas over which they had no jurisdiction.[23] The growth in permanent settlement in the late eighteenth century had brought increasing complexity to merchant dealings in the Island. The legal system no longer functioned effectively as much of its structure rested on an improperly constituted legal system. Decisions made in Newfoundland civil cases could be, and were, struck down by courts in England. In 1791 the first Judicature Act was created and in the following year, 1792, new courts, rooted in statutory law and legally constituted, were developed to deal with increasingly difficult civil cases.[24] Matthews has observed that by the end of the eighteenth century, "criminal and constitutional law were adequately provided for and rested either on English practice or parliamentary legislation."[25]

In 1824, Newfoundland became an official colony of Britain. The laws protecting private interests developed during early use and settlement of Newfoundland were rescinded. A civil governor, Sir Thomas Cochrane, and an official council were appointed and the Supreme Court was revised and extended.[26] Finally, in 1832, Newfoundland became a self-governing colony of Britain. A House of Assembly, under a system of Representative Government was established.[27] Statute laws were passed by the legislature of Newfoundland, and vetted in Britain before being given formal royal assent. The governors of the colony, appointed by Britain, kept the British government abreast of developments, so few laws sent to Britain for approval were refused.[28]

On November 18, 1837, the governor, council and assembly of Newfoundland enacted An Act to extend the Criminal Laws of England to the colony under certain modifications.[29] By this enactment, Newfoundland adopted the criminal laws of England then in force, and applied them to Newfoundland. As well, any criminal laws passed in England after 1837 were to be extended to Newfoundland twelve months later. Fines and penalties imposed by criminal laws were to be distributed in the following manner:

> . . . one half to the Informer and the other Half to her Majesty, Her Heirs and Successors, to be paid into the Public Treasury, to and for the use of this Island.[30]

With the adoption of England's criminal laws, Newfoundland had the basis of its legal system in place. During the next one hundred and twelve years, until Newfoundland became part of Canada in 1949, the local government would enact new laws, amend some of those inherited from England and repeal others. It is important to note, however, that the criminal laws of England prevailed in Newfoundland until 1949. No Newfoundland statutes pertaining to criminal law were enacted.[31] In 1949, Newfoundland joined Canada and came under the Canadian Criminal Code.

The evolution and development of law is an intricate process. Common law, based on custom, usage and judicial decisions, may be changed in two ways: through case law as judges interpret current laws and write decisions which set precedents for future cases; by statute law enacted through legislation in response to changing social conditions and public opinion. Statute law is then interpreted by judges in the same manner as case law.[32] It has long been recognized that the personal attitudes held by judges are reflected in the severity of sentencing and the building of case law.[33] In 1985, writing on the experiences of women in New Brunswick, Elspeth Tulloch noted:

> Like all law, English common law reflected attitudes towards women which were narrow and riddled with misconceptions and prejudices. As those attitudes slowly changed, so did the law.[34]

At every stage of a woman's life, civil and criminal laws have a direct impact. These laws determine women's rights and status in society, whether single or married: the right to own and dispose of personal property; the right to vote; to be protected from violent actions against them; the right to a fair wage in a job for which they are qualified, and much more. In establishing these rights, the law has reflected society's view of women. Women have been treated differently than men in our society. We have been seen as passive creatures, requiring the protection and guardianship of men. Many women have led lives circumscribed by this restrictive, stereotypical view of females as weaker vessels, less competent in the world than their male counterparts. Numerous laws are rooted in the belief that women were, and are, the chattels of men, possessions to do with as men wished. With this prejudicial view, male legislators gave to men responsibilities considered too onerous for women: the right to vote, to sit on juries, to have custody of children, control of property and money or to run for public office. In this way the patriarchal attitudes of the general public, judges and legislators have shaped the legal rights, and therefore, the lives of women.

However, while women have been barred from participation and control in the legal process for many years, we have been present as the accused, the accuser and as witnesses in the courtroom. Women's lives have been radically altered by their experiences with the law. This essay looks at some of those experiences and major developments in law from the seventeenth to the twentieth centuries in Newfoundland.

III. THE CHILDHOOD YEARS

In her father's house, a female child, like her brothers, gained whatever security and status was accorded their father's position in society. The rights and liabilities of children were similar, regardless of sex. Under English common law, children were considered "infants" until they reached the age of twenty-one, and so lived under the sole legal guardianship of their father.[35] A mother retained no rights to custody or to determine the religious education of her children. In November 1891, the Honourable Mr. Justice Pinsent upheld the father's right of custody in a decision regarding the custody of nine-year-old John Congdon. John's father, Richard Congdon, was declared to have "first title," while the mother, Catherine Congdon, was declared to have "the second." The judge ruled, in part that:

> The right of the father is considered so paramount that nothing can deprive him of it nor afford an answer to his suit for delivery of the person of his children . . . .[36]

In this case, Richard Congdon had died and thus the judge ruled that the rights of the surviving mother were absolute. Catherine Congdon retained both legal custody and the right to determine the religious education of her son, John.

A father's proprietorship over his children is also reflected in a court case from 1915. In November of that year, Thomas Laracy of Harbour Main sued the magistrate and police sergeant of Harbour Main for two thousand dollars for the wrongful arrest and imprisonment of his twelve-year-old daughter Nora and her two sisters. A complaint had been laid against the sisters alleging that they had broken glass in a Harbour Main house. Laracy's lawyer argued that "no money verdict could satisfy the parents for the wrong done to the children."[37] The emphasis during the trial was the redress to the parents, not to the children. The jury agreed and awarded Laracy the verdict.

In 1922, Sir William Horwood, administrator, Government House wrote to Winston S. Churchill in London, England regarding the matter of joint guardianship of children:

> . . . in relation to the guardianship of infant children, I have the honour to intimate that the Department of Justice reports that we have no legislation of this character—the joint guardianship of father and mother over infant children is not practised in this Colony.[38]

In the absence of legislation stating otherwise in 1922, the authority of the father was still deemed paramount in Newfoundland. Although legislation stipulating joint guardianship did not exist, some courts took into consideration the happiness and welfare of children when deciding custody cases. As early as the mid-1800s, children of sufficient age were consulted to determine their wishes in their own custody cases.[39] Chief Justice Brady, ruling in the 1849 custody case of thirteen-year-old Sarah Jane Harvey, noted in his written decision that upon discussing her life with Sarah Jane, she stated "she was as happy as she could wish to be, and she expressed the strongest desire to remain with her [aunt and uncle]."[40] Guardianship was awarded to Sarah Jane's aunt and uncle. Another reported case from 1861 also supported the welfare of the child, four-year-old Harriet Sophia Rutherford, by awarding guardianship to her grandparents on the basis of the "tenderness and care" displayed toward the child.[41] Crucial in both of these cases was the consideration by the courts of its duty toward an infant ward of the court. In the Rutherford case, Justice Robinson noted that "it is a well understood and obvious principle that the court will not suffer its ward to be carried beyond its jurisdiction" in order that the court should retain control over the fate of the child.[42]

Subsequent court cases reflect an evolution in the application of the rule of guardianship. Over many years, and through litigation rather than legislation, guardianship evolved to custody, and the welfare of the child was given paramount consideration.[43] In custody cases heard in 1927 and in 1929, the welfare of the child was given prime consideration rather than the right of the father.[44]

Legislation was eventually introduced to address the question of custody of children, initially through the Health and Public Welfare Act of 1931.[45] In 1952, the Newfoundland Judicature Act established the equality of parents in application for custody.[46] In the case of a young child, "the natural love and confidence of a child towards its mother" was deemed to weigh heavily in favour of the mother's custody.[47] Finally, in 1964, the Child Welfare Act[48] brought Newfoundland legislation concerning custody of children into line with other jurisdictions. This Act asserts ". . . the welfare of the child as the first and paramount consideration . . . ."[49]

Newfoundland appears to have lagged behind other jurisdictions regarding the enactment of equitable custody legislation. In Canada, judicial decisions of the 1880s indicated a changing attitude toward the role of mothers and their right to custody. In 1887, Ontario introduced An Act respecting the Guardianship of Minors which included a requirement for judges "to consider 'the welfare of the infant,' 'the conduct of the parents,' and 'the wishes as well of the mother as of the father.'"[50] Children were no longer viewed as simply property of the father. In the evolution of child custody laws we can glimpse the power of individual judicial decisions in the lives of children and the place these decisions may have had in establishing precedents for change.

Patriarchal attitudes were evident not only among the legislators or in the courts. The authority of the father over his children was reinforced and supported by the views of society. Respected institutions in the community often echoed the feelings of the majority. In a discussion of amendments to the Welfare of Children Act of 1944, the Right Reverend G.F. Bartlett of St. Michael's Presbytery on Bell Island addressed the question of children and the authority of the father:

> . . . many fathers leave their homes in the evening seeking the comradeship they have missed during the day. Since it is largely the father's authority which rules and governs most homes, in his absence the children must be less rigorously reared.[51]

That a mother would be capable of responsible rearing of her children was not considered by Reverend Bartlett. Her role was to provide offspring and heirs for her husband, not to have authority over them.

Given the legal control allowed fathers for so long, it appears logical that children also derived their citizenship from their father. Until 1977, with the introduction of The Canadian Citizenship Act, this was the case. With this act, the mother was given the right to choose Canadian citizenship for her children.[52]

Even if their legal status was similar, the roles male and female children played in the family were quite different. In the outport family home, children of both sexes often had work to do, indoors and out. For girls and young women, housework occupied a great deal of time. Bread making, polishing the family shoes, cleaning cutlery on Saturday and scrubbing the floors and the threshold with sand and a spruce bough scrubbing brush were the main tasks assigned to girls in many outport homes. Tending younger sisters and brothers was an ever-present duty. Outdoor work for females included "picking" grass, weeding the garden, berry-picking and, if the family fished, working on the fish flakes or drying caplin.[53] One Stephenville woman who never married, recalled her mother's philosophy regarding these chores. She commented, "'Mother said it was all good practice for when you got married and had babies of your own.'"[54] All of these activities also contributed to the family economy. By law, a child's labour and any wages or earnings arising as a result of their labour were the father's to appropriate.[55] Throughout the nineteenth century, suits to obtain the wages of female workers certainly occurred.[56] Both fathers and individual women resorted to the courts for settlement. However, because a father's name appears in the court records as the complainant, we should not assume that the father claimed the wages on his own behalf. Given the patriarchal structure of the court system, a male complainant may have had a better chance for success in pressing for the restitution of wages than a female. As a result, it is the father's name which appears in the court record. Unfortunately, court records do not provide an insight into the final dispersement of any settlement.

If her mother was incapacitated or dead, a young girl may have been required to assume the role of woman of the family. She may have taken on the responsibility of providing her father, brothers and sisters with food, clothing and nurturing normally undertaken by her mother. Some women have described their responsibilities in this regard as "regular maid's work."[57]

Young women may have found the constraints of home life under their father's rule somewhat of a trial. A woman from Stephenville, born in 1903, reflected on her lot as a young woman.

> My father was awful strict with the girls. I cried my heart out more than once having to stay home from a wedding or garden party to look after the house and the little ones. Here in Stephenville not too darn many women were allowed to go anywhere farther than Church on Sundays.[58]

The limitations of an early life spent tending to the needs of others could be deeply felt. The Evening Herald ran a four paragraph story on one young woman's bid for greater freedom in 1895.

> A young girl, 17 years of age, left her home at Petty Harbour Sunday morning and walked to the city. She had no cause for leaving beyond the fact that she desired more freedom in her movements than could be obtained under the argus eyes of her relatives.[59]

In an effort to return her to the family home, her father went to St. John's. She was eventually returned home by her father after the police arrested her in the city.

Freedom for females was not the rule. Work in the home began early in life and was firmly enforced. As sole legal guardian, a father could give his children up for adoption or apprentice them to others. He also had the liberty to provide them with whatever formal and religious education he wished.[60] In some communities, female children were often removed from school, if they attended at all, and put to work under the supervision of female relatives.

There were few formal restrictions prohibiting education for women. However, it was not always the custom for women to receive extensive education. Not every family placed a high value on schooling. Nor could every family afford the loss of a child's labour or wages during the school term or the outlay of cash to provide an education. Further, with education at the discretion of the father, the importance of education for young girls may not have been recognized. For instance, in Elliston, Bonavista Bay, one young girl was allowed to attend school only during the winter when she lived with her aunt or married sister. When she reached grade two, "her father decided she was educated enough and kept her out of school although she wanted to stay." By the time she was ten, the young girl was doing "women's work" in her family.[61]

Formal schools existed early in the 1800s in Newfoundland, generally located near larger population centres. Many provided only a minimal education with reading, writing and arithmetic, some grammar and composition as the main subjects. Even at school, the young women were often required to perform traditional "women's" tasks such as sweeping and dusting. Sitting in cold classrooms, on hard wooden benches, with few textbooks, little paper and no blackboards, made education an arduous task for even the most favoured child.[62]

The Presentation Order of Sisters established a school in a converted St. John's tavern, the 'Rising Sun,' in October 1833. When it closed in December of 1833, a new convent and school was opened on Nunnery Hill in St. John's. This school ran for eight years and educated over one thousand students.[63] However, despite the existence of schools, there were no compulsory attendance regulations in force and only a privileged few could afford the fees for their children's education. As noted above, low enrolment in early schools may also be attributed to the lack of desire on the part of parents to have their children educated, particularly their female children.[64]

As early as 1836, the legislature of Newfoundland was concerned with the promotion of education in Newfoundland. Under An Act for the encouragement of Education in this Colony passed in May of 1836, the Government set aside monies for "the establishment and support of Elementary Schools throughout this Island . . . ."[65] The individual grants of money were distributed in several electoral districts. This was followed in 1844 by An Act to Provide for the Establishment of an Academy at St. John's because it was deemed "desirable that an Academy should be established at St. John's for the instruction of youth in the several branches of Scientific and Classical Learning."[66]

Shortly after the enactment of the Education Act of 1844, the Church of England founded an educational institution solely for young women. The Diocesan Girl's School established in 1845 became The Church of England Girl's School in 1857, and then the Synod Girl's School after 1887. Following the Great Fire of 1892, Bishop Spencer College was built[67] and provided a place of education for thousands of female students.

Ellen Carbery (1845–1915), businesswoman and poet from Turk's Cove, Trinity Bay, was educated by the Presentation Sisters at the Convent School in Harbour Grace between 1856 and 1863. This school was based on the National School system of Ireland and received special accolades for its high standard of education. The curriculum was extensive for the day, including "Reading, Writing, Arithmetic, Grammar, Geography, Spinning (both flax and wool), knitting (both plain and fancy), and embroidery. Weaving is taught also . . . ."[68] Practical accomplishments for women were still very important. Ellen Carbery was fortunate to live with her uncle William Talbot, who was very active politically, culturally and socially during the 1850s. Thus Ellen was exposed to an extensive education, both formal and informal, usually accessible only to the upper class of Newfoundland society in the nineteenth century.

The situation of schooling in Newfoundland for the wealthier classes was improved somewhat by the late 1800s. In 1884, Littledale Academy, a Roman Catholic boarding school for girls was founded in St. John's. Prior to this time, it had become common practice for children of wealthier families to attend private schools in England or Canada.[69]

For working class children in St. John's during the 1920s and '30s, without compulsory education laws nor the money to pay school fees, formal education was often a brief interlude in their lives.[70] One school which provided scholarships for young women whose families could not afford school fees was Bishop Spencer College.[71] Run by Miss Violet Cherrington between 1922 and 1952,[72] the pupils came from a variety of class backgrounds.

> We had children of plumbers, we had children of stevedores and workers down in the shipping place on Water Street, we had children of electricians, we had fishermen's children from the Battery, some very good children, too . . . I don't think you could leave out any social background here in St. John's that wasn't in that school.[73]

Bishop Spencer College emphasised what might be termed "feminine" virtues. Violet Cherrington liked her pupils "to be able to express themselves and the girls to be able to help in the community, to help in the school; she stressed good manners, good speaking." Being good wives and mothers was Miss Cherrington's goal for her students. The very practical curriculum included domestic science, to make good homemakers, and a secretarial course.[74]

Children of both sexes living in more rural areas of Newfoundland often did not have the same year-round access to a school or teachers. The seasonal variations in the family economic cycle could mean that the family would be elsewhere than their home harbour during the school year. Greta Hussey writes of her experience with schooling in the 1920s in rural Newfoundland and on the Labrador coast.

> We had to leave home before school ended in Hibbs Cove and didn't return home until after classes had started. This caused us to miss about two and a half months of our school year. Some summers, we went to school at Batteau; that is, when the Newfoundland school board could get a qualified person to come to that isolated harbour to teach the Labrador children to read and write. My sister and I went along and this helped to supplement our meagre education.[75]

Greta Hussey notes that in order to pay for tuition and board, fathers of children attending schools cut wood to supply the school.[76]

In their home communities, the organization of work within families, especially fishing families, often meant that female students were the most consistent in their attendance in school. The young men tended to be more transitory, often working in the fishery with their fathers. Both the Wesleyan Methodist Missionary Society and the Society for the Propagation of the Faith established schools in outport communities during the nineteenth century. Unless the family relocated, women's work kept them in the community during the fishing season, so they were the focus of missionary activity.[77]

In Elliston, Bonavista Bay, schooling was a somewhat different experience. Girls and boys appear to have had equal opportunity to attend school in that community. During the early 1900s, well-qualified female teachers taught in Elliston. Children started school at any time in the course of the school term and promotion through the grades was based on the teacher's knowledge of her students. Often female students excelled in their school work, while their brothers dropped out of school.[78] Still, the state of the family finances was reflected in which children attended school. If older children were needed at home to support the family, only the younger children attended school; a poor fishing season might mean none of the children went to school.[79]

It wasn't until 1942 that the School Attendance Act compelled all children over the age of seven and under the age of fourteen to be enroled in school. The minister of St. Michael's Presbytery, Bell Island, noted in 1947 that "the majority of children in our community leave school as soon as possible after their fourteenth birthday and frequently obtain employment . . . ."[80] Under the 1942 act, no child between seven and fourteen years of age was to be "employed for remuneration during school hours" when the school was open for classes.[81] Given the need for additional income to support the family, the curtailment of child labour must have been keenly felt. Undoubtedly, children continued to work in family related labour, even if they did not openly engage in paid labour outside the home.

In 1944, the Welfare of Children Act specifically prohibited "women under the age of seventeen from employment in restaurants and taverns, and waged work for all women between 9 at night and 8 in the morning."[82] The Daily News of October 7, 1947 observed that this provision was included "to assist in the enforcement of the Compulsory Education Act [of 1942] and to protect the morals of young girls, many of whom are said to be constant visitors to certain types of cafes."[83] Once again, as in the days of early settlement, a belief in the inherently immoral potential of females was used to curtail their activities in the community. No mention was made in the news article of the behaviour of young males.

Poverty or early death from accident or epidemics often left children without any means of support. The Newfoundland government found it necessary to pass a statute in 1840: An Act to defray certain charges that have arisen for the support of Aged and Infant Paupers up to the First of February, 1840. In the year of the legislation, fourteen of the twenty-two women who received financial support under this legislation had cared for orphan or poor children. For example, widow Jane Meany received four pence per day for three hundred and six days for her support of Rebecca Ricketts. Mrs. Millon received three pounds, one shilling and four pence for support of Sarah King, a pauper child. In all, the government paid out three hundred and fifty-three pounds, seventeen shillings and seven pence up to February 1840.[84]

Financing individuals in this manner to look after orphaned or destitute children was possible while the population remained relatively small. However, long-term solutions for the care of children were soon required. Religious and charitable institutions played an active role in the development of early orphanages. In 1854, the Sisters of Mercy established the first orphanage in Newfoundland, St. Clare's, on Military Road. Belvedere, the former residence of Bishop Fleming, was opened as an orphanage in 1859 and operated for one hundred and ten years in that capacity.[85]

Sometimes the treatment of indigent children was unduly cruel and insensitive. If parents were absent from the home or deemed unfit, children might be taken away. In Labrador during the late nineteenth and early twentieth centuries, harsh methods were sometimes employed. Wilfred Grenfell, doctor, missionary and influential man of the time, simply took children rather than leave them to the future their own parents could provide.

> He would often take children from their parents . . . Some went to his orphanages; others to foster families in America or Britain. He would persuade destitute families to "sell" him their children in exchange for clothing. Many a screaming child was carried off in this way. Once he took children to a lecture and auctioned them off to the highest bidders in order to raise funds for the Mission.[86]

It is not clear exactly when Grenfell engaged in such activities, nor is the source of the legal authority which allowed him to do so. However, we do know that Grenfell was a man of great power in Labrador. In a 1908 volume of letters written from Labrador, George F. Durgin describes Grenfell as clergyman of the Church of England, a physician and surgeon, and a master mariner. To all these competencies, Durgin adds, "with his powers of magistrate, conferred by the Newfoundland government, he represents the force of the law and brings the guilty to punishment . . . ."[87] Perhaps in his role as magistrate, Grenfell gained the authority to decide the course of children's lives.

In large part, a childhood of carefree play and little responsibility did not exist for children in Newfoundland between the early nineteenth and mid-twentieth centuries. As early as age nine or ten, young women were expected to contribute to the family support, working both in the home and outside of it. In *More Than Fifty Percent*, Hilda Chaulk Murray describes the turn-of-the-century childhood experience of an eighty-one year old woman from Elliston, Bonavista Bay.

> Before the girl had reached her teens she had started to work for a woman who was a practical nurse in the community . . . Whenever there was sickness, she was there to render what help she could, and her "servant girl" usually accompanied her on her rounds.[88]

In some communities, young women were sent to neighbouring communities or as far away as Nova Scotia to work as domestic servants in the homes of relatives.[89]

In Newfoundland, during the first four decades of the twentieth century, there were few child labour laws and no compulsory education laws restricting children's entry into paid labour. Nancy Forestell has noted that:

> Prior to World War II, there was only one piece of legislation in Newfoundland which dealt with minimum age requirements for employment, and none at all covering age of school leaving. The "Mines (Regulation) Act" of 1908 stipulated that no boys under thirteen and no girls or women of any age were allowed to work underground in mines.[90]

According to Wendy Martin, author of a history of mining in Newfoundland, the first recorded mining attempt was in the 1700s, but earlier English explorers had documented the discovery of specific minerals such as pyrite.[91] It was in the nineteenth and twentieth centuries that major mining activity occurred. Zinc, gold, nickel, copper, coal, fluorspar, uranium and iron ore were all successfully mined in Newfoundland at various times. Martin notes, "[N]early every major bay around the Island contains at least one abandoned mine . . . ."[92] Thus, mining may have employed thousands of people in Newfoundland throughout the last two hundred years.

We know little of the intent of the section of the Mines Regulation legislation which pertained to the employment of women and children. There appears to be no record of women being employed underground in Newfoundland mines. Photographs reveal only male faces; boys, some looking less than thirteen years of age are often members of the photographed group of miners.[93] Whether these boys were working underground or at the mine's surface is not entirely clear.

The Proceedings of the House of Assembly reporting discussion prior to the passage of the 1908 Mines Regulation Act reveals concern only for the duties of mine management and the use of explosives. No mention is made of the section prohibiting women and children working underground.[94] That Newfoundland did not originate the legislation is evident. In response to a question regarding the specifics of the legislation, the Minister of Agriculture and Mines responded, "[T]hey simply adopted the form of procedure in England."[95] This may account for the section referring to women and children.

The English Mines and Collieries Act, prohibiting women and girls from underground work had been enacted in 1842.[96] It was passed in response to the national furore raised by the publication of the Children's Employment Commission Report. In the Report, the horrendous working conditions of women in English mines was detailed. Backhouse observes that rather than the harsh working conditions being the subject of public outrage, "femininity and morality were the chief rallying cries."[97] The Report described women who:

> . . . wore a dress more than half masculine, and who talked loudly
> and discordantly, and some of whom, God knows, had faces as hard
> and as brutal as the hardest of their collier brothers and husbands
> and sweethearts.[98]

Female mine workers did not comply with the accepted vision of femininity in nineteenth century England. Licentious behaviour in the mines would surely result if women were allowed to continue their work.

Further prohibitions on the working hours and meal breaks for women in mines were introduced in England in 1872. British Columbia introduced similar legislation in 1877 and Ontario barred women from both underground and surface work in mining in 1890.

There is no indication that similar public outrage or concern motivated the 1908 legislation in Newfoundland. It appears that the government of the day simply adopted the current English legislation in order to deal with a spate of serious mining accidents in Newfoundland.[99] Whether the legislation seriously affected women in Newfoundland is unknown; further research into the history of mining would be required to provide a richer picture. However, the English legislation and its complete adoption, unamended by the Newfoundland government, points to a paternalistic, perhaps class-based, view of some women as innately immoral creatures requiring prescriptive legislation to keep them in an appropriately feminine role.

In the later twentieth century, census records provide further evidence of young women's work in Newfoundland. In 1921, some

69 percent of working women in St. John's were between the ages of fourteen and twenty-four.[100] About 1.7 percent were fourteen years of age and under in 1921. By the 1935 census, only 1 percent of working women were under fourteen years of age. The reasons for young women entering the workforce did not vary much between the census of 1921 and 1935. Although fathers were considered the primary wage earners in the household, most young daughters living at home contributed their earnings to the household in order to supplement their father's wages. In 1926, at fourteen years of age, Jenny Fogwill went to work in a small confectionery store.

> "I went to help out our family. I was the oldest girl and my older brother couldn't get work. Times were hard so I went out to work and it seemed as if that was all I did." Her earnings alone had to feed the family when her father went on strike in the fall of 1932.[101]

In 1915, fifteen-year-old Mary Taylor Norris had begun work at the Newfoundland Knitting Company factory, sewing knitted garments for $4 a week. Her daughter, Dorothy Norris Froggot, went out to work in the Browning-Harvey confectionery factory when she was twelve years old, in 1934. Dorothy's $3.50 a week wages occasionally sustained the Norris household during periods of her father's unemployment in the 1930s. If a family had children deemed to be of working age, they were sent outside the home to engage in paid work. Their mother's labour, which might have brought higher wages, was required in the home to maintain the household and family.[102]

Many young women were employed as domestics in middle- and upper-class homes during the 1920s and 1930s. The 1921 census records 2 percent of the female domestic servants were under the age of fourteen; an amazing 40.7 percent were between the ages of fifteen and nineteen. By 1935, these figures had dropped considerably to less than 1 percent under fourteen and 23.8 percent between fifteen and nineteen.

In St. John's, by the time young women reached the age of seventeen or eighteen, they were often working at adult employment. For example, when Jenny Fogwill was eighteen, she began work on the cash desk with Ayre and Sons.[103] At nineteen, Stella Wiseman began work at the Imperial Tobacco Company in 1937. She worked packing cigarettes for three years.[104]

The lives these young women led, both urban and rural, were not unusual for working class children in the twentieth century. Although childhood was viewed as a distinctive stage of growth and development during this period, those families with fewer financial resources often could not afford to relinquish a child's labour. With the advent of compulsory education laws and the Welfare of Children Act of 1944, a broader range of legislation allowed greater state intervention in the lives of children. The prolonged childhood of today, with early years primarily given over to play and up to twenty years or more of schooling, is quite different from the childhood experienced by many Newfoundland children in the nineteenth and early twentieth centuries.

IV. IN AN ADULT WORLD

Although the legal age of majority varied from fourteen years of age for compulsory school attendance to twenty-one or even twenty-five years for the right to vote, it appears that in Newfoundland most young women had left childhood behind by their mid-teen years. Many, especially working-class women, sought wage employment outside their family home, contributed to the upkeep of the family or married and had families of their own. If they came from middle- or upper-class circumstances and were more financially secure, some young women went on to further education or training.

Generally, women's legal and civil rights have never matched those held by men in our society. The rights of single women approximated those of men, with some distinct qualifications and exclusions. Few laws were drafted to affect single women in particular, although single women were obviously affected by more sweeping legislation. A woman's rights changed drastically upon marriage. In the nineteenth and twentieth centuries, most women in Newfoundland married, thus the legal inequities which limited the rights of married women affected most women.

One of the most profound legal inequities was the denial of "personhood" to women. With this restriction, women, whether married or single, were not permitted to sit on juries, vote or hold public office. These prohibitions rested on the definition of "persons" as exclusively male. An example of the inequity of this definition is jury duty. To be eligible for jury duty in St. John's, potential jurors had to possess personal property worth two thousand dollars, or own or rent a house, land or tenement to the value of two hundred and forty dollars per year. Other court districts outside of St. John's required less evidence of financial stability in potential jurors, but personal and real property was always included in the criteria for jurors. Single women, though perhaps few in number, might have qualified under this provision. However, there was an additional clause in the 1892 act of the Newfoundland legislature pertaining to trial by jury, which stated "'Persons' in this chapter shall mean male persons."[105] This short sentence meant that women were not considered persons, and were therefore excluded from jury duty by this piece of legislation.

Eventually, in 1973, women were allowed to sit on juries, but they were still permitted to exempt themselves from this duty. Although there were a number of grounds available for exemption from jury duty, women in particular had a right to exemption simply because they were women. Women's groups argued against this exemption for women on the basis that "[E]quality of women with men in our society carries with it responsibilities as well as rights."[106] In addition to the responsibility argument, women recognized the importance of jury duty as confirmation of their citizenship. The exemption for women, based on sex, was eventually dropped.

The denial of personhood to women had wider ramifications, especially regarding the issue of enfranchisement. In Newfoundland, the campaign to gain the vote for women, whether single or married, was a long one. It was not until 1921 that women were legally permitted to vote in municipal elections, providing they had the necessary property qualifications. Finally, in 1925 women were granted the right to vote in all elections. However, even the 1925 amending act, passed to permit women to vote, contained discrimination. Section 2 of the act states, in part:

> Every male British subject of the full age of twenty-one years and every female British subject of the full age of twenty-five years of sound understanding and resident in this Colony . . . .[107]

Evidently women of twenty-five were deemed to be only as competent as men of twenty-one.

In December 1925, the St. John's Municipal Elections were held. Julia Salter Earle, Fanny Knowling McNeil and May Kennedy exercised women's newly-acquired right to run for public office. They ran for election to St. John's city council. None were elected but some accounts of the election state that Julia lost by a mere eleven votes; others claim the figure is more like two hundred. Writing in 1965, Eleanor McKim noted the lack of information from the papers of the period.

> Indicative of the time or the prevailing sentiment is the fact that neither of the two daily newspapers carried a whisper of their campaigns.[108]

The fascinating story of the suffrage movement in Newfoundland and the colourful women who led it is chronicled in Margot Duley's essay elsewhere in this volume.

Another first for Newfoundland women was recorded with the election of Lady Helena Squires to the Newfoundland House of Assembly in the May, 1929 by-election for the District of Lewisporte. She won by a majority of over 81 percent of the votes. In commenting on her momentous election win, the *Newfoundland Quarterly* went to great lengths to describe her education, charm, hobbies and family. Of Lady Squires' first day in the House, the *Newfoundland Quarterly* observed:

> The new Lady Member took her seat on the opening day of the Legislature, and enlivened the proceedings with a flash of wit which won approval from both sides of the House, and indicated future possibilities of keen and incisive readiness in debate.[109]

The election of Lady Squires seems an odd turn of events, since she had vigorously opposed the activities of the Women's Franchise League in the preceding years. One New Brunswick newspaper noted:

> . . . in reality Lady Squires was elected as one of the supporters of Sir Richard, her husband . . . There is always the possibility that, by exercising the ancient privilege of her sex, she may change her mind and be in opposition to his government.[110]

Sir Richard was, of course, Sir Richard Squires, in his third term as Prime Minister of Newfoundland when Helena Squires was elected.

The election of women to the House of Assembly or the House of Commons is still an event worthy of comment in the 1990s. Although women are 52 percent of the population, our representation in municipal, provincial or federal governments remains marginal.

Single Blessedness: Women and Work.

Nancy Forestell has noted that for a large part of this century women worked in paid employment outside the home for only short periods of time:

> . . . for the vast majority of women, work was just a temporary interlude between school and marriage or until the birth of their first child.[111]

Once married or a mother, women were usually expected and sometimes required to resign from their paid work outside the home. But until then, young women worked in order to support themselves and their families. Unlike her married sisters, a single woman had somewhat greater freedom in employment. A single woman could own and manage her own property and business and enter into contracts in the same manner as men.[112] Clara Brett Martin of

Ontario, the first woman lawyer in the British Empire observed in 1900:

> Single women amongst us have from time immemorial bought and sold, kept shop and farm and inn, driven to market, collected their rents, made their investments, sued their debtors, compounded with their creditors and in a word lived their life exposed to nothing worse than a good deal of time-honoured and heavy jesting about their "single blessedness."[113]

Despite having many of the same property and business rights as men, single women may not have been able to avail themselves of a wider range of employment possibilities. Access to the finances and property required to establish a business was not readily available to most women. In Newfoundland society, especially in rural fishing communities, women did not inherit portions of the fishing household goods as did her brothers. Generally, the father's property was divided and passed on to the sons, so they could establish themselves as independent workers in the fishery. Without the means to establish a business, and with other work options limited, single women could gain little from their rights to property and business. A closer examination of the reality of life for single women is needed before we can assume their legal rights in this regard were of any benefit.[114]

Single women were subjected to the same prejudices and discrimination other women faced. This was particularly true in the area of employment since there were limited job opportunities available to women before the onset of industrialization. Class background, age and marital status influenced whether a woman worked or not, the type of employment she sought and was able to acquire. In 1921, 93 percent of the female workers in St. John's were single and noticeably young; the majority of workers in St. John's were between the ages of fourteen and twenty-four.[115]

> Working-class women were far more likely to work than middle-class women, primarily because of the necessity for them to contribute to the household economy.[116]

For these single, working-class St. John's women, tailoring, waitressing, factory work, sales and stenography were the main employment options. Women from the outports often relied on domestic service for employment in St. John's. These jobs usually paid low wages for long hours in poor working conditions.[117] In contrast, middle-class women were more likely to choose "professional" employment as teachers, nurses or other occupations which required a higher level of education, more time spent in school or training and considerably more money to accomplish.[118]

Professional employment as doctors or lawyers was not readily available to women, whether single or married. Until recent years, there were few female lawyers or medical doctors. For a female doctor, acquiring a licence to practise in Newfoundland at the turn of the century was not easy. In 1902, Dr. Carrie Lemon was accorded very different treatment than her husband Dr. A.E. Lemon. Both had trained in Michigan with Dr. J.H. Kellogg at the Battle Creek Health Institute. When they arrived in St. John's, Dr. A.E. Lemon was immediately granted permission to practise. However, Dr. Carrie Lemon was forced to acquire permission from the Department of Justice of the Newfoundland government in order to assume her rightful role as a medical doctor. The Medical Board vigorously opposed a female doctor being allowed to practise.[119] It wasn't until the first decade of the 1900s that Newfoundland produced its first woman doctor. Edith Weeks, born in Bay Bulls on the Southern Shore and educated at Trinity College in Toronto, graduated in 1906 with her M.D. As the first Newfoundland-born female physician, Dr. Weeks returned to St. John's to practise for several years before emigrating to Australia.[120]

Until 1911, the legal profession was closed to women in Newfoundland. It was only when challenged by a determined young woman that the regulations of the Law Society Act were changed. In 1910, Janet Miller (Ayre Murray) petitioned the Law Society to allow her to enter under Articles of Clerkship. She was eighteen years of age and possessed an excellent academic record. Her petition was rejected. To open the legal profession to women, a legislative amendment to the Law Society Act of Newfoundland had to be passed, thus striking down the exclusion of women. The Benchers of the Law Society itself engaged in a "spirited discussion" on the issue of the right of women to practise law.

> The majority of Members present felt that they were ". . . not satisfied as to the necessity or the expediency of any such radical change in the Constitution of the Society . . . for this and other reasons this Society desires to place on record its dissent from the principle of the measure proposed."[121]

Despite the decision on the part of the Law Society, the Legislature passed an amendment extending the word "person" "to include a female person,"[122] thereby "permitting women to become articled clerks, students-at-law, solicitors and barristers."[123] In October, 1910, the Benchers of the Law Society acquiesced and granted Janet Miller the right to become Newfoundland's first woman law student, articling with her uncle in his law practice. That the government of the day acted quickly to pass the amendment may have been

Edith Weeks (Hooper)—the first Newfoundland-born female physician.

Credit: Medical Audio Visual Services. The General Hospital Corporation, Health Sciences Centre, St. John's, Newfoundland.

Louise Saunders—the first female lawyer admitted to the Newfoundland Bar.

Credit: *Newfoundland Quarterly.*

influenced by the fact that Janet Miller was the niece of the then Attorney General, the Honourable D. Morison, K.C.[124] Janet Miller's class position and connections may well have aided her in securing the articling position. Although she passed second year exams, Janet Miller left her legal education with the advent of World War I and her subsequent marriage.[125]

It wasn't until 1929 that the first woman lawyer was admitted to the Newfoundland Bar. Louise Maud Saunders, of Greenspond studied law with the firm of Squires and Curtis and acted for many years as confidential clerk and private secretary to Sir Richard Anderson Squires, Prime Minister of Newfoundland. She also held the position of Supervisor of Debates in the Legislative Council and acted as its official reporter. The July, 1929 issue of the *Newfoundland Quarterly* described Louise Saunders as possessing "a well stored mind" and "a quiet but engaging disposition."[126] Louise Saunders became the first woman solicitor in 1933 and later, in 1964, she was appointed as Queen's Counsel. She died in St. John's, June 14, 1969, still a practising lawyer at seventy-two years of age. Her death marked the cessation of the law firm of Squires, Saunders and Carew.[127]

In the early years of the twentieth century, nursing became an option for single women. If the tone of the items found in the newspapers of the day is any reflection of the public attitude towards nursing, then the work was highly, though patronizingly regarded:

> The profession of nursing is coming into favour here, no fewer than four young ladies of this city leaving shortly to be properly trained in American Hospitals. It is much pursued in England and America and the supply of graduates, by no means equals the demand, a well-trained, intelligent nurse being rightly regarded as a treasure.[128]

In 1898, one Miss Rendell was appointed Matron of the General Hospital in St. John's. Miss Rendell, the first Newfoundlander to be admitted to the profession as a trained nurse, was a graduate of Johns Hopkins Hospital in the United States. Then, in 1903, two Newfoundlanders, Miss Mary Southcott and Miss Hannaford were appointed nursing superintendent and matron of the General Hospital. With their appointments, a training school for nursing was established in Newfoundland. Today, Miss Southcott is renowned for her contribution to nursing in Newfoundland.[129] In 1921, there were ninety-seven women working as nurses in St. John's, with fourteen more women in training for the nursing profession.[130] Mary Southcott died in 1943.

Margaret Rendell, matron of the General Hospital, 1898 and the first Newfoundlander to be admitted to the profession as a trained nurse.

Credit: Medical Audio Visual Services. The General Hospital Corporation, Health
Sciences Centre, St. John's, Newfoundland.

By the turn of the century, increasing numbers of young women were devoting themselves to teaching. Advertisements of the day indicate that in St. John's women were usually teaching at the primary level and included music, both vocal and instrumental, in their accomplishments and training. In 1895, the Reverend W.C. Shear, Chairman of the Board for the High School in Bay Roberts West advertised for an assistant female teacher. The salary offered ranged from $130 to $140 per year.[131] By 1921, 5.8 percent of the female labour force in St. John's were teachers. While the total number of female teachers had increased by 1935, the percentage of women in teaching fell to 4.8 percent.[132]

Teachers, both in St. John's and outport Newfoundland, often taught their first classes when they were still in their teens. Eleanor Tizzard of Twillingate, first taught on Trump Island in 1932, at the age of eighteen. She boarded in a house next to the school, at a cost of $10 a month. At that time her monthly salary was $19. Her sister, Vina, began teaching in 1935 in Boyd's Cove. She had obtained her Grade II Teacher's Licence by attending the Teacher's Summer School in 1935 at Memorial College in St. John's. Vina taught in seven different schools between 1935 and 1943.[133]

The salaries of teachers were augmented according to their level of educational attainment. In 1890, the augmentation payments for first, second and third grade were $20, $12 and $6 respectively. Both female and male teachers received the same amount. However, by 1930, the situation had changed radically. The augmentation scale differentiated between women and men in the amount of money they received. For example, for second grade, women received $160–$200 and men $200–$250. This was repeated at each level of the scale, with the top of the women's augmentation scale equal to, or just above, the bottom of the men's payment scale.[134] This inequitable treatment of women continued until the 1940s.[135]

Single women also held positions as principals in St. John's girls' schools. In 1895, Miss De La Mare was the "Lady Principal" of Bishop Spencer College, a private Church of England Girl's School in St. John's. She was followed by other female principals, including Violet Cherrington. The school offered "a full collegiate course, including English, French, Needlework, Drawing, Swedish Drill, and Elementary-Kindergarten work" at the Synod Hall Building on Queen's Road.[136] The course list indicates the prevailing middle- and upper-class notion of women's education. Such educational opportunities were not open to every young woman.

Many single, working-class women employed outside the family home took work requiring less education or training. In her study of working women in St. John's, Nancy Forestell observes:

> From the late nineteenth century onwards there were increasing employment opportunities for women as domestic servants, sales clerks, factory operatives, and typists in towns such as Harbour Grace and the growing city of St. John's.[137]

To obtain some types of employment, enterprising young women advertised their services in the daily newspapers. The *Evening Herald* of September, 1895 carried the following ad:

> Wanted—By a young lady, a situation as governess. For terms, address "teacher," this office.[138]

Another young woman sought work in a family home in 1890.

> SITUATION WANTED—Wanted—a situation as a HOUSEMAID; Can furnish references. Apply at this office.[139]

Prospective employers also took advantage of the daily papers to locate and hire servants for work in Newfoundland, Canada or the United States of America. Some young women preferred to work in Canada or the U.S.A. since wages were generally higher outside of Newfoundland. In the 1920s, domestics in St. John's earned $16 or $17 a month, while their more adventurous sisters earned approximately $40 per month in Montreal or Boston.[140] Ads like this one for domestic service were extremely common in the first three decades of the twentieth century.

> Wanted, a good general servant to proceed to Nova Scotia (immediately). Must have good references. Good wages and passage paid. Apply at this office.[141]

If a single woman lacked paid employment outside the home, she often served the family in her father's or a relative's household.[142] In Newfoundland, young women might be sent to serve others, usually people known to their families, in the same or a neighbouring community.[143]

With industrialization in Newfoundland, many single, and some married women, sought employment in factories. Employment opportunities existed in the expanding clothing, boot and shoe, tobacco, cordage and confectionery factories in the city.[144] In addition, companies such as the Dominion Textile Mills, located in Nova Scotia and New Brunswick, frequently advertised for "girls" or "families . . . consisting largely of girls fourteen years and over" to work in their mills. In one advertisement from 1909, the Dominion Textile Company of Windsor, Nova Scotia included information on wages, low cost of living and amusements for young people as enticements.[145] Other ads were direct and to the point:

> 25 GIRLS TO WORK IN Dominion Textile Company's COTTON MILLS AT MONCTON, NB AS WEAVERS. GOOD WAGES GIVEN WHILE LEARNING AND PASSAGE MONEY ADVANCED; APPLY IMMEDIATELY TO EDWARD J. SPRY, 78 CASEY STREET.[146]

Of course, local businesses, many of which were centred on the fishing trade, also employed young single women. The *Evening Herald* noted in 1890 that "quite a deal of employment is given to a number of young girls in the wareroom of M. Munroe, labelling tins of lobster canned at the various factories in which he is interested."[147] While not the most exciting work, young women were able to earn wages of their own. The fishery in rural Newfoundland employed many thousands of young women in shore work. Generally, they worked in support of the household economy, contributing their labour to the family.

In more urban centres, like St. John's, other small businesses such as drapery, millinery and dry-goods shops sought single female employees as well. Not unlike today, employers expected previous experience, good recommendations and hand-written letters to accompany an application.[148]

Occasionally, there would appear more intriguing ads:

> WANTED. Four Ladies, to take part in Dramatic Entertainments. Good Salaries will be given to competent persons. Apply to T.M. White, Manager.[149]

As today, women continued to work out of their homes. Selling homemade foodstuffs and flowers at local markets or perhaps giving piano lessons during the morning hours provided a limited income for some women.[150]

With the advent of World War I, more factory work opened up for young women. As men went off to war, women were needed to fill their positions. This is not to suggest that women's work options were suddenly unlimited. Societal norms for what was considered men's work or women's work still operated to constrain women's entry into some fields.[151] With the return of men after the war, women resumed their more traditional roles.

The depression of the 1920s and 1930s severely reduced women's employment. Factories, shops and offices closed; women were laid off in large numbers. Suffragist Julia Salter Earle, in her position as a trade unionist in St. John's, tried to remind the public that many women were being put out of work. In 1921, she wrote to the Newfoundland House of Assembly, reminding them of ". . . the hundreds of girls also out of work on account of the factories closing."[152] Despite the fact that many of these young women supported themselves and others in their families, attitudes towards women and paid work meant that little attention was given to their plight. The prevailing ideology of the male breadwinner as the only wage earner in the family undermined the employment of women. Even with single women, the common assumption was that "they would have a father or husband to support them."[153]

In the 1930s, the Depression led to massive layoffs and wage cuts in traditional male occupations in the mining, forest and fishing industries. Many men were unemployed and families had little to eat.

> The winters of 1931, 1932, and 1933 were ones of appalling misery in Newfoundland as the numbers of people totally destitute and receiving the dole rose to a maximum of 90,000, approximately one-third of the country's total population.[154]

In the winter of 1932, a crowd of unemployed had forced a confrontation with Prime Minister Sir Richard Squires. Squires promised a better distribution of relief in order to calm the crowd. The financial situation in Newfoundland was so bad that the Squires government fell and the incoming government, under F.C. Alderdice, instituted a restricted program of relief. No relief payment was to exceed $1.80 per month per person, or six cents a day.[155] By 1949, the relief allowance had crept up to $5 per month per person.

Some relief from unemployment and poverty came with World War II. In 1940 the American military leased land in Newfoundland for ninety-nine years and constructed facilities at St. John's, Argentia, and Stephenville.[156] By 1942, there were over ten thousand American military personnel in Newfoundland. Construction work and, later, maintenance, support and office jobs employed almost twenty thousand Newfoundlanders. Wages were high for the time, averaging $1,500 annually for males in St. John's and $627 annually for females. Wages in the rest of the island averaged $901 for males and $496 for females.[157] In the fishery ten years earlier, wages had averaged $333.

Near the American military base in Stephenville, single women had an opportunity for employment outside the home. As in other areas, the labour market was segregated along gender lines with women performing traditional roles of cooking, cleaning and typing. Single women worked in the mess halls for about $8 a week, as barmaids in the Non-Commissioned Officers club or tavern, or keeping house for officers. One observer noted, "Women were never promoted, rarely received pay increases, or were given an opportunity to learn trades, to unionize . . . women's wages were still far below those of their male relatives."[158] A woman's physical appearance received special attention and was thought to be an asset in gaining a well-paying job. At the Stephenville base, ". . . the best looking girls got special pay for working in the offices, bookkeeping and typing."[159]

Social life in communities near the bases was considerably enlivened during the early 1940s. When the first Americans arrived, hundreds of young women were there to greet them.

> The taverns were filled to capacity every night mainly due to the soldiers themselves, but also due to the girls they were dating.[160]

Although the marriage rate did not increase in the Stephenville area, according to the census of 1945, the rate of illegitimate births rose. Between World War II and 1949, the American government provided special welfare benefits to single women who had become pregnant. With the end of World War II and the subsequent phasing out of military operations, women were no longer needed to work on the bases. The chance for military employment disappeared and women again took up familiar occupations such as domestic labour.

As newspaper advertisements attest, many young women worked in domestic service as housekeepers, cooks, maids and general servants. The St. John's census of 1921 reports 958 females employed in domestic service, totalling 33.8 percent of the female labour force of St. John's, many of them young and single. This was a much higher percentage than in other North American cities; domestics in Halifax constituted 20 percent of the female labour force in the 1920s.[161] By 1935, there were 1329 women in domestic service or 34.4 percent of the female labour force.[162] Despite these figures, domestic service was not highly prized by women from St. John's.

> Because this type of work entailed long hours of hard physical labour, offered meagre wages, and severely limited the freedom of workers, many young women, particularly those from the city, attempted to avoid domestic service if at all possible.[163]

In St. John's, middle-class women did not consider domestic service as potential employment. Working-class women ventured into service only if factory or shop work were not available to them.[164]

Young outport women may have viewed domestic employment differently for they often sought domestic work in St. John's. They had many reasons: lack of employment in their home communities; need for money to supplement their family's income; relieving their families of another mouth to feed; or perhaps a desire to see the "big city."[165] With room and board paid by their employers as part of the domestic's work situation and a measure of security for a young woman far from home, live-in domestic work may have suited outport women. Forestell notes that many of these women would seek employment in St. John's at the end of the fishing season in September. As daughters of fishermen, their labour would be required at home during the summer fishing season.[166]

As we might expect, not all situations led to happy conclusions. With no legal rights or protective legislation covering domestic work, young women were occasionally exploited by their employers or cheated of their wages. Nettie Parsons found herself in a difficult situation over wages.

> In 1923, a domestic servant named Nettie Parsons was charged with striking her mistress. When the case came to court, it became clear that the action had been provoked because Nettie had not been paid.[167]

The court fined Nettie one dollar for striking her mistress and ordered Nettie be paid a full month's wages by her mistress. Some domestic servants were forced to resort to suing their employers for the wages that were rightfully theirs. Annie Pike did so in 1938. She was awarded two months wages amounting to $16.[168] According to the census of 1935, 8 percent of all domestics received no wages, only room, board and some clothing. The average annual income was only $100.[169]

Between 1890 and 1915, the local newspapers reported a number of cases of theft or larceny involving young female domestic servants. Although little information is available on many of these cases, the sentences reveal the court's attitude regarding the theft of an employer's property. Sentences ranged from fourteen days imprisonment for the theft of $6,[170] to a $100 fine or six months in jail for the theft of $200.[171]

Domestic servants were in a very vulnerable position in their employer's household. They could be subjected to abuse, harassment or assault at the hands of their employers. In April 1890, a domestic charged her employer with ill-treating her on the 13th, 14th, and 15th of April. Many witnesses gave testimony on behalf of the domestic. The employer argued that his servant was "a very refractory character," and he found it necessary to use violence against her. Judge Conroy ruled that both had very bad tempers and imposed a fine of $20. The victim's conduct was taken into consideration by the judge in his verdict.[172]

Being present in the home of an employer on a full-time basis allowed the domestic to be privy to her employers personal affairs and livelihood. Occasionally, this meant testifying in court. Catherine Kelly was called by the prosecution in an 1890 trial regarding the presence and use of liquor in the home of her employer, Mr. Henry Johnson of George Street, St. John's. She described her role in collecting "a jar of Jamaica and 2 bottles of whisky, sometimes twice a week." In those days of strong temperance agitation, the use of liquor, paid for and consumed in the home, was illegal. No doubt Catherine Kelly's testimony did little to help her employer. One wonders in what position Catherine found herself once the trial was concluded; loss of employment may have been the least she endured.

If a young woman left or was fired from her job, she often found herself in a difficult position. According to Forestell:

> St. John's newspapers frequently reported court cases involving unemployed domestics charged with vagrancy or loitering because they did not have a place to stay. The judge usually ruled for the woman to be taken to the penitentiary for a brief period of time as a means of "safe-keeping."[173]

A woman could receive eight to ten days imprisonment in the penitentiary for "safe-keeping" or as much as thirty days for vagrancy.[174]

In the female labour force of the 1920s and 1930s, domestic service was accorded the lowest status and remuneration in a limited range of occupational choices. Low wages were common for women employed as domestics as they had no trade unions or labour legislation in place to protect them.

Unfortunately, even when legislation does exist, it is not always progressive. Low wages for domestics continued for many years because they were specifically provided for in provincial government legislation. The Labour Standards Act of 1977 provided for a "special" minimum wage for domestics which was about half of that paid to other workers.[175] While this law was not directed specifically towards women, the end result was discriminatory since most domestics are female. Finally, in April 1991, the provincial government eliminated the lower wage for domestics. Now, legislation requires that all employees over the age of sixteen receive at least minimum wage for their work.[176]

Women who made their living from prostitution or running "a house of ill-fame" could be treated harshly by the Newfoundland justice system. The first mention of a known prostitute appeared in 1757. Eleanor Moody was convicted, not for prostitution, but for robbing one of her customers. Moody was sentenced to be put into a "whirlygig" for one hour and then banished from the island, as she was deemed to be "a Nuisance to the Publick."[177]

Occasionally the local newspapers contained stories on the discovery and closing of local houses used for prostitution. In 1890 the Police Court column of the *Evening Herald* noted the following story:

> Johanna Hilliard, aged forty years, residing in Springdale Street, for keeping a house of ill-fame, was sent to the penitentiary for three months. In delivering judgement his Honour Judge Prowse said he had gone to the fullest extent, and that if the law would permit him he would make the sentence longer.[178]

Five years later, a married couple were arrested for "keeping a house resorted to for prostitution."[179] The husband, Timothy Vivian, was convicted of the charge. He was given three months hard labour. A warrant was issued for the arrest of Mrs. Vivian on the same charge. During her trial, her lawyers argued that she did not own or operate the house. It is interesting to note that Judge Prowse, still on the bench, ruled that a married woman, "if knowing anything of the proceedings in the place would be presumed to be acting under the influence of her husband and therefore not responsible."[180] Mrs. Vivian was discharged. It could be said that in Mrs. Vivian's case marriage served her well.

In Newfoundland at this time, charges of prostitution and keeping a brothel were covered by the Criminal Code in force in England.[181] Judge Prowse was constrained by the penalties stipulated in the Code: the convictions called for "any term not exceeding three months, with or without hard labour."[182] The newspaper articles do not tell us if Johanna Hilliard or the Vivians were first or repeat offenders; according to the law, the penalty becomes increasingly harsh with each conviction. Perhaps Judge Prowse's desire for a harsher sentence reflected his personal bias regarding prostitution and related charges.

The history of 19th century prostitution law in Canada has been more fully explored in recent years by Constance Backhouse.[183] She notes that sentences for prostitution differed from those for keeping a common bawdy-house or house of ill-fame. In the late 1800s in Canada, prostitutes could receive sentences ranging from seven days at hard labour to six months. The keepers were sentenced to three or more months regularly.[184] As we have seen in the items from the *Evening Herald*, notoriety usually accompanied a conviction, singling out and marking those convicted in the eyes of society.

Prostitution laws in Canada appear to have been primarily directed at women as few male customers were ever arrested or charged.[185] This has been attributed to sex discrimination. Women

> ... were seen as failing in the society's expected standards of feminine behaviour ... [T]hey were not at home, nurturing a family or properly domesticated; their perceived deviance endangered the maintenance and propagation of the moral order, the family and the training of children.[186]

Not unlike the women working in mines, prostitutes were seen as acting contrary to approved moral and social behaviour for women. Whether the policing and sentencing of women working as prostitutes or keepers of brothels in Newfoundland matched the treatment received by women doing similar work in Canada remains to be documented.

Protective Legislation and Benefits

Many jurisdictions in Canada enacted protective legislation in the late nineteenth and early twentieth centuries to govern the hours and working conditions of women and children who worked in factories.[187] Ontario introduced the Ontario Shops Regulation Act in 1888, and New Brunswick passed the Factories Act in 1905.[188] Newfoundland does not appear to have passed similar laws at that time.

This gap in protective legislation had serious repercussions. Workers were expected to work overtime without pay, for example. In 1899, young women employed at Ropewalk Factories refused to work unpaid overtime and were subsequently fired and replaced with other workers.[189] Without protective legislation, women workers were at the mercy of their employer.

In a bid to secure better wages and working conditions, the first all-female union was formed in August, 1918. The Ladies Branch of the Newfoundland Industrial Workers Association grew to four hundred members by November of 1918. Women factory workers from Newfoundland Cordage, British Clothing, Imperial Tobacco, Knitting Mills, Standard Manufacturing, Colonial Cordage, F.P. Wood and Browning's joined the union.[190] The first strikes involving the union took place in November 1918. They struck for higher wages at Browning's and, in a separate action, the women struck in order to maintain a closed union shop at Colonial Cordage Company.[191] How successful these actions were for the women is not documented.

In the spring of 1931, a petition urging passage of protective legislation regarding shop closing hours was signed by twelve hundred sales clerks, most of the women and men working in city retail shops. This petition was presented to the House of Assembly. After repeated defeats in the House, the Shop Closing Hour Act, St. John's, was passed in 1936. It addressed the working conditions of store salesclerks, but only those who worked in larger shops on Water Street.[192] Water Street, located in the heart of St. John's, was lined with shops and businesses selling goods of all descriptions. For hundreds of years it was the mercantile centre of the city. Throughout the rest of the city, numerous small shops operated as groceries and confectioneries. The 1936 act specifies the type of goods sold in the stores covered by the act and those in stores exempt from it.[193] The stores exempt from the act carried goods which indicated smaller shops, those not generally located on Water Street.[194] Thus the act mainly affected sales clerks employed on Water Street.

The act provided that where an employee was either female or under the age of eighteen, that employee was not to work more than eight hours a day or fifty-four hours in any one week.[195] An immediate amendment was passed in 1936 to reduce the number of working hours per week to forty-eight, "except on the one day in each week on which the shop in which he or she is employed remains open after 7:30 p.m."[196] Clearly the conduct of business was not to be hindered by excessive concern for employees. Indeed, earlier attempts to pass a shop hours act had been reviled as efforts to restrain trade, not to aid weary shop workers.[197]

Another amendment was introduced and passed in 1940. This amendment, The Shops Act, restricted work for employees under eighteen and all females, regardless of age, to eight working hours in a day and no more than forty-eight hours per week (exclusive of "relief periods").[198] As well, the maximum hours of work for young or female employees was not to exceed sixty hours of work during the Christmas season. The maximum for other employees (male, over eighteen) during this season was sixty-five hours a week.[199]

A further amendment to the Shop Closing Act in 1941 again detailed the working hours on a specifically gendered basis. Males could work one half hour per day longer than females and in January could work up to two and one half hours per day more.[200] This legislation may have been influenced by the belief that male wages constituted a family wage which needed to be protected. Wages for female workers may have been seen as secondary earnings rather than primary support for a family or individual. As indicated earlier in this essay, it was commonly assumed that women were supported by a husband or father.

There was a separate Shop Act for St. John's, passed in 1942, which stipulated that female employees were not to work more than eight hours a day, or eight and a quarter hours if the shop was not on Water Street.[201] This provision was included in the general 1941 Shop Closing Act as well. Again, male employees were able to work a half an hour per day longer than females. No explanation is given for the extra fifteen minutes work required of shop clerks not working on Water Street.

All of these acts also required that seats be provided for female clerks, and these requirements were reworded and included in the 1963 Hours of Work Act:

> In all rooms of a shop where female assistants are employed in the serving of customers the occupier of the shop shall provide seats behind the counter . . . and the seats shall be in the proportion of not less than one seat in each room to every three female assistants employed in the room; and no employer or occupier shall take any means to hinder or restrict the reasonable use of the seats by the female assistants.[202]

This type of protective legislation may have been motivated by the commonly held view of women as "the weaker sex," who were unable to work as many physically demanding hours as their male counterparts. For many shop workers, this kind of legislation protected them from some forms of exploitation at the hands of their employers. Of course, many of these women also worked in the family home long after the shop work day was through and must have been thankful for the counter stools to ease their weariness.

Wages were low for shop clerks: saleswomen on Water Street earned $5 a week in 1925; in 1935, the average annual income for female retail workers was $277, or less than $25 per month. Female office workers earned $8 to $20 per week, depending on their skills and bank employees earned about $17 per week during the 1920s.[203]

In 1944, the government passed legislation designed to prohibit the payment of wages in goods or services.[204] Section (e) of this act outlines the workers who are covered by the act. It specifically excludes domestic workers. As we have already seen, many domestic servants were female and were paid in room, board and clothing for their services. This legislation did nothing to help domestic workers. The only occupational category detailed in Section (e) in which women were likely to be found in the early 1940s was clerical work. The numbers of women so employed may have been fairly small.

According to a confidential memo from 1946, the law was designed to raise the sub-standard rates of pay received by unorganized workmen in sawmills and fishing premises.[205] Perhaps some women working in fishery premises for pay would have been covered by this legislation.

Finally, in 1947, the Commission of Government passed An Act to Provide for the Fixing of Minimum Wages for Workmen.[206] The definition of "workman" is fairly broad.

> . . . "workman" means any person who has entered into or works under a contract with an employer by way of manual labour, clerical work or otherwise . . . .[207]

Whether many women in the labour force were engaged in manual labour or clerical categories in the 1940s remains to be discovered. The extent of employment covered by the word "otherwise" in this legislation is not clear. Until the effect of this type of legislation on the daily working lives of women is known it cannot be said that these acts provided fair wages for them.

The Minimum Wage Act certainly did not help those few women who were part of organized labour. The government resisted extending the minimum wage rates to organized labour, saying that the "[G]overnment should not do the work of Trade Union Leaders"[208] and that "[O]rganized labour can fight its own battles."[209]

Traditionally, the areas in which women have been employed have been the areas in which wages were lowest. Benefits such as health, unemployment insurance and pensions have been virtually non-existent. Indeed, women were not usually specifically referred to in laws concerning pensions, unless it was in the capacity of widow or wife of an employee. Provisions stating that a widow was to receive her husband's pension usually stipulated that the pension would cease if the woman remarried.[210] The underlying assumptions of pension legislation are familiar ones. All women married and were dependents of their husbands and thus would be provided for under his pension. That some women did not marry, that marriage did not guarantee financial security for women or that marriages could end in separation and divorce was not considered in pension laws. In addition, no provisions were made for women who stayed home to care for their children. Women who worked outside the home and left their jobs to raise their children, returning to work after the children were older, usually lost those pensionable years from their earlier work. This resulted in women having fewer pension benefits when they retired. When women did receive a pension it was often lower than that of male workers since women on the average

earned, and still earn, less than men.[211] Thus, early pension legislation was inequitable in its treatment of women and men.

Women and Relationships

Laws specifically directed towards single women sought to regulate
their relationships with men before marriage. These laws included
those that prevented them from marrying, before the age of majority,
without the consent of their father. In some jurisdictions the consent
of a father was required up to the mid 1970s. As with guardianship
of children, a mother's consent was not permitted to be substituted
unless the father were dead or otherwise unavailable.[212] In Newfoundland by the 1950s, the law required the consent of "parents or
guardian" for the marriage of a female under twenty-one, but if the
woman or girl were pregnant, or had already had a child "out of
wedlock" and was under the age of twenty-one no parental consent
was necessary.[213]

Unwanted Pregnancy, Infanticide and Concealment of Birth

Unwanted pregnancies or "out of wedlock" births were not uncommon, although in the early 1900s such pregnancies were not openly
discussed. Customary attitudes toward illegitimate births varied
from community to community. In Elliston, Bonavista Bay for
example, the birth of a child out of wedlock "might be referred to
casually as a 'merry-begot'" but the situation was tolerated. The
mother would not be "discriminated against and might later marry
successfully."[214] In Stephenville, women who found themselves in
such a position were ostracized as "bad" women.[215] No doubt, over
time and across communities, response to children born outside of
legal marriage varied to a considerable degree.

Sometimes the child was raised by the mother's family but
additional financial support was often required. In June, 1834 the
government of Newfoundland found it necessary to pass An Act to
Provide for the Maintenance of Bastard Children.[216] This act allowed
for the apprehension of the man named as father of the child and
the ordering for "the relief and keeping of such Bastard Child" so the
Colony would not be required to provide financial support.[217] The
expectant mother was liable for up to six months in jail if she was
thought to be making a false accusation against a man.[218]

Under the Health and Public Welfare Act of 1931, fathers were
still required to provide financial support. The director of Child
Welfare had the right to enforce child support; a negligent father
could be brought before a magistrate. The magistrate at Clarenville

in 1938 received letters from mothers seeking such support. He, in turn, wrote to the offending fathers and ordered payments be made. This wasn't always an easy task, but occasionally his efforts were rewarded.

> I am rather pleased with the way in which this young man Pritchett is making his payments. He is always on time and thus far I do not have to write him asking for the payment toward the support of the child. I hope others would follow his example.[219]

Mr. Pritchett's support payments totalled $30 a year.

A woman's reputation in the community could affect both the strength of her demand for maintenance and the view the court took of that demand. In the 1800s, if a woman were judged to be "of ill-fame or a Common Whore," the man charged could appeal to the justices and seek to have the case heard by a jury in the court.[220] One can only imagine how the reputation of a woman might be used in such a trial.

To be single and pregnant, perhaps forced to leave precious employment, was not an enviable position for any young woman. A woman's moral character could be severely judged and found wanting in such unfortunate circumstances. Faced with an unwanted pregnancy or simply out of ignorance regarding pregnancy and childbirth, some women found themselves charged with concealment of birth or infanticide.

> A woman who by wilful act or omission causes the death of her newly born child shall be deemed not to have committed murder or manslaughter if at the time of the act or omission she had not fully recovered from the effect of giving birth to such child and by reason thereof the balance of her mind was then disturbed, but shall be deemed to have committed an indictable offence, namely infanticide.[221]

So reads the description of infanticide provided in the English Infanticide Act of 1922. As early as the 1600s, British law dealt severely with women accused of concealment of birth or infanticide. The first English statute enacted to deal with infanticide appears to have been An Act to prevent the destroying and murdering of Bastard children in 1623.[222] Under this act, it was only necessary to prove that a woman had given birth, that the child had died, and that the woman had tried to conceal the event. There was an automatic presumption of the woman's guilt, and she could be charged with murder and sentenced to death.[223] The act only applied to "bastard children," those born out of wedlock, and not those born to married parents.

This statute was repealed in 1803, and under the new law presumption of guilt was dropped.[224] Instead, it had to be proven that a child had been born alive in order for the mother to be convicted. If a woman was acquitted of murder it was possible to convict her for "concealment," for which the penalty was two years imprisonment.[225] This was a considerable improvement over the death penalty.

The English law on infanticide was amended again in 1828, and was extended to cover married women who committed infanticide or concealment.[226] Since Newfoundland had adopted the criminal laws of England these statutes applied in this province after 1837. When Canada enacted criminal legislation in 1867 it retained the death penalty if murder of the child was proven and provided a penalty of two years imprisonment for concealment of birth.[227]

Although few offenders were charged, the crime was considered to have been prevalent, not only in Newfoundland but in England and Canada.[228] In a 1984 article on infanticide in nineteenth-century Canada, Constance Backhouse argues that court records indicate judges and juries held lenient attitudes towards women accused of infanticide. She states that in most Canadian cases women were discharged and released.[229] As we will see, this was not generally the case in Newfoundland.

Although the killing of an infant seems a drastic step to take, most of the newspaper accounts in Newfoundland appear to document the actions of unmarried servants. Backhouse notes that in Canada this was also true.[230] Most of these women could not have afforded to support a child, even had they been allowed to keep their jobs once their employer discovered their condition. The disgrace of being an unwed mother, as well as the lack of money to support the child, would have worked together to make infanticide appear as one of the only options. Other factors also played a role:

> The general acceptance of infanticide may have been related to the ineffectiveness or unavailability of other methods of fertility control; when circumstances made child rearing impossible, infanticide was adopted as a last resort. Furthermore the fragility of infant life in an era of limited medical knowledge must have helped create an environment in which the death of newborn children was a customary feature of daily life. Deliberate child murder must have seemed less reprehensible under these conditions.[231]

At the turn of the century, cases cited in the court columns of local Newfoundland newspapers included both concealment of birth and the general term infanticide. Although the crime is generally termed infanticide, there were a number of charges which could be laid under this heading: murder, manslaughter, or concealment of birth. There are more reported cases of concealment of birth, but still relatively few reports given the apparently large numbers of such offences.

One newspaper account of infanticide, which resulted in a charge of manslaughter, details the trial of Bridget Fitzgerald. In 1889, Bridget was an unmarried domestic who concealed her pregnancy from her employer. She gave birth, alone, in a passageway outside the house and then left the child alone to return to the kitchen. Bridget stated at her trial that when she returned the child had died, and she buried it later that night on a road beside a farm. She was charged with manslaughter rather than murder.

> Here the accused is charged with manslaughter only, the charge being reduced to this, the Prisoner at the Bar, although not intending the destruction of life, was guilty of such unlawful acts as resulted in death . . . .[232]

Mr. Greene, Q.C., acting for the Crown, observed that infanticide, due to the "cruelty and neglect of the mother," was a fairly common crime.

> The crime of infanticide is, I regret to say too prevalent amongst us, and it behooves us by all legitimate means to stamp it out both by punishment of the offender and by deterring others from its committal.[233]

After a long deliberation, the jury found Bridget guilty of manslaughter but recommended mercy in the sentencing. Justice Pinsent dealt with the case as if the charge were concealment of birth, not manslaughter, and sentenced Bridget to twelve months imprisonment and hard labour.[234]

Twelve months imprisonment seems to have been a fairly standard sentence for women convicted of infanticide or concealment of birth in Newfoundland at that time. Letters to the Governor in 1899 and 1900, regarding Jane Pye and Thurza Elson, indicate that these women received sentences of fourteen months and twelve months respectively, having been convicted of concealment of birth. Both women earned a one month commutation of their sentences for "good behaviour, diligence and industry."[235] These sentences are in sharp contrast to those meted out in Canada in the 19th century where the most common sentence was three months.[236]

In May of 1900, a young girl from Bryants Cove was charged with infanticide. She had been a servant in a St. John's home for over a year. One day the mistress of the house returned home to find the young girl in a bedroom with the body of a dead baby. Although the incident was reported to the local police by the attending doctor, it is not clear whether the young girl was tried or found guilty.[237] A second case in February of that same year found Clara Anne Rogers of Newmans Cove, Bonavista Bay charged with concealing the birth of her child by "secreting its dead body in the woods."[238] Again, the sentence imposed is not known.

It appears that juries were reluctant to convict a woman on a charge of murder or manslaughter under infanticide and were more likely to convict on a charge of concealment of birth. Possibly this was due to the severe penalty for murder and manslaughter, and perhaps the juries felt some degree of sympathy for these unfortunate women. Other reasons have also been suggested for the leniency of judges and juries in these cases.

> The male legislators, lawyers, judges and jurors who controlled the legal system did not have to be concerned about these women in order to ensure the proper continuation of male blood lines or to supervise the descent of male property to the next generation . . . [These women] were insignificant in terms of the overall balance of power between the sexes. This then provided a conspicuous and ideal platform upon which the courts could well afford to exhibit compassion towards desperate women.[239]

Still, the severity of women's prison sentences in Newfoundland and the absence of prosecution of the fathers of the illegitimate children attest to the moral outrage levelled against women in these cases. Clearly the penalty for sexual freedom was paid by only one sex.

Nevertheless, not all men escaped without punishment, even if the law courts were not involved. The *Evening Herald* reported the following incident in October, 1895:

> Last night a neatly dressed woman called at the residence of a well-known professional gentleman in this city, and left a parcel for the proprietor. On being opened it was found to contain the body of a still-born infant, and there is a big sensation accordingly.[240]

Unfortunately, further details of the incident, including the fate of the well-known professional gentleman, were not reported.

The Canadian Criminal Code continued to include the crime of infanticide, although by 1955 the penalty had been reduced to five years imprisonment. A woman could not be convicted of murder or manslaughter if it were proven that the balance of her mind had been disturbed by the birth and that she had not fully recovered when she killed the child.[241] Concealment of birth was punishable by two years,[242] but neglecting to obtain assistance at the birth was punishable by five years in jail.

A female person who, being pregnant and about to be delivered, with intent that the child shall not live or with intent to conceal the birth of the child, fails to make provision for reasonable assistance in respect of her delivery, if the child is permanently injured . . . or dies immediately before, during or in a short time after birth, as a result thereof, is guilty of an indictable offence and is liable to imprisonment for five years.[243]

These provisions were still in place in 1976 when a case was heard by Justice Cummings of the District Court in Burin-Burgeo involving a young girl charged with infanticide.[244] The seventeen-year-old girl delivered a child by herself, in a bedroom of her family home. Her young brother who shared the room with her apparently remained asleep during the birth, as did the rest of her family. The girl stated that neither she nor any members of her family were aware that she was pregnant. After giving birth the girl had placed her hand over the baby's mouth to keep it from crying out, and when she removed her hand the baby was dead. She was charged with infanticide. The judge dismissed the charges, stating that there was no evidence that she had intentionally caused the death of the child. The crime of infanticide had become far less common by 1976, as Justice Cummings noted:

In the 28 years since the creation of this crime of infanticide there have been only three cases dealing with the offence as far as I can ascertain.[245]

Infanticide is still an offence under the Criminal Code, with a maximum sentence of five years imprisonment. Problems with this offence have been noted, including the fact that the Crown has the discretion to charge a woman with murder instead of infanticide. The woman would not then be able to use the defence set out in the Criminal Code section on infanticide, arguing that she had not recovered from the effects of the birth. As well, conviction for the offence could result in a woman being imprisoned for a crime she committed while "unbalanced," and it has been suggested that some form of treatment would have been more appropriate than imprisonment.[246]

The risk of unwanted pregnancies and the birth of illegitimate children sometimes existed in the course of the work in which women were engaged. These risks and the morality of women involved in the Labrador fishery each summer became the subject of public debate and pressure for legislation in the early 1900s in Newfoundland. One observer wrote, "[E]ighty per cent of the illegitimate children spring from this class of girls."[247]

Four maid servants outside a cabin probably in Labrador. Credit: Centre for Newfoundland Studies Archives, Memorial University of Newfoundland.

Historically, women and girls, many of them single, were employed in the Labrador fishery to tend to the physical comforts of the male fishers. Sometimes the female fishery servants were as young as thirteen years old.[248] Women's work in the Labrador fishery was described in two surveys conducted in 1900. Prominent men, including clergy, merchants, doctors, master mariners and captains responded to the survey.[249] One return stated that the women's work was "mainly washing, cooking and cleanlieness [sic], their work about fish is only a secondary."[250] Mending clothes, darning and rudimentary nursing of colds, cuts or blisters were considered part of the women's tasks.[251] Women were hired "to make life more bearable for men,"[252] and to increase men's comfort in difficult conditions. Their work was thought to be peripheral to the role of the male fishers and a potential drain on profits for a season's fishing effort. Thus women could be dispensed with by the owners or captains if their work in the fishery became a problem or uneconomical.

Not every young woman's experience of work in the Labrador fishery was a positive one. Women in the Labrador fishery often had to work in extreme conditions "which made modesty and privacy impossible."[253] It appears that more than one girl came home from the fishery "in the family way," a condition that was regarded as a result of "exposures and temptations to young girls."[254] A newspaper account from 1899 comments upon the death of a girl who committed suicide by drowning herself at Merchament's Harbour, Labrador.

> What privations those poor girls have to endure from the time they leave here in the spring until they return again. What insult they have to endure from men who should be leaders of men but instead choose to be misleaders of women.[255]

In the newspaper accounts and the governor's correspondence there is a decided emphasis on the moral degradation of women placed in a vulnerable position in the course of their work. Governor Sir Henry McCallum wrote to the Honourable Chief Justice on the matter. It was, he said:

> . . . not only shameful to those responsible for the continuance but also detrimental to social order seeing that the future mothers of young Newfoundland should be rescued by both Government and employers from evil surroundings rather than exposed to impurity, temptation, and to the hot passions of stalwart fishermen.[256]

Fishermen are clearly represented as subject to unbridled passions directed toward the nearest available woman. Women, on the other hand, were again thought to be weak creatures, capable of slipping into coarse and indecent habits given the first opportunity and therefore requiring protection from themselves as much as from the stalwart fishermen. This is by now a familiar theme in the rhetoric surrounding legislation which prohibits women from entering specific lines of work.

Moreover, some prominent men of the day harboured a critical opinion of any young woman who worked in the Labrador fishery. Wilfred Grenfell, the Labrador doctor and missionary, wrote to the governor in 1900 on the subject.

> I must however in justice to the men state that I have known the women the first to incite to immorality, and indeed I don't think they are one whit less to blame.[257]

Grenfell believed that "*none* of these girls or women who are the future mothers of this country, can possibly retain that natural modesty so absolutely essential for the welfare of their future responsibilities."[258]

Under an existing 1892 law, vessels carrying females, servants or passengers were to provide separate cabins and sanitary facilities for them.[259] Clearly this law was not being enforced, for women were found to be living in generally bad "moral conditions" in the 1900 survey.[260] Space on these vessels was at a premium and separate accommodations may have been physically impossible as well as costly to the ship's owner.

Another economic consideration may have played a more prominent role. Little was made publicly of the fact that women were paid only one quarter to one half the wages of men doing the same work. In the survey responses this economic consideration was raised by the captains of the vessels when they noted ". . . a boy may be employed as cook, but his wages may be higher than that of a girl"[261] and "females are better than two men and half the expense."[262] One response noted that "the captains can get a girl to do the work and cooking for from $20 to $28 while a man would cost $80 to $90."[263] The surveys indicate an ambiguous response to the issue of women in the Labrador fishery. Men in the Labrador fishery appear to have held a double standard: some decried the immorality of women's position in the fishery but others maintained it was the only economical course to take.

Some who worked regularly on the Labrador objected strongly to the characterization of it as a place of immorality. Isaac Mercer, ship captain, was one of the individuals who disputed the claims.

> I have been for the last 15 years carrying females to the number of 40 and about 120 males. I have never known one girl in my employ get into trouble on Labrador . . . The females are wrongfully slan-

dered and I know some of them feel it very keenly, as they dont [sic] deserve such odium thrown upon them.[264]

Nevertheless, in 1901 a report from the Fisheries Board, which had conducted the survey in 1900, was forwarded to the governor. The board recommended that "a law be enacted prohibiting the carrying of females to Labrador in green fish schooners."[265] However, Governor Henry McCallum, who was ending his term, wrote to the Honourable Chief Justice on March 4, 1901, expressing pessimism that the government would ever pass such a bill.

> Mr. Murphy [minister of marine and fisheries] who handed me the Resolution also informed me that he did not believe the House of Assembly would pass any Bill which would provide for dealing with what is really a shameful traffic. This observation leads me to suspect that political considerations may unfortunately be at work . . . . [266]

McCallum's suspicions may have proven correct, for no record of the passage of a law restricting or prohibiting females in the Labrador fishery is to be found. The practice appears to have continued, as Kate Knox of St. Brendan's, Bonavista Bay, testifies in her reminiscences of 1912 on the Labrador.

Kate Knox remembered well her days in the Labrador fishery from 1911 to 1915. Between the ages of sixteen and nineteen, she travelled the Labrador coast as a cook on fishing schooners. Her memories describe a routinized, yet happy experience of the work and the life. Every day had a set meal—beans for breakfast, fish for dinner and salmon, salt meat or pea soup, along with potatoes, cabbage, pudding or cakes for supper.[267] For her work between early June and the end of September she would be paid thirty dollars. Although alone amongst a group of men, she enjoyed her life.

> It wasn't lonely for a girl like me. There were a lot of other boats and we had so much to do. We had to do the wash, make the bunks, get the men up and make their breakfast when they came back from fishing. I never got to see the other girls very much, but we would talk to each other because sometimes the boats were anchored pretty close. There was no music on the boats . . . . Only when the men would sing. But it was the best kind of life. I only wish I was as healthy now as I was then.[268]

Kate Knox's recollections do not tell us whether she worked for relatives or friends in the Labrador fishery or whether the potential immorality of her position was even an issue in the second decade of this century. The actual circumstances of her work would have had a profound impact on her experience.

Kate Knox of St. Brendan's, Bonavista Bay.

Credit: *Decks Awash*, October 1977.

Common-Law Relationships: A Civil Inconvenience

Lawmakers took little interest in women who chose to live in a common-law marriage arrangement. Sir William Blackstone, an eminent British jurist of the 1700s, termed such alliances "a civil inconvenience." In this form of union, a couple lived together openly, had a sexual relationship and represented themselves to the community at large as being in a married state.[269] The law safeguarded some rights of the individuals and their children but only for limited purposes. This general lack of legal status in common-law unions grew out of a concern for the morality of such unions and for the rights of inheritance. Suzanne Boivin, a Montreal lawyer, describes this concern as:

> . . . fear of legitimizing behaviour that would deviate from the moral order imposed by Church and State in order to uphold the patriarchal system of right to property ownership. The existence of a monogamous family unit that is easy to classify and control by means of legislation facilitates the acknowledgement of paternity, which is the key to the transfer of a man's wealth to his heirs.[270]

It should come as no surprise then that children of common-law relationships had no right to inherit their father's money or property. However, as far back as 1834, an act of the Newfoundland legislature attempted to ensure that such offspring would be supported financially by the Colony.[271] Similarly, a common-law wife was not usually able to inherit from her husband unless he had made a will specifically naming her as one of the beneficiaries.[272] If there was no will the woman would not be entitled to anything from the relationship unless it was in her name. A common-law wife did have claim to her husband's pension as far back as 1919 in some jurisdictions.[273]

Newfoundland's Workman's Compensation Act of 1970 defined a common-law wife:

> . . . a woman who, although not legally married to a man, cohabits with him and is recognized as a wife in the community in which they live . . . .[274]

Under this act a common-law wife was entitled to benefits that her common-law husband would have received. There is no mention of common-law wives receiving benefits prior to 1970 in Newfoundland.

Although common-law relationships did exist, marriage was the accepted practice for women and men. By entering into marriage, women surrendered most, if not all, of the legal rights they had as single women. Marriage was viewed not only as a personal relationship, but also "a legal and economic institution through which the community imposes a certain order on society."[275] Within this legal and economic institution women were subordinate to their husbands.

"So Great a Favourite": The Married State

> Even the disabilities that the wife lies under are for the most part intended for her protection and benefit—so great a favourite is the female sex with the laws of England.[276]

So wrote Sir William Blackstone in an early commentary on English law. Being a "favourite" in a patriarchal society meant that upon marriage, women were relegated to a dependent and subordinate role that was enshrined in the law.

Since biblical times, marriage has symbolized the joining of husband and wife to become "one flesh" embodied in one person— the husband. With the 17th century adoption of canon law into English common law, the husband and wife were also one in law.

> In practice, legal and civic rights could be given only to one of the two. Since society viewed the male as superior, those rights were given to the husband. When a woman married, her separate legal identity merged with her husband's and she became invisible.[277]

This "unity of the person" principle had far-reaching ramifications for women. It meant that a wife could not own her own property, enter into contracts or business without her husband's approval, charge her husband for rape or theft of her property, sue him for slander, libel or compensation for assault, or give witness against him since it was deemed that one cannot commit these acts against "oneself."[278] The limitations this principle imposed on women and the latitude it afforded men are obvious.

The "unity" principle provided the basis for the courts' decisions in cases involving married women's property in English case law. Courts in Newfoundland followed the example of the English courts in deciding that married women were not legally separate persons in the eyes of the law. As we know, the adoption of the laws and procedures of England was due to the "settled colony" doctrine which held that where English settlers founded a colony without first conquering it, they brought with them the common law and statute law in place in England at that particular time. Thus, from the early English settlement of the 17th century in Newfoundland, English common law prevailed. Any later legislation had to be specifically adopted by the local legislature to be applicable.[279]

Under English common law, men were the legal owners of any property that their wives had owned prior to the marriage, as well as any that they acquired during it. The term "property" was not limited to land and money but also included personal belongings such as ornaments and clothing.[280] This personal property could be disposed of by a husband during his lifetime, although he could not leave the property to someone else through his will.[281]

By the seventeenth century in England, attempts were made to soften some of the harsher effects of a woman's lack of separate legal identity under English common law. The concept of equitable ownership of property, real and personal, was developed under separate equity rule. By written or verbal agreement between a husband and wife, property could be held in trust for the wife by an appointed trustee. Although restrictions on use or disposition of property could be written into the agreement, the property would not belong to the husband and was out of his power to control. It was held for the married woman's separate use even though she didn't exercise direct control over it.[282] A leading English case from the mid-nineteenth century between Lady Jodrell and Sir R.P. Jodrell, illustrates how this was enforced.

> By the law of England the very existence of the wife is considered as merged in that of the husband. The exceptions which have been introduced have not gone further than to allow a wife to have property for her separate use, independent of her husband; and secondly to give her separate rights through the intervention of trustees upon an actual separation but which altogether terminates by a reconciliation.[283]

The purpose behind the concept of equitable ownership was somewhat undermined during the nineteenth century because courts recognized the husband as trustee over his wife's property where no other trustee had been specifically appointed. It was feared that this would allow husbands to persuade their wives to sign over their property to them. To counteract this possibility, the courts began to allow the families of women contemplating marriage to insert a clause into a marriage settlement agreement that would prevent a married woman from signing over her property. The marriage settlement agreement specified what property a woman would bring into the marriage with her. These added clauses could also state that the woman could not sell or otherwise dispose of property that was held in trust for her.[284] Toward the end of the nineteenth century, a husband's right to his wife's personal belongings was no longer being enforced by the courts, which held that women were entitled to their personal effects.[285]

Unfortunately, to acquire the protection afforded in equity agreements required money. It was not deemed practical to enter into such legal arrangements unless a great deal of property was involved, so such agreements were only useful to wealthy families. The appointment of a trustee was often an attempt by a woman's family to retain control over family property that the woman had been given before or upon her marriage. Therefore, the development of trustees for women's property may have been less an attempt to extend women's property rights than a way to keep property within a family's control from one generation to the next. Under these class-specific circumstances, only one-tenth of the marriages in England involved marriage settlements in equity.[286]

The Newfoundland court's adherence to the principles of equitable ownership is illustrated by the comments of Chief Justice Carter of the Newfoundland Supreme Court in 1880. His comments are based on the settlement of the estate of Mary and Thomas Spracklin.[287] At the time of her death in 1880, Mary Spracklin possessed property and money separate from her husband. Those contesting the estate claimed that the money held in a bank account in Mary Spracklin's name, under general rule of law, belonged to her husband.

> This may be the general rule of law derived from the unity of person which was formerly held to render a married woman incapable of taking a gift . . . the moment she took it it was her husband's property; but that rule of common law has long since been controlled by the intervention of the courts of Chancery . . . .[288]

At a later point the Chief Justice stated:

> It is satisfactory to know that by the local enactment of 1876 "relating to the property of married women" a similar question . . . is not likely to arise . . . .[289]

This "local enactment" was the Married Women's Property Act of 1876 in Newfoundland. This act followed similar legislation which had been passed in England in 1870. The act gave a married woman, who did not have a marriage agreement, the right to acquire property as if she were not married. A married woman could retain for her own separate use the wages, money or property gained by her from her own employment, skills or investments. A condition for this was that the married woman publish a notice in the *Royal Gazette*[290] and one other local newspaper announcing her intention of carrying on this portion of her life separate from her husband. Once this was done, a married woman could sue, and be sued in her own name, take out life insurance policies if she wished and inherit, as next of kin, property and goods for her own use.[291]

A revision of the 1876 act occurred in 1883.[292] In this revision, a married woman was permitted to acquire, hold and dispose of real or personal property as if she were a *femme sole*, or single woman.[293] The right of inheritance still held.

In 1883, Joseph Legrandais of Bay St. George, Newfoundland wrote a last will and testament which clearly specified the distribution of his property to his sons and daughters. The will also provided for the retention of the property within the family line. In the will he bequeathed "an equal share of all my real estate, personal property, cattle, goods and money" to his three children, Josephine, Louisa and Joseph. Special stipulations were made regarding the share left to Louisa and her daughter, Bessie. Louisa's legacy was "for her own sole support as long as she lives, the principle [sic] to be placed in a safe Banking Company and the interest to go to her support." Louisa's husband was not to receive any benefit from the will.

If Louisa died, her one-third share would be redivided among the remaining sister and brother and Bessie, with Bessie receiving one-third. Again, the legacy contained restrictions on its use.

> And her daughter Bessie's third of her mother's legacy is to go to her support until she comes of age and no part thereof to be made use of by her father or his relations . . . .[294]

Any portion of the legacy remaining should Bessie die before coming of age was to revert to her aunt and uncle, Josephine and Joseph or their heirs. In this rather complex fashion, Joseph Legrandais protected his property and money, retaining it within the family control while providing for the support of his children and grandchildren.

Although under the 1883 act married women could control their own property, many women did not possess much property before marriage. Some women did receive a settlement of property from their families upon their marriage, or inherited property as in the case of the Legrandais family, but these families were generally those belonging to the middle and upper classes. Those less fortunate possessed little. Elizabeth Goudie, writing of her life in Labrador as a new bride, described the personal property she brought to her marriage in 1920. She said, "[W]hen I got married I did not have much money of my own. I had saved enough to buy myself a washboard."[295]

The Married Women's Property Act of 1876 formed the basis of the Married Women's Property Act of 1970. The 1970 act provided that whoever had paid for property brought into the marriage was

the legal owner of that property. Thus each spouse retained ownership of any property they had brought into the marriage, and any
property acquired during the marriage became the property of
whoever had paid for it. If the marriage ended, the husband and wife
were entitled to whatever property they purchased.[296] This apparent
broadening of the law did not grapple with the reality of many
women's lives within marriage. At the time when this act came into
effect it was still common for men to be the sole wage earner in a
marriage. Most women, if they had been employed prior to marriage,
left that job to devote themselves to home and family life. They
usually had no separate personal income with which to purchase
goods or property. Any property acquired would be purchased by
the husband and registered in his name. Therefore, at the dissolution of the marriage, the husband would generally be considered to
own virtually all of the property acquired during the marriage.

A woman's contribution to the marriage in the form of housework
and child care or work on the family farm, in the family fishing
enterprise or other family business was not usually considered
sufficient to entitle them to an equal share in property ownership.
The Murdoch and Rathwell cases in western Canada made clear that
under the law wives would not share in the "family" property.[297] The
comments of Mr. Justice Mifflin of the Newfoundland Supreme
Court sum up the state of the law at that time.

> I can readily appreciate the view of the [wife] that she feels she has
> a claim to the home, because if it were not for her prudent
> management of the household while bringing up a large family the
> [husband] would not have been able to build [the home] . . . The
> work that she did in connection with the construction of the house
> is not unusual for any wife in Newfoundland and it does not create
> a proprietary interest in the house and land . . . .[298]

Women's groups in Newfoundland and Labrador were very
aware of how the Married Women's Property Act of 1970 affected
women upon the breakdown of a marriage, and they lobbied the
provincial government on this issue. Women asked the legislature
to make changes to the existing act or draft a completely new piece
of legislation. The Royal Commission on the Status of Women also
lobbied for changes, recommending that the government "recognize
the concept of equal partnership in marriage."[299]

In 1976 the Newfoundland Status of Women Council presented
a brief to the provincial government that included among its requests a recommendation that matrimonial property be divided
equally between spouses if a marriage failed. The Newfoundland
courts, when hearing cases involving the division of matrimonial

property, were also recommending that changes to the current legislation be introduced. The comments of Mr. Justice Noel Goodridge were quoted in a local newspaper, the *Evening Telegram*, in 1977. His remarks upon the situation existing for women should their marriage break down arose out of a written court decision.

> The wife in most cases sacrifices her economic value to the husband even if it consists only of housekeeping; in other cases she will work and contribute her earnings to the marriage. Unless she can establish a trust—a difficult task—she is turned out at the end of the marriage wiser perhaps but penniless. The situation will prevail until the jurisdiction of the court is enlarged to order property settlements.[300]

Finally in 1979, the Newfoundland legislature passed the Matrimonial Property Act which came into force July 1, 1980. The provisions of the act were based upon the concept of an equal division of property upon separation or divorce, or in other words, a "fifty-fifty" split. Husband and wife were entitled to an equal share in property considered to be a matrimonial asset, such as the family home. This is currently the law regarding matrimonial property in Newfoundland and Labrador.

A Proprietary Interest

A husband was not only entitled under common law to possess his wife's property once they were married, he was also entitled to possess his wife as his property. Possession of a wife could increase a man's chances for success, especially in the fishery.

> A woman's role . . . is not enviable. A man without a wife is like a man without a good boat or a good horse and a woman is, in the division of shares of a voyage, considered an item of her husband's capital, just as a cod trap or an engine.[301]

With this view of the useful place of women, it is not surprising that male lawmakers sought to secure a man's right to his wife. Thus, the old common law held that a husband "had a proprietary interest in his wife which gave him a right to her services and company."[302] This encompassed sexual and domestic services, including the bearing and raising of children.[303]

The sexual ownership of women was intimately linked to property ownership and inheritance. It was deemed crucial for the male to be assured of the legitimacy of his heirs, principally, that his sons were his sons, in order to ensure the smooth inheritance of property. To safeguard his exclusive rights to a woman, a man had grounds to take another person to court if that person had negligently or otherwise deprived him of his wife's "consortium," or the "affection, companionship and services" of his wife.[304] There were a number of actions that a husband could take against loss of consortium, but generally a woman did not have the same right to sue for the loss of her husband's consortium.

Actions for loss of consortium could include a suit for "criminal conversation," or relations between a wife and a third party.[305] A husband had a right to sue another man who had taken his wife away and committed adultery with her. The man defending against such a law suit could argue that the woman had little value to the husband and thus no damage had been done to either the husband's feelings or his honour. This form of action existed in England before divorce became available in that country under the Matrimonial Causes Act of 1857.[306]

Husbands could also sue a party for "enticement" if he thought that person had persuaded his wife to leave him. The husband, deprived of his wife's companionship and services, could have grounds to take the offending person to court.[307] In an unusual 1950 legal case heard in England, a wife sued her husband's employer for enticement. In *Best* v. *Samuel Fox & Co., Ltd.*, the plaintiff's husband was injured in an accident.[308] A result of these injuries was the loss of marital sexual intercourse. The wife was therefore deprived of a "normal marital relationship" and was said to suffer ill effects as a result. The case was argued on the basis of enticement—that "each spouse had a right to the consortium of the other." This enabled the wife to take action against the third party who interfered with the consortium,[309] in this case the employer. The final decision, rendered on July 31, 1952 by the House of Lords, was to disallow the use of loss of consortium as grounds in the legal action by the wife. They stated:

> . . . while it was anomalous to grant such a right to the husband and not to the wife, the real anomaly was the husband's right to seek such an action and there was no reason to extend such an anomaly by granting a like right to the wife.[310]

Norman Marsh, author of an article reviewing the case in the *Law Review Quarterly* of 1951 stated that the wife had "a strong case, the force of which was not fully appreciated by the trial judge."[311] This was an unusual case in that it reaffirmed the exclusive right of husbands to the argument of loss of consortium.

"Harbouring" was yet another action that a husband could pursue if his wife left him. A husband could sue someone for giving his wife a place to stay after she ran away from him. The court would not allow his lawsuit to be successful if it was proven that the woman had honestly been in need of protection from her husband.[312] Such appears to be the case in *Rose* v. *Kavanagh*, 1946.[313] The plaintiff, Rose, and his wife had been married for thirty-six years and had fourteen children. In the last few years of the marriage, the couple argued repeatedly and Rose assaulted his wife on at least two occasions. A neighbour of the Rose's, Kavanagh, had become increasingly friendly with the couple over the course of fifteen years. During this time, Kavanagh paid a great deal of attention to Mrs. Rose, which Mr. Rose resented. Finally, the situation in the Rose household forced Mrs. Rose to leave and reside in St. John's in April, 1945. Mr. Rose then sued Mr. Kavanagh for loss of consortium and harbouring Mrs. Rose. Justice Brian Dunfield commented that this was an unusual case as no others like it had ever gone to trial in the Newfoundland courts.

Justice Dunfield ruled that Mr. Rose's conduct toward his wife was reprehensible, and that he did not have much to lose in the form of pleasant consortium. Dunfield believed Mr. Rose's suit was motivated by animosity, not desire for compensation. Rose was awarded only $1, but Dunfield noted that this award was still in recognition of the husband's proper assertion of his rights.

Not only did a husband own his wife's property and her person, she was also an adjunct to him under citizenship regulations. A woman's own citizenship derived from her husband. Until 1949 all Newfoundland citizens were considered to be British citizens and under the British Naturalization Act of 1914 a woman who married a British subject became a British subject herself. If her husband died she retained his British status, but if a woman then married an "alien" (the citizen of another country), she lost her status as a British subject and took on her new husband's citizenship. Children also took their father's citizenship.[314]

The 1914 act stipulated that "any person under a disability could not receive a certificate of naturalization." Disability was specifically defined to mean "the status of being a married woman or minor, lunatic or idiot."[315] Therefore, married women were ineligible to receive their own certificate of naturalization. In this way, a woman's identity was firmly tied to the man she married.

Early in the twentieth century, Newfoundland found itself embroiled in a debate regarding the admittance of "alien" Chinese immigrants into the country. Laws created to restrict Chinese immigration had a profound impact on the lives of women. The first documented evidence of Chinese presence in Newfoundland is a notice advertising the opening of a Chinese laundry on New Gower Street in August 1895.[316] After a series of violent clashes with local people in 1897 and 1900, the government of the day introduced a bill in 1904 to prohibit the immigration of Chinese or Japanese labour into Newfoundland. This bill seems to have died when it did not pass the Legislative Council.[317] From this point on, the Chinese community found itself under increasing scrutiny. In 1905–06, more negative comment on the Chinese and further press coverage occurred.[318] Finally, in 1906, anti-Chinese legislation was re-introduced and passed.[319] This legislation copied the current Canadian law, but charged a "head tax" of $300 instead of $500 on all Chinese wishing to enter Newfoundland.[320]

The 1906 act and subsequent amendments affected women in different ways. First, Chinese women whose husbands were not Chinese, were considered by the Newfoundland government to be of the same nationality as their husband. Their children took the father's nationality as well. For all intents and purposes, these women and children were not considered Chinese. Second, a 1907 amendment to the act allowed the wives and children of Chinese merchants to be exempt from the $300 head tax.[321] This provision made the entry of selected Chinese women possible, since it waived the high tax. Finally, although no separate statute existed specifically restricting the entry of Chinese women into Newfoundland, in 1947 the chief commissioner of immigration stated in a memo that the Department of Immigration "never permitted Chinese women to enter Newfoundland."[322] This overtly racist act was in direct contravention of the government's own legislation.

In 1947, the issue of the immigration of Chinese women to Newfoundland in order to join their husbands in the country was again raised.[323] Mr. Davey Fong requested that his wife, Seto King, be allowed to join himself and his son Hayford, both naturalized British subjects, in their home in Newfoundland. Howell, Chief Commissioner of Immigration, writing to the Secretary of Justice requested that they "look into this matter at your earliest convenience and advise us what action we can take under existing law to prohibit the entry of Chinese females."[324] It is clear from ensuing correspondence[325] that the government was seeking ways to restrict the entry of Chinese women into Newfoundland. It was feared that a decision on Chinese women would have "repercussions on the position regarding immigration"[326] H.L. Pottle, commissioner for home affairs and education, notes in a 1948 confidential memorandum:

> Several applications for naturalization as British subjects have been received from Chinamen resident in Newfoundland and the solicitors acting for the applicants are pressing for a decision . . . .

It is quite possible that if these applications are granted a number of others will follow from Chinese who are watching the outcome.[327]

In the end, Pottle called upon the Commission of Government for a decision. No further laws appear to have been passed on the subject until Confederation with Canada in 1949.

After Newfoundland joined Canada the province came under the country's Canadian Citizenship law, enacted in 1947. Women no longer lost their citizenship by marrying someone from another country. Regrettably, the act did not reinstate the citizenship of women who had married "aliens" before the act was passed. Women from other countries who married Canadians could become citizens of this country after living in Canada for a year, but men marrying Canadian women had to wait five years to become citizens.[328] In 1950, families of Chinese men resident in Newfoundland were allowed to come to Newfoundland, and finally, in 1951, seven Chinese residents of Newfoundland became citizens of Canada.[329]

After 1976 the law was amended to allow women who had married non-Canadians to be reinstated as Canadian citizens, and the residency requirements for males and females were equalized.[330]

A Home and Family

For most Newfoundland women, married life was simply an extension of life in her father's house. The training of childhood prepared her for the duties and responsibilities of a home and family of her own. Marriage age varied from community to community between 1900 and 1949, but usually young women married by their late teens. In some communities, if a woman reached the age of twenty-five and had not yet married, it was thought "she might as well 'hang up her hat.'"[331]

Once married, a woman would be expected to begin a family. Motherhood was considered to be a woman's major role in life. In Stephenville, if she were not pregnant within the first year of her marriage, a young woman was considered to be sick or, worse still, not pleasing her husband.[332]

It was very difficult for a woman to avoid pregnancy. The absence of reliable birth control did not allow women to separate pregnancy from sexual activity. Some women passed on information on birth control to new mothers, but such lore was only marginally successful in the prevention of pregnancy. Prior to 1969, birth control was not legal in Newfoundland. As a result, women resorted to home remedies to end a pregnancy: herbal treatments, stomach salts, jumping from a high place in order to induce a miscarriage. Some attempted self-administered abortions or sought abortions from others.[333] With such unreliable and dangerous remedies for pregnancy, large families were common in Newfoundland.

> The Stephenville women remember that it was common to see twelve to fifteen children from one couple. Of course, many died young in child-birth or from contagious diseases which periodically spread through the area . . . [334]

Midwives, usually older, widowed mothers, who felt a calling to their community role as midwife/healer, served as the birthing support to expectant mothers.[335] Doctors were usually unavailable in rural communities, and many families could not afford the cost of their services. Virtually all deliveries, especially in rural Newfoundland, were made at home with the midwife in attendance.[336] Often midwives gained their skills and their knowledge of techniques and herbal cures from other women.

> I first learned to doctor women by going about with my aunt who was widowed . . . . My only real law was to confine the mothers for ten days to the bed. Poor souls, it was their only true holiday, if you don't mind to call it that.[337]

In St. John's, doctors usually attended a birth only if the midwife called upon them for assistance. This may have created animosity on the part of some doctors who felt that midwives were usurping their medical role. Indeed, at the turn of the century, with the growing emphasis on professionalization of health care and increasing concern over child welfare, some doctors and nurses took a dim view of practicing midwives. Nurse Rogers, a public health nurse from New York City commented in 1918:

> . . . at present there are all too many engaged for obstetrical service who are grossly ignorant, personally untidy, ever dirty in appearance, and their teachings and practices are altogether questionable and disgusting.[338]

In light of the antipathy of doctors and nurses and the concern for safety and cleanliness in childbirth, legislation to control and regulate midwifery was introduced in the House of Assembly.[339] An Act Concerning the Registration of Midwives[340] was passed by the House of Assembly in 1920. The governor of Newfoundland at that time, C. Alexander Harris and his wife, Constance, were personally interested in the passage of this act. Four months prior to the passage of the act, Harris indicated their interest to Sir Richard Squires, then prime minister of Newfoundland.

The Act deals exclusively with the qualifications of what is commonly known as a medical practitioner and section 42 of the Act distinctly lays down that nothing in the Act prevents the practice of midwifery by women whom you describe as the "grannies" which [t]he doctors of St. John's are most anxious to control and therefore my wife and I shall look forward to hearing from you again on the subject.[341]

However, the 1920 act was vaguely worded and engendered no debate in the House of Assembly.

In 1921, the Squires government appointed a voluntary group, the Newfoundland Midwives' Board, to define and oversee the act of 1920. However, in 1922, the Board was declared to have no authority under the act. After years of lobbying and at the insistence of the Board, the legislature passed the 1926 Act to Secure the Better Training of Midwives and to Regulate Their Practice. This time, the act provoked much debate in the House of Assembly, but it eventually died "in a tangle of red tape."[342] In 1931, the Public Health Act included a section requiring the names of practising midwives to be published in the *Royal Gazette*. Perhaps due to the urgent financial difficulties in which the Squires government found itself, and the lack of priority given to midwifery concerns, the 1931 section was never enforced. Finally, in 1936, An Act to Govern the Practice of Midwifery[343] was passed. Under this act, midwives were required to be licensed. Again, the law was not fully enforced by the government:

. . . the public health bureaucracy was not heavy-handed or punitive in dealing with midwives. In the 1940s and '50s, efforts were made to urge women already established as midwives to attend public health training and acquire licences. But women who were unable to do this practised into the 1960s without certification . . . .[344]

In an effort to increase the medical knowledge and skill of midwives, The Midwives Club was founded in 1920, in St. John's. Lectures and courses were provided and in the spring of 1922, the first class of midwives graduated. Few outport women participated in this training. It wasn't until 1935, under Commission of Government, that the first course of lectures and practical instruction for outport midwives occurred. The practice of training and licensing midwives ceased in 1961.

Janet McNaughton, in her 1989 dissertation on midwifery in Newfoundland, notes:

Successive governments trivialized the role of midwife in Newfoundland, by not publishing lists of individual practitioners, by depriving them of the right to reimbursement for charity work, and by educating them to be doctor's assistants, although most worked independently, but no efforts were made to eliminate empirically trained midwives.[345]

McNaughton reports that the financial reward for midwifery was slight as money was scarce in the nineteenth and early twentieth centuries. Compensation for services rendered was often "in kind": fish, hay, bread, quilts or hooked mats. By the 1930s midwives were beginning to receive cash for their assistance—from two dollars to ten dollars. Most midwives were married or widowed women who relied on financial support from husband or extended family. While a woman might not be able to support herself or her family on her midwifery earnings, the role of midwife was a way to share her knowledge and skill in the healing arts and to attain a more public profile in her community. It was acceptable and available work for married and widowed women who desired such a role.[346]

With the birth of a child, mothering was considered a woman's prime responsibility. She was to bear and raise her husband's children, yet have no legal right to make decisions regarding their future. As we have seen, for decades legal guardianship rested solely with the father. Sir William Blackstone commented in 1765 on the legal position of mothers, "Mothers as such, are entitled to no power, only reverence and respect."[347] It is questionable how much reverence and respect women were accorded for their home work. A woman was expected to devote her energies to maintaining the home and family, particularly her husband. A Stephenville woman, born in 1898 and mother of ten children recalled her married life:

> You were born to work and tend on the men and you lived with it. Work was your story and so you bit your lip, tied your shoe laces and got on with it. We women had what it took to make a good frame. Sometimes I wonder, as I sit here getting old, how I conquered it all.[348]

The quantity and type of work a woman was expected to do in the home varied with the class background and geographical location of the family. Generally, women were responsible for keeping the house, feeding the family and nursing the sick. On top of these daily tasks were seasonally variable duties including, in rural Newfoundland, care and tending of animals, planting and keeping of gardens, making hay, picking and bottling berries, baking bread daily, helping "make" the fish, and much more. If the family moved in the spring to fishing grounds, the women were required to prepare the family for the move and establish a new household at the fishing station. In a more urban setting, women might still be required to care for animals or chickens, keep a garden, bake bread, take in laundry or mending, and make ends meet. Only those women in the middle and upper classes could afford to employ many servants, whom they then had to direct, to maintain their households. For these women, involvement in social causes and church work were added to their list of responsibilities. Most women learned their duties when they were children, watching and participating in their own mother's household work.

Since most married women did not engage in paid work outside the home, financial support for the family had to come from the husband's work or the wages contributed to the household by working children. Married women might earn some money by taking in laundry or sewing, tasks they could manage while still attending to their own home. At times, additional money was needed. In 1949, the Mothers' Allowances Act was passed by the Commission of Government. The act provided for the financial support of dependent children. Under the act, a Mothers' Allowances Board was established to screen applications for allowances and to determine the amount to be paid to the applicant. Unmarried mothers and widows could also apply for financial assistance and under certain conditions an "incapacitated" father could apply for an allowance.[349]

Work and Marriage

In the first half of this century, a woman's marital status affected whether or not she worked outside the home. As Nancy Forestell has noted, most women worked for a few years until they were married. According to St. John's employment statistics for 1921, only 1.4 percent of the female workers in St. John's were married. By 1935, 2.6 percent of the working women in St. John's were married. Forestell points out that a woman's age and the presence and age of any children had "a direct relationship on their participation in the workforce."[350] Childcare and home work fully occupied most married women.

Although there was not a wide range of employment possibilities for any woman, the married women recorded in the census for the 1920s experienced even more limited prospects.

> The small number of older, married working women that show up in census records appear to have confined themselves primarily to being owners of confectionery or grocery stores, hotel keepers, boardinghouse keepers, and in one instance, a hairdresser.[351]

In the late 1890s and early 1900s, advertisements and stories appearing in local newspapers indicate women pursued a few other employments: washer woman, bookstore owner, landlady, milliner

and dressmaker.[352] Notable in all of these business endeavours is
the fact that they could be conducted in close proximity to the family
home. Women were thus able to bring wages into the household
while still maintaining the upkeep of home and family. This ten-
dency appears to remain throughout the 1920s and 1930s as well.
Women coupled their waged labour with their household responsibilities once their children were in school. It appears from census
records for the 1920s and 1930s that "part-time work was relied
upon by a significant proportion of married and widowed working-
class women in the city."[353] It may be that middle-class women, not
being as dependent on outside wages to sustain their families,
participated less in wage labour outside the home than did working-class women.

Prevailing attitudes of the day also shaped women's expectations
regarding work outside the home. The concept of separate spheres,
public for men and private for women, was a strong force. Indeed,
during the suffrage campaign of the 1920s women's position in
society was made abundantly clear to one female campaigner.

> One well-known old gent told Mrs. Mitchell: "Go home, madame,
> and learn to bake bread." "I bake excellent bread," was her reply.[354]

Society deemed women's proper role to be that of tending to home
and family concerns.

In an experience closer to our own time, Ruby Cabot of West St.
Modeste, Labrador described her active life in 1975 as a housewife
and as co-owner, with her husband, of a community store.

> I have seven children, from 10 to 20 years old. I have two finished
> school. I get up around 8:00 in the morning, get breakfast for my
> family, do a few chores before I leave for the store at 9:00 a.m. I
> rush back at noon, and sometimes wash the breakfast dishes
> before I lay the table for lunch. Usually I cook something at night
> for lunch, if not, I cook something quick for lunch . . . . On wash
> day I usually wash when I come back from the store after 6:00 p.m.
> When it's baking day, I get up early and mix my bread before the
> children wake up. Then I go home at noon and knead the bread.
> And at 1:00 p.m. before I go back to the store, I put it in the pans
> to rise. . . . When the time comes to do spring cleaning, I set the
> alarm for 6:00 a.m., which gives me about two hours before the
> children get out of bed.[355]

The "double day" of many women workers is evident in Ruby's
description. Until recently, women were unable to make a claim
based on their labour in a family business such as Ruby Cabot
co-owned. Often years of hard work were ignored by the court in
separation or divorce proceedings.

Certain areas of business were the exclusive right of men and single women. Prior to the enactment of the Married Women's Property Act in 1876, married women could not enter into contracts, either with strangers or with their husbands. Under the "unity of the person" principle, a husband and wife were one person, and the law ruled that a man could not contract with "himself."[356] As a result of this principle, a woman lacked the separate legal identity to enter into her own contracts. Thus, if a wife entered into a contract, either with her husband or a third person, during her marriage, that contract would be invalid in the eyes of the law. Neither the woman nor her husband could be sued by the other person who had signed the contract if the woman did not fulfil her duties under the contract. Even if a woman had separated from her husband, neither the woman nor her husband could be sued.

Before 1876, if a single woman signed a contract prior to her marriage, all of the benefits from that contract automatically accrued to her husband once she married. If someone wanted to sue the woman for not fulfilling the terms of the contract, that individual would have to sue both the woman and her husband. If the husband died while the contract was still in effect it was possible to sue his wife.[357]

Married women who wished to get involved in business had to have their husbands sign all contracts. In the absence of a formal contract, the explicit or implicit agreement of the husband could be taken as authority for the wife to engage in business. An 1883 Newfoundland case illustrates the problems that this system could create. Mrs. Walsh had managed her husband's shop and boarding house businesses in St. John's for many years, and eventually she started her own business in Holyrood. She ran into debt with the Holyrood business, and her creditors attempted to sue her husband for payment of her debts. Mr. Walsh argued that he wasn't responsible for the debts that his wife had incurred, and that he had expressly forbidden his wife to start up her business venture. The court decided that Mr. Walsh was responsible for the debts since creditors would have assumed that he would make good on his wife's debts based on the years his wife had managed his businesses under "his sanction and authority."[358] That the debts were run up in relation to her own business in Holyrood, rather than her husband's in St. John's, made no difference in law. Even if Mr. and Mrs. Walsh had entered into a written contract between themselves, which would have been legally binding if entered into between strangers, the court might hold that such an agreement was not binding.[359] Husband and wife were firmly one in the eyes of the law.

As a result of the Married Woman's Property Act of 1876, a married woman could be sued in her own name for the property which was hers before her marriage, and had remained so by written agreement between husband and wife after their marriage. Her husband would not be held liable for any debts she accrued prior to their marriage.[360] Whether written marriage settlement agreements between husband and wife in Newfoundland were used largely by the upper classes remains to be investigated.

The general assumption that a woman's main responsibility was to care for the family home and children was sometimes enshrined in law, as with the 1947 Civil Service Act.[361] The act provided that female civil servants were to be retired upon their marriage, unless it was in the "interests of the public service" that they be retained.[362] In 1964, a section was added to this act which stated that if a woman occupied the position of "Confidential Secretary and Personal Assistant to the Premier or to any Minister of the Crown" she was not required to retire when she married, or when she reached the age of 60.[363] Presumably, these women were deemed too valuable to male politicians to be retired merely because they had married or aged. Both of these sections concerning women were repealed in 1979 by the Human Rights Anti-Discrimination Act.[364]

Other specific references to women contained in provincial legislation were sometimes included where it might have been assumed that women were to be excluded. Thus, for example, The Memorial University Act of 1949 stated that, "Women may be members of the Board of Regents and of the Senate."[365] This section of the act was not altered by the provincial legislature until 1988, when it was repealed by the Charter of Rights Amendment Act.[366]

With marriage, motherhood and the responsibilities of a home, women have traditionally spent less time in the workforce than men. This is reflected in the size of pensions many women receive. If a woman has not held a pensionable job, perhaps engaging only in part-time work for example, she may have forfeited any pension security. Historically, lack of daycare options in rural and urban Newfoundland and the antiquated and paternalistic view of women's proper role in society have kept many women in a subordinate and economically dependent position. Current legislation in many areas still proves unsatisfactory for women and inadequacies in laws concerning equal pay, daycare, pensions, and working conditions remain.[367]

V. SEEKING THE PROTECTION OF THE LAW

Marriage was supposed to last forever, providing a safe haven emotionally and financially for a woman. Marriage was deemed permanent and indissoluble. If a woman chose to leave a marriage that was intolerable to her, she faced the loss of economic security, her children, and her reputation. There was a widely held belief that if a couple knew they could separate, licentious and unreserved immorality would be the result. In 1790, Sir W. Scott, a noted English jurist observed:

> In this case, as in many others, the happiness of some individuals must be sacrificed to the greater and more general good.[368]

In reality, it was generally the woman's happiness that was sacrificed since her husband retained economic and social control in their relationship.

Women, within society and marriage, were, and are, vulnerable to the greater physical and economic power of men. Between 1890 and 1949, local Newfoundland newspapers continually reported cases of physical assault and mental cruelty committed by men, usually husbands, on women, usually their wives.[369] Beatings, assaults, threats of violence, arguments resulting in assault, ill-treatment—all appear in the public record. Doubtless many more remained unreported.

In the late nineteenth century, the law and public opinion seemed to shy away from discussions of the domestic difficulties experienced by couples. As Backhouse comments, it was less the cruelty toward women involved in these difficulties, than the public nature of the difficulties which the judges, the courts and the citizenry disliked.[370] In Newfoundland, the Evening Herald reported in its "In and Around the City" column in 1890 that:

> Judge Prowse is to be recommended for his efforts in trying to get cases between husband and wife settled outside of Court, instead of scandalously making public every little grievance between man and wife.[371]

Judge Prowse is notable for his apparent lack of concern for women in his courtroom judgements. Earlier that year, he had tried a case of ill-treatment and wounding with a knife charged against a husband by his wife. The Evening Herald commented on the trial in their "Police Court" column.

> The defendant denied the knife-cutting, but admitted to kicking and striking, which he made an effort to justify. As the case developed, it was shown the couple was not living very harmoniously, and the husband had a great deal to contend with. Judge

Prowse stated that as a judge he could not excuse the man for
kicking or beating his wife, and fined him $20, or 10 days, at the
same time strongly admonished the woman as to her future behaviour.[372]

Evidently, Judge Prowse was torn between upholding the law
and his personal opinion regarding the appropriate behaviour of a
wife toward her husband. Until the late 1800s, English common law
gave the husband the right to beat his wife, to "discipline" her, so
long as he did not endanger her life or health, if she did not obey
him.[373]

Indeed, Judge Prowse was noted for his negative opinion of
women. In one case heard before him in 1890, the Evening Herald
reported the Judge's words.

The case was dismissed, as the judge said, since the days of the
ten years war in the time of Pliny, to the days of the racket at the
Rope-Walk, women were the cause of every trouble. He . . . warned
the women that in the future they should conduct themselves in
such a manner as to prevent a breach of the peace . . . .[374]

But the peace could not always be kept when women were subjected
to cruelty, abuse and violence at the hands of their husbands.
Moreover, some violent treatment of women was not considered
illegal.

Violent attacks such as rape committed on women by their
husbands were not chargeable offences in civil law because under
the "unity of person" principle, "one" could not rape "oneself." A wife
had no recourse against her husband in civil law. Under English
criminal laws adopted by Newfoundland,[375] it was possible for a
convicted rapist to be subjected to the death penalty or a sentence
of three years to life imprisonment. However, this penalty did not
apply to a man who raped his wife. The Criminal Code of England
clearly stated:

A man cannot be guilty as a principal in the first degree of rape
upon his wife, for the wife is unable to retract the consent to
cohabitation which is part of the contract of matrimony.[376]

It was assumed that a wife's consent to sexual relations with her
husband was a permanent part of the marriage vows and could not
be retracted.[377]

The right of a husband to sexual relations with his wife was also
enshrined in the first Canadian Criminal Code enacted in 1892. This
code was modelled on a well-publicized draft of an early Criminal
Code of England which was never enacted by the British Parliament.[378] This would explain the similarity between the two codes.

The adopted 1892 code contained a complete definition of rape for the first time. Rape was:

> . . . the act of a man having carnal knowledge of a woman who is not his wife without her consent, or with consent which has been extorted by threats or fear of bodily harm, or obtained by personating the woman's husband, or by false or fraudulent representations as to the nature and quality of the act.[379]

Thus, with the 1892 Canadian Criminal Code it became legally impossible in Canada for a woman to charge her husband with rape. The sentence for rape by other than a husband in the 1892 Criminal Code of Canada was life imprisonment or death.[380] In the 1955 Criminal Code the maximum sentence was life imprisonment plus whipping. Attempted rape was punishable by ten years imprisonment plus whipping,[381] but there is no evidence to suggest that it was ever imposed.

Indeed, the 1970 Canadian Criminal Code showed little change from almost a century earlier. The section that dealt with rape stated:

> A male person commits rape when he has sexual intercourse with a female person who is not his wife,
>
> (a) without her consent, or
> (b) with her consent if the consent
>   (i) is extorted by threats or fear of bodily harm
>   (ii) is obtained by false and fraudulent representations
>   as to the nature and quality of the act.[382]

Eventually, a man could be charged with raping his wife where they were no longer living together, but this was not provided for under the law until 1978.[383] Finally, a 1982 amendment to the Criminal Code of Canada provided for a man to be convicted of raping his wife.

Constance Backhouse has suggested that the introduction of spousal immunity from rape charges in the 1892 Canadian Criminal Code reflects a conception of rape as an offence against male property, an assumption long held in rape cases.[384] Rape laws originated as a form of property law, in that rape was seen as a crime against a woman's husband or father instead of a crime against the woman herself. Men were to be compensated for a woman's loss of value if she had been raped, particularly if she had been a virgin. The Statute of Westminster in 1275 was one of the earliest codifications of rape laws and formed the basis of later and present day laws.[385] In 1275, the penalty for rape was a maximum of two years imprisonment and a fine.[386]

While the Statute of Westminster provided for equal treatment for those who raped virgins or married women, and included rape as a crime against the state, the Statute also provided for a lesser offence in which a victim would bear part of the blame for the offence. This lesser offence was applied where it was felt that a wife, in particular, did not attempt to fight off her attacker as strenuously as she could have in the circumstances. In these cases the husband was considered the real victim, and the woman would be "stripped of her dower" or marriage settlement.[387]

The 1970 Canadian Criminal Code also contained a section dealing with sexual intercourse with a female who was "feeble-minded, insane, or is an idiot or imbecile."[388] A male who had sexual intercourse with such a female, "in circumstances which do not amount to rape" was liable to a penalty of five years imprisonment. This section apparently had its origins in an 1886 Act of the Parliament of Canada entitled An Act to Punish Seduction and like Offences and to Make Further Provision for the Protection of Women and Girls.[389]

Proving a case could be an ordeal for the victim. A woman who attempted to have her rapist convicted had a heavy burden to bear in terms of proof and in enduring the public shame that such an attempt would bring. Sometimes the victim would be exposing herself to community censure and ridicule. Usually the defence counsel attempted to defame the victim in court, using her previous relationships to undermine her credibility in the rape charge.

A letter written in 1907 to the Attorney General for Newfoundland, Sir E.P. Morris, illustrates the way many influential male citizens viewed the victims of rape. The letter was written by T.P. O'Donnell, a magistrate who heard a rape case at the court on Bell Island:

> . . . and I had not the least doubt on my mind then or now but that she was a willing, nay a soliciting victim and that it was not her first indiscretion.[390]

The "willing" victim in question was a fifteen year old orphan. O'Donnell further commented that the young girl's "whole demeanour throughout the trial was one of cold defiance and shameless indifference."[391] Not surprisingly, given the comments of the magistrate, the alleged rapist was not convicted. Such misogynist sentiments must have precluded many a woman receiving a fair and sympathetic hearing of her case.

Concern over the sentencing of convicted rapists was occasionally expressed, as in the House of Assembly in 1920. The Honourable P.T. McGrath questioned the seriousness with which Magistrates treated rape cases. He noted that a Magistrate had recently fined a rapist "$20 or $25 . . . when he should have got three years."[392]

Comments such as this reveal the leniency with which male perpetrators of rape were treated in the courts. Newfoundland courts may not have been alone in this approach to rape cases. Constance Backhouse notes that prosecution for the crime of rape in nineteenth-century Ontario rarely resulted in a conviction.[393]

Even when a man was convicted of a sexual offence he might still retain the respect of the community. In 1918 a reputable local merchant wrote to the governor, Sir Charles A. Harris, on behalf of Captain James Belbin, who had been convicted of indecent assault and sentenced to two years imprisonment. W.J. Button, of M. Button & Sons of New Melbourne, asked that Captain Belbin's sentence be commuted, and that he be pardoned. It is worth noting that the argument for his release is based on the honour and justice of the law being satisfied, not on justice for the assault victim.

> Perhaps the honour and justice of the law would be fulfilled seeing he has had his punishment . . . in Grand Bank where he resided he had a pretty good reputation previous to this offence, where he was known to be a successful banker. We hear since his imprisonment his conduct has been pretty good.[394]

The governor was not inclined to release Captain Belbin. He replied, "It seems to me that this case is a bad one and there are no grounds for the exercise of clemency."[395] Shortly thereafter, the Minister of Justice pointed out to Governor Harris that there were problems obtaining men willing to undertake voyages to war zones at that time. More in the name of political expediency than justice, James Belbin was released on condition that he immediately join the mercantile marine.

In another case the family of a man convicted of rape circulated a petition in the man's hometown asking that the man's sentence be commuted. In August of 1900, William Strickland of Dildo Road, Trinity Bay wrote to the governor on behalf of his son Benjamin, who had been convicted of rape and sentenced to eighteen months hard labour and imprisonment.[396] William stated that Benjamin had been the sole support of his father and seven brothers and sisters. He asked that his son be released so that Benjamin could find a job and continue to support his family in the coming winter. Mr. Strickland added that Benjamin had always been a good son and attached a petition, listing the names of sixty-three men from the town of Whitbourne, asking for the governor's clemency in releasing Benjamin Strickland from prison. Subsequently, Governor McCallum wrote to the presiding judge, Mr. Justice Emerson of the Circuit Court at Harbour Grace, asking for his opinion in the matter.

Justice Emerson indicated that Benjamin Strickland had been convicted of attempted rape of a sixteen-year-old-girl. He commented upon the letter written by William Strickland.

> Upon a consideration of the petition and the recommendations of the inhabitants of Whitbourne and the vicinity, I have only to say that the indigent circumstances of the petitioner and the fact that he has seven helpless children to support . . . are not sufficient reasons to weigh with me to recommend to your Excellency the favourable consideration of the petition.[397]

Justice Emerson commented further on the incidence of sexual assaults against women, saying, in part, that:

> . . . offences against women in this country are becoming so common that to release a prisoner under a sentence of 18 months, after a lapse of six months, would , in my opinion, be placing a premium upon such crimes.[398]

Governor McCallum informed William Strickland that his request had been denied and repeated Justice Emerson's comments about the frequency of attacks against women. The governor stated offences such as rape were to be suppressed with the "utmost rigour of the law" and the family's personal circumstances were not to be taken into consideration when dealing with petitions for clemency:

> . . . the law recognizes no distinction between classes, and the adoption of such a position would place a premium on crime amongst the poorer members of the community.[399]

However, the law did make a gender-based distinction between the victim and the defendant. The female victim of a sexual offence was treated differently by the courts. Her evidence had to be corroborated by another person in order for that evidence to be accepted. A patriarchal morality and scepticism regarding the truthfulness of women are evident in the reasoning behind this practice. They are clearly outlined in this 1962 statement on the need for corroborating evidence.

> There is sound reason for this, because sexual cases are particularly subject to the danger of deliberately false charges resulting from sexual neuroses, phantasy, jealousy, spite or simply a girl's refusal to admit that she consented to an act of which she is now ashamed.[400]

This prejudicial understanding of women's testimony was echoed by the Newfoundland Supreme Court in 1960 when Chief Justice Furlong stated in a judgement:

> One cannot help feeling that the common sense warning that an unscrupulous, or untruthful, or an hysterical woman can bring

grave charges against man . . . has been blown up into too techni-
cal a matter. It would surely be an extraordinarily stupid jury to
which . . . the point would not occur anyway.[401]

The requirement that a rape victim's testimony be corroborated
by another source was not changed until 1975.[402] Technically, after
1975, a rape victim's evidence did not have to be "backed up" by
other sources, but judges still had the prerogative to warn a jury
about convicting an accused rapist on a victim's uncorroborated
evidence.[403]

A rape victim's past sexual history was long considered pertinent
in deciding whether a woman had in fact been raped. Until 1976 a
defence counsel could question a victim in great detail about her
sexual history. This was considered crucial in deciding whether the
woman had actually "consented" to sexual intercourse. Presumably,
if a woman had consented to sexual intercourse in the past then she
was more likely to have consented in the situation before the court.

> These judges reason that if a victim admits some form of previous
> sexual contact, it can be inferred that she is a woman of bad moral
> character. If she is an immoral person then it can be inferred
> further that she would not have conscientious scruples about lying
> in the witness box . . . [404]

This practice was used to discredit victims of sexual assault in the
eyes of the judge and jury.

Thus it was possible for a woman's past sexual partners to be
rounded up and brought to court to testify that the victim had not
previously been of chaste character, as was done in one 1976 case
involving a sixteen-year-old girl. In that case the victim testified that
she had been offered a ride home from the beach by a twenty-five-
year-old-man who was the brother of a former boyfriend.[405] On the
way home he had parked his van on a deserted road and attempted
to assault her. She escaped from the van and ran home. Two men
had seen her running away from the van, but the accused had told
them that the girl was under the influence of drugs.

The defence counsel for the accused attacker brought in two
witnesses, including the brother of the accused, to testify that they
had engaged in sexual intercourse with the girl in the past. Justice
Steele of the Newfoundland District Court held that this had no
relevance to the attack in question and convicted the accused. The
man was sentenced to six months imprisonment, a fine of $200 and
two years probation. Justice Steele stated that he hoped that this
sentence would " . . . deter a large number of young people in the
Conception Bay area from committing these sexual offences."[406] The
relevant section in the Criminal Code was changed in 1976. The

amendment was introduced by then Minister of Justice Otto Lang, who stated:

> The existing laws do not ensure a fair trial. Indeed one often wonders whether it is the accused or the victim who is on trial . . . I do not believe that the moral integrity of the complainant is on trial.[407]

However, the reforms made in this area could be largely ignored by the courts if judges allowed a certain line of questioning as relevant to the case.[408] Since 1983, and new changes to the law, this line of questioning has been more clearly forbidden although it has been challenged by accused rapists on the grounds that excluding evidence of a victim's past sexual history does not allow the accused a fair trial.[409]

Changes in the law still do not prevent judges from interpreting law in ways which work against women. This is clearly demonstrated in the infamous 1984 case of *R. v. Chase*. Chase was found guilty of the sexual assault of a fifteen-year-old girl and sentenced to eight months' imprisonment. Chase appealed the decision. The New Brunswick Court of Appeal allowed the appeal, reduced the conviction to common assault and the sentence to six months' imprisonment. The Court of Appeal, referencing the dictionary definition of "sexual," held that touching a woman's breasts did not amount to a sexual assault because breasts, like a man's beard, were a "secondary sex characteristic." The court said that if touching a woman's breasts were to be considered sexual assault then they would also have to hold that touching a man's beard was sexual assault.[410] In an annotation to the summary of the case found in Criminal Reports for 1984, Christine Boyle notes:

> . . . equating the beard with the breasts is an excellent example of a proposition which is abstracted to a gender-neutral level even though gender is a significant aspect of the context.[411]

Since 1982, under the amended Criminal Code of Canada, rape has been termed sexual assault in order to underscore the violent nature of this crime against women. The new code also recognizes that sexual assault may occur within marriage. The code provides for the imposition of sentences ranging from ten years to life imprisonment for the crime of sexual assault. These changes indicate a shift away from a view of rape as an offence against a man's property to one of women deserving protection from sexual assault in their own right. Newfoundland is governed by this amended Criminal Code.

Loosening the Bonds Of Marriage

Until the 20th century, if the husband withdrew all financial support, the wife had almost no assistance from the legal system in enforcing her right to be supported. The law became involved only after assessing the conduct of the spouses, and determining whether or not the husband had cause in withdrawing his financial support. Only the blameless wife was considered to deserve the protection of the court.[412]

Under English common law a husband had a duty to support his wife even if they were separated, although wives did not owe the same duty to their husbands. However, where the separation between husband and wife had occurred as a result of her desertion, the husband did not have a duty to support her. As well, if the wife committed adultery in the years following the separation she would no longer be entitled to any support from her husband. Once the couple was divorced, the husband's obligations to support his wife were ended, although it was the custom for a husband to make some provisions for his wife's continued support if she had not been unfaithful during the marriage or after the separation.

The successive governments of Newfoundland had never wished to have the Colony be financially responsible for the maintenance of family members left destitute. In 1834, Newfoundland passed An Act to Afford Relief to Wives and Children, Deserted by their Husbands and Parents. The act gave deserted wives and children the right to sue husbands and parents for support. If the court had made an order for maintenance that had not been complied with, the person who had defied the order could be imprisoned for a month and given only bread and water.[413] The act also provided that where a husband would not work to support his family, or where he drank away the family earnings, he could be sentenced to do hard labour for two weeks.

This act expired in 1856 and was replaced two years later by another enactment. The new act included a procedure for attaching the wages of a deserting husband or father. Thus the man's employer could be ordered to pay part of the employee's wages to the wife and children. This act was repealed in 1865 but replaced with the same provisions, as well as a new provision for the maintenance or elderly or infirm parents.[414] Some of the provisions of the original 1834 act continued to remain in force, with some changes and new provisions, until 1989 when a new Family Law Act was proclaimed.[415] Women would have to continue to prove that they had been deserted in order to qualify for maintenance, a requirement that was often difficult to meet and one that caused hardship for many women.

While the effect of these maintenance laws was to provide deserted wives and children with some means of recourse against starvation, the intent of the law was to prevent these women from becoming a "charge" on the Colony by forcing the government to provide for them. Instead, wives had to sue their husbands in an attempt to secure some form of maintenance from them. Often violence accompanied the woman's suit for support. The *Evening Herald* of 1915 reports a typical case in its "Events and Echoes" column.

> This morning a woman on George Street has her husband before court for assault. An agreement was entered into by the parties to separate. The husband to contribute five dollars a week for the support of his wife and children.[416]

The court's action to impose responsibility for financial support on the husband may or may not have ensured the continued maintenance of the woman and her children. Other news items testify to the difficulty women had in obtaining compliance with the court order.

> . . . No. 5 proved to be a case where a husband refused to support the woman he had taken "for better or worse." She thought he was going to leave the country and had him arrested. The defendant will have to find sureties for his faithful compliance with the unwritten law, or go to jail for thirty days.[417]

Some women resorted to desperate measures. In 1927 a woman was arrested in St. John's and returned to her home town. It seems that the woman had had her husband arrested for non-support of his family but this action had no effect on his behaviour. As a result, the woman left her family and travelled to St. John's. Her husband then had a warrant issued for her arrest on the grounds of desertion of her family. Unfortunately, the sparse details of such news accounts do not tell us the results of this unhappy experience.

In 1931, the sections of the act that dealt with deserted wives and children were no longer the basis of a separate act but were included in the Health and Public Welfare Act of 1931.[418] The deserting husband could be charged with desertion and the court could demand that he provide a security by bond for the support and maintenance of his wife and children. If the husband defaulted on the court order, he could be sentenced to thirty days, with or without hard labour.[419]

The 1931 act stipulated that the wife's "behaviour and moral character" be taken into consideration by the judge. The judge was not bound to make any order for support if he determined that the wife was not deserving by virtue of her behaviour and morality.

Further, if the wife had left her husband, his behaviour and moral character would be scrutinized by the judge. If the judge were not satisfied that the woman was justified in deserting her husband, the judge could refuse to award support.

In 1937, Governor Humphrey Walwyn wrote to the secretary of Dominion Affairs to inform him about the recorded cases involving deserted married persons.[420] He advised the secretary that one hundred and ten cases were heard in 1936. Of these, approximately sixty couples were reunited, a further twelve cases were heard by the judge of the Central District Court, and the majority of the remaining cases were settled to the satisfaction of the parties involved. Most of the one hundred and ten cases arose in St. John's. Walwyn noted that while cases of desertion did arise outside of St. John's, they did not equal the number of cases in the city. Of course, Walwyn's report covered only those cases known to the courts; many more may have been resolved in a very different manner than he described.

Eventually, in 1952, the Newfoundland legislature passed the Maintenance Act.[421] This was intended to provide an inexpensive and relatively uncomplicated procedure for deserted wives and children to obtain a court order that would require a deserting husband or parents to make maintenance payments.[422] A wife was eligible to apply for a court order if she could prove that she had been ill-treated or deserted by her husband. A woman could attempt to establish that she was a victim of assault, cruelty, adultery, or that her husband had refused to supply her with food and clothing. Cruelty was defined as:

> . . . such conduct as creates danger to life, limb or health, or in any course of conduct which in the opinion of the court is grossly insulting or intolerable or is of such a character without proof of actual personal violence that the wife . . . could not reasonably be expected to be willing to live with the husband . . . after he had been guilty of same.[423]

The word "deserted" had a variety of meanings under the act. Even where a husband and wife were still living together, a woman could claim that she had been deserted where her husband refused to support her although he had the means to do so.[424] Although the grounds for desertion appeared reasonably broad, the actual application of the Maintenance Act to a woman's personal circumstances did not necessarily achieve the results sought in the action. An order for support might not be issued by the court, or, conversely, the support payments requested could be substantially increased.

The discretion of the judges affected the final decision and ultimately, the support settlement awarded.

In 1949 Lucy Rideout applied for maintenance under the Health
and Public Welfare Act of 1931 on the grounds that she had been
deserted. She and her husband, Ernest Rideout, had been married
for four years, had three children and had lived in Back Harbour. In
1948 Lucy left her husband, taking the children with her. She gave
evidence in court that her husband had threatened her on a number
of occasions, telling her that he kept three loaded guns in the house
and that he would like to shoot her. On another occasion the
husband had:

> . . . knocked her down, grabbed her by the throat and wrung her
> ears, and that while she was nauseated he pushed her off [the
> porch], took a stick and walked behind, threatening her.[425]

The magistrate in Twillingate, where the case was heard,
awarded Lucy Rideout $50 per month for the support of herself and
the three children on the grounds that Ernest Rideout had failed to
support his dependents. The husband appealed the decision to the
Newfoundland Supreme Court. Chief Justice Walsh finally accepted
Lucy's version of these events but with some reservations. He stated
in his judgement that:

> . . . in the view of this court the incidents referred to are not
> sufficient to permit the magistrate reasonably to reach the conclu-
> sion that the behaviour and moral character of the husband are
> such as to justify her refusal to live with him . . . It is undesirable
> unless for sufficiently grave cause that the wife should be aided in
> living apart from her husband . . . There is no evidence of unfaith-
> fulness or insobriety on the part of the husband and the wife agrees
> that he worked hard on the farm.[426]

Life-threatening violence was apparently not sufficient cause to
warrant a separation and a support settlement for Lucy Rideout and
her children.

Some cases were resolved in favour of the wife and resulted in
larger maintenance settlements. Florence Skinner of Boxey, near
Harbour Breton, applied for maintenance for herself and children
on the grounds that her husband, Ralph, had deserted her. The case
was heard by Magistrate Eric Jones in 1952. A summons was served
on Ralph Skinner but due to the fact that he was working on a
trawler out of Harbour Grace he asked for a postponement. He did
not, however, say that he would attend later, nor that it was
impossible for him to attend on the date that had been set. Magistrate Jones proceeded to hear the case without him being present
and ordered Ralph Skinner to pay $100 a month in maintenance for

Florence and their three children. The husband appealed on a number of grounds, one of which was that the couple had made a separation agreement stating that Ralph would pay $60 a month if they separated.

Justice Brian Dunfield of the Newfoundland Supreme Court heard the Skinner appeal. He looked at the evidence of Mr. Skinner's income as a mate on a dragger. Finding that it was in excess of $1,800 a year and noting that Mrs. Skinner was unable to support herself and three children on $60 a month, the court upheld the original order of $100 monthly in support. The appeal was dismissed.[427]

Perceptions of a woman's behaviour could render her ineligible for support as well. Where a woman applied for permanent support, the court was expressly permitted to take her "conduct" into consideration. If the court considered the wife's conduct undesirable she could be denied permanent maintenance support. Heterosexual liaisons outside the marriage were considered adultery. If a woman had committed adultery either before applying for a maintenance order or after receiving such an order, a judge could refuse to allow her application for support or rescind an order already given. Even in recent years a judge ordered that a woman was no longer entitled to support from her husband after six years when the husband discovered that his wife had committed adultery some years after their separation.[428] The historical proprietary interest held by the husband in a marriage continued to hold sway in some case decisions.

Even where a woman succeeded in obtaining an order for maintenance she could not be sure in advance how much would be awarded for the support of herself and her children. The old English Ecclesiastical Courts allowed alimony in the amount of one-fifth of the husband's income. Later this was changed to one-fifth of the combined income of husband and wife, and still later, amended to one third of the spouses' combined income. The economic outcome of separation and divorce for women was often a severely reduced standard of living. Socially, women might face isolation and ostracism. It is little wonder that many women chose to remain in unhappy marital situations rather than face an impoverished and difficult life.

Severing The Ties

There was a striking contrast between the lawyers and their clients: the lawyers exuded an air of glamour . . . The clients were, with one exception, women. They were all, except me, living on social assistance or unemployment insurance. Most of them had young children and couldn't go out to work. They were at the very bottom of the social ladder, in terms of sheer poverty.[429]

The remedy of divorce has its origins in English ecclesiastical laws. A divorce *a mensa et thoro*, or separation from bed and board, had been available since a proclamation by the Roman Catholic Church at the Council of Trent in 1563. Those who were granted this remedy could live apart, but were not permitted to remarry. By 1603 legal separation was part of England's Canon Law.[430] Couples might also obtain an annulment of marriage, *a vinculo matrimonii*. This form of divorce would declare a marriage void from the beginning. Unfortunately, any children of the union would be declared illegal or bastard children.[431]

In Britain, legal divorce was regulated through the passage of the English Matrimonial Causes Act in 1857. Lord Lyndhurst, during the second reading of the Matrimonial Causes Act, commented on the state of a married woman seeking a divorce.

> From that moment the wife is almost in a state of outlawry. She may not enter into contract or, if she do, she has no means of enforcing it. The law, so far from protecting, oppresses her. She is homeless, helpless, hopeless, and almost destitute of civil rights.[432]

Prior to the 1857 enactment, a legal divorce in Britain was only available through a private act of the British Parliament. This was a remedy available only to the rich, however, with only two hundred and twenty-nine divorce statutes passed between 1603 and 1857. The Matrimonial Causes Act also replaced the Church divorce *a mensa et thoro* with a legally recognized judicial separation. The jurisdiction of the Church in this area was thus replaced by the courts.[433] Although Newfoundland had adopted many of the acts of the English Parliament it did not adopt the Matrimonial Causes Act of 1857. Thus the act had no application in Newfoundland and divorce was not a legal option at that time.

Between 1832 and 1949, no legislation in Newfoundland assigned jurisdiction over divorce to local courts.[434] The only remedy available to those seeking a divorce in Newfoundland was a judicial separation, *a mensa et thoro*, which was possible because Newfoundland acquired English common law with early settlement of colonies.[435] Anyone seeking such a divorce in Newfoundland prior to 1949 had to go through the English Parliament by way of a Private Member's Bill.

It was not until 1948 that an application was made for a divorce *a mensa et thoro* in Newfoundland. In the 1948 application, Mrs.

Hounsell took an action against her husband, claiming that he had deserted her and expelled her from the family home. She asked for alimony, or alternatively, the restitution of conjugal, or marital rights. The husband claimed that the court had no jurisdiction to hear the matter, but the Newfoundland Supreme Court held that it had the same powers to hear cases as the 1832 Ecclesiastical courts of England. The court therefore had authority to hear applications for divorce *a mensa et thoro*, or judicial separation, and applications for the restitution of conjugal rights. The court did not, however, take upon itself the authority to hear divorce applications.[436] The court ordered the restitution of conjugal rights, but stated that if Mrs. Hounsell could prove that this order hadn't been complied with within thirty days she could apply for a judicial separation and make a claim for alimony.[437]

Prior to 1930 in Canada a woman automatically acquired her husband's domicile when she married. This was another result of the "unity of the person doctrine." Divorce proceedings had to be initiated in the province or country where her husband resided. If she did not reside in the same province or country, the domicile requirement could create serious economic hardships for the wife. After 1930, Parliament enacted the Divorce Jurisdiction Act, which permitted a woman who had been deserted by her husband for two years to apply for a divorce in the province the couple had lived in before the desertion, if she was still living there.[438] After Confederation this also applied to Newfoundland couples.

Some Newfoundland couples availed themselves of another alternative, that of going to the United States or another foreign jurisdiction to obtain a divorce. This was only available to those few residents who could afford the financial costs of the action. There were difficulties inherent in leaving Newfoundland to obtain a divorce. Some of these divorces were not considered valid by the Newfoundland courts. This is illustrated by the case of *Downton v. Royal Trust Company*.[439] Marion and Raymond Downton were married in St. John's in 1948. In 1960 they agreed to live apart from each other and entered into an agreement whereby Raymond paid Marion $2,000 outright and then $300 a month to support herself and their two children. In 1965 Raymond went to Las Vegas and obtained a divorce. He then remarried. Difficulties with the divorce arose in 1969, after Raymond's death. His will left $6,000 to each child and the remainder of his estate to his second wife, which came to about $125,000. Marion applied for relief under the Newfoundland Family Relief Act, on the grounds that the Las Vegas divorce was invalid and therefore she was entitled to relief as Raymond's widow. Chief Justice Furlong of the Newfoundland Supreme Court, Trial Division, held that the divorce was invalid because neither Marion or Raymond were residents of Nevada when the divorce was obtained, and ordered that Marion receive $20,000 from Raymond's estate. This was appealed by Raymond's executors and the case eventually went to the Supreme Court of Canada which upheld the decision of Chief Justice Furlong.

It is not certain how many residents of Newfoundland left the country to obtain divorces in the United States before the enactment of the Divorce Act in 1968, or whether they subsequently had difficulties with the validity of those divorces in Canada. It is likely that the numbers were relatively few given the expense involved and the rarity of divorce in the province at the time. The majority of out-of-Newfoundland divorces were obtained prior to Newfoundland's confederation with Canada.[440]

After 1949, applications for divorce by Newfoundland residents had to go through the Canadian House of Commons on a private member's bill. Statistics show that sixty-nine such private member's bills were passed on behalf of parties domiciled in Newfoundland.[441] These bills dissolved marriages in order to allow for remarriage, but did not provide for custody of children or maintenance of women or children.[442]

In 1963 the procedure of applying for divorce through the House of Commons was altered so that divorce and annulment petitions first went to the Senate, with applicants having a right to appeal to the House of Commons after the Senate's decision. Forty-six petitions on behalf of Newfoundland couples were passed by the Senate.[443] In such petitions, proof of adultery was generally required for a divorce to be obtained, although it was possible for a divorce to have been granted on any grounds.[444] Applying to the Senate or House of Commons involved a number of expenses for residents of Newfoundland, including travel costs and legal counsel in Ottawa and Newfoundland. This restricted Parliamentary divorce to the relatively affluent or influential sector of the population.[445] The heavy economic burden attached to either of these procedures is partly reflected in the number of divorces sought in Newfoundland between 1949 and 1968. During those years only one hundred and fifteen divorces were obtained by Newfoundland residents.[446]

The Divorce Act of 1968, which broadened and clarified the grounds for divorce and separation, applied to all Canadian provinces. It also reduced some of the economic burden. For the first time a three year separation between husband and wife was considered grounds for divorce. Other grounds included the permanent breakdown of the marriage due to the long-term addiction or imprisonment of one partner.[447] Many Newfoundland couples took advantage of the new legislation and applied on the basis of a three year separation. Between 1968 and 1971, the number of divorces obtained by Newfoundland residents jumped to 686. Of these, 411 were petitions filed by wives.[448] Thus in the early '70s there was an initial rash of divorce applications heard by the courts in Newfoundland.

Additional grounds for divorce included both "matrimonial offences" and specific types of marriage breakdown. Marriage offences included sodomy, bestiality, rape, homosexuality, bigamy, adultery, and physical or mental cruelty.[449] As well, the 1968 Divorce Act empowered the courts, for the first time, to make orders regarding custody of children and maintenance. Thus the financially more secure spouse, usually the husband, could be ordered to support the remaining spouse. For the first time in Canada, wives could be ordered to support their husbands.[450]

The 1968 act did not set out any specific formulas and relied a great deal upon the discretion of judges.

> The [1968] Act required sums of interim orders to be such as the court "thinks fit and just" and sums of permanent orders to be what the court thinks "reasonable."[451]

Courts looked at the particular circumstances of each case, and considered factors such as "means" and "needs." While some formulas were available for use in determining support, there is no real evidence to demonstrate that they were actually applied by the Newfoundland courts.[452] Both the husband and wife were obliged to disclose their income, assets and debts in order for the court to determine an appropriate sum for maintenance.

One Newfoundland case from 1971 illustrates the procedure that a court might follow in determining the amount of an order for support. Dr. and Mrs. Sharpe had been married for almost twenty years, and the woman was seeking a divorce on the grounds of physical cruelty. Mrs. Sharpe was claiming maintenance for herself and the couple's four children in the amount of $1,401 per month. This was to cover all the requirements for herself and her children. Her husband was earning an annual income of $42,000, but informed the court that the most he could pay to support his wife and children was $740 per month, due to other debts. Justice Higgins of the Newfoundland Supreme Court reviewed the finances of both parties and made the following statement:

> Counsel for the [husband] . . . submitted that the petitioner and
> her children should be prepared to accept a lower standard of living
> than that to which they have been accustomed while the family was
> united . . . inasmuch as the [husband] has accustomed his de-
> pendents to a particular standard of living, he cannot now be heard,
> in the absence of evidence of his inability to pay, to say that the
> living standards of his dependents are unrealistic.[453]

The court awarded Mrs. Sharpe more than she had actually requested, giving her a maintenance order for $1,663 per month. We should not assume that the Newfoundland courts regularly awarded large sums of maintenance, nor that it was common for a woman to receive more support than she had actually requested. Since the judges had a great deal of discretion, the amounts that the courts awarded for support could vary greatly from one judge to another.

The 1968 act was succeeded by the new Divorce Act of 1985. In a paper accompanying the 1985 bill, the minister of justice noted that:

> . . . nearly 40 percent of marriages now ended in divorce and that
> the length of marriages ending in divorce has dropped from 16
> years in 1969 to 12 years in the latest figures [1984].[454]

The 1985 act included changes recommended by a number of provincial Status of Women Advisory Councils, including an amendment that reduced the three year separation period to a one year separation period in order to obtain a divorce. With each new amendment to the Divorce Act, divorce actions have become potentially more accessible for women and settlements more equitable and responsive to a woman's contribution to the marriage.

VI. THE LATER YEARS

Little has been documented historically about women's later years in Newfoundland or Canada for that matter. How were older women cared for through the centuries? Who did the caring? What were their economic circumstances? What types of work did they perform, under what conditions? Much remains to be understood about the circumstances in which older women found themselves. However, some general statements, based on what we do know of women's lives, can be made.

> The low wages of many husbands, the fact that men frequently
> pre-deceased their wives, women's ability to command only rela-
> tively poor remuneration in the paid labour market, and the
> absence of pension arrangements for the vast majority of Canadi-
> ans all added up to widespread penury.[455]

This situation of older working- and middle-class women in Canada was undoubtedly echoed in Newfoundland. A woman's health, age, education or skill level and employment opportunities were also crucial factors in determining the standard of living a woman could attain for herself.

For women of any class background who found themselves alone through desertion, separation or divorce, economic security for themselves and their families was of utmost concern. Financial support from an absent husband might not be enough to feed the family. Older working children may have aided in family support, contributing their wages to the household income.

If a woman was widowed by the death of her husband, her situation often worsened. A letter to the *Fishermen's Advocate* in 1912 described the plight of one elderly woman.

> . . . the subject on which I wish to write on is the treatment which our wornout fishermen's wives receive. I shall write on one only. The old lady's husband . . . has been dead upwards of two years. She has sons, but all of them are married. Her youngest son has a wife and six children to support . . . she is living alone and is between 75 and 85 years of age. She receives from the government the large sum of $8 for 12 months. With this money she must provide fuel, provisions, clothing etc. . . . [456]

Doubtless many women found themselves in a similar position in their later years.

Governments in Newfoundland had long been aware that there was a need to provide for relief for the poor. In 1840 the Act to Defray Certain Charges that have Arisen for the Support of Aged and Infant Paupers provided sums of money for the care of the destitute.[457] The act lists those persons providing care and those receiving support; six of those listed are described as aged or widowed women. In one case, a Catherine Supple was paid three pounds, five shillings and six pence for one hundred and thirty-one days care and support of an aged woman and one pound, twelve shillings and one penny for laundry expenses. After the woman died, Catherine Supple continued to care for her and was paid five shillings for washing the body of the woman in preparation for burial.

Two widows, Ann Dwyer, with three children, and Bridget Oats with six children were supported for ten months each at twenty and twenty-five shillings per month respectively. A third widow, Jane Meany, earned some income at various times for supporting "a lunatic," a child and a sick man. She received fifteen pounds, eleven shillings for her work.

In 1861, perhaps realizing payments to individuals were insufficient for the impoverished population of St. John's, a pauper's home was built in the west end of St. John's to accommodate the poor. The Poorhouse or Poor Asylum, as it was called, housed the aged and infirm for over one hundred years until it was demolished in 1965.[458] Both women and men were housed there, and were expected to work in the asylum or on public works to earn their keep. People from across the island were sent into St. John's to live out their lives in the Poor Asylum. A typical case is one reported in the *Evening Herald*, May, 1895. The article reports that a seventy-eight-year-old woman from Brigus, named Keats, was brought into town to "spend the balance of her days in the Poor Asylum."[459]

Faced with an impoverished life, perhaps needing to maintain the family, women turned their hand to different sources of income. In the late 1890s and into the early 1900s, a number of cases involving the illicit sale of liquor appeared in the local newspapers.[460] Many were charges against older married women, found selling liquor or "Garden Beer" from their homes. In one case the lawyer's argument for leniency on the part of the court was based on the fact that "his client was a widow, who admitted to selling the beer, it being her only means of support." The judge fined her $20.[461] This fine seems to be at the lower end of the scale; some fines reached as high as $200.

Judge Prowse intervened in a similar case in 1905, when he met an impoverished widow, Bridget Gunn, on the train. He describes her as "a poor ignorant woman of her class,"[462] who had been sentenced to one month in the Harbour Grace jail for selling liquor without a licence. This was her first offence and even the constable escorting Bridget sympathized with her plight. He informed Judge Prowse of her impoverished situation:

> ... she had only half a barrel of rotten flour for food in her miserable house, and her children were almost naked. Her sickly husband had died two years ago and she had 12 children 7 alive all delicate.[463]

Judge Prowse revealed this information in a letter to the governor, and appealed to him for the release of Bridget Gunn in the name of humanity and justice. In making his case, Prowse stated that "selling liquor is not a crime but an artificial offence created by statute"[464] and that the justice of the peace trying the case had erred in his judgement. The justice had awarded the costs of the case to himself, an action which Prowse felt was "opposed to all legal principles."[465] The governor agreed with Prowse and sent a telegram to the jailer at Harbour Grace ordering Bridget Gunn's release and the payment of her passage home, to be billed to the minister of justice.[466] Although many cases for the illegal selling of liquor were reported in the newspapers of the day, few seem to have had such a positive resolution.

A woman might not be very old, yet still be a widow. Those whose husbands were fishermen faced this possibility almost daily since fishing was, and is, a dangerous occupation. In Grand Bank, Newfoundland, between 1862 and 1936, one hundred and eighty vessels from the community were lost, most with all hands. Grand Bank became known as "the widows' town," with every family involved in the fishery reporting the loss of relatives at sea.[467] Following some sea disasters, a small pension might be collected by the family of those lost. In Grand Bank of the 1950s, a pension could amount to very little. Laura Barnes recalled the money she and her two small children received after her husband drowned in 1956.

> . . . my son only used to get $17.50 a month, right, and my daughter $15, and I only used to get $10, so that weren't very much money.[468]

Under such impoverished conditions, women struggled to make ends meet. When a South Coast woman was in her thirties, her husband died at sea. To feed and clothe her family of seven young children, she "took in laundry, sewing and a boarder." Eventually she began living in a common-law relationship with the boarder so they could both continue to collect their full pensions.[469]

Small sums of money could be granted to widows by the Protestant Society of United Fishermen (1863) or the Catholic Star of the Sea Society (1871). These organizations took it upon themselves to work for the economic betterment of their members by providing death benefits for widows out of membership dues. However, because the dues were collected from fishermen, whose incomes were often sporadic, the benefits were irregular as well.[470]

Some widows, particularly those in an urban area, supported themselves by continuing work in a trade such as millinery or taking in washing. Others worked as domestics, going to their employer's home in the morning and returning to their own home in the evening.[471] In the St. John's census of 1921, 5.1 percent of urban working women were widows, the bulk of them between fifty and fifty-four years of age. By 1935, widows accounted for 5.4 percent of urban working women, with the slightly larger proportion being forty to forty-four years of age.[472] The majority of these women, in both the 1921 and 1935 census, recorded some or all of their children were sixteen years of age and over.[473] Clearly, most widows went outside the home to work after their children were older. These widows were heads of households with perhaps some children at home, contributing to the household income.

As we have seen, the role of midwife was an ill-paid occupation for some widowed women. Many practised until they were quite elderly. In 1939, Ilka Dickman, a doctor practising as a nurse in outport Newfoundland, observed of one midwife:

> She is seventy-eight years old and has been a midwife in New Harbour for sixty years. All by herself she has brought up six children, which job included spinning the wool and sewing all the clothing for these kids; has grown vegetables and potatoes, taken care of goats and chickens, whenever there were any . . . She has come over the mountains to sell a few onions, to bring a few eggs . . . and has never in her life seen an easy day.[474]

Ingenuity, strength and perseverance were required to keep body and soul together, as well as to support children.

If a woman's husband had personal property or land holdings and had provided for her in his will, she was usually assured of some security. As well, English common law had developed a method of protecting a widow's rights to a limited degree. A married woman retained dower rights to one-third of the real property owned by her husband during their marriage.[475] This property would only become hers on the death of her husband. Court records from the early to mid-1800s in Newfoundland reveal the difficulties entailed in a widow receiving her rightful share of her husband's estate.[476]

In what has been termed "patriarchy from the grave," a husband's will could stipulate that his widow was entitled to her dower rights only as long as she remained tied to him as his widow.[477] If she remarried, a woman could lose her dower rights. As we might expect, a woman could also lose her dower if she were divorced or separated from her husband at the time of his death, was deemed to have committed adultery or was judged to be mentally incompetent.[478] Of course, a husband's conduct would never affect his right to a share of his wife's property.[479] If a man did not provide for his wife in his will, "his estate had no obligation to her until laws in some parts of Canada in the 20th century enabled her to assert a claim to his estate through dependent's relief legislation."[480]

During the 1920s and 1930s, the Newfoundland government provided a small payment of $5 a month to widows who were deemed "deserving."[481] While this amount might help to support a widow on her own, it would not support a family. In 1931, the Newfoundland Legislature passed the Health and Public Welfare Act. This act, in part, stipulated that a child, leaving their parent or parents destitute and a burden on the funds of the Colony, could be required to provide a bond of support for the parent(s). To fail to do so could mean a sentence of thirty days imprisonment with hard labour for the deserting child.[482]

Financial support was also available from the Newfoundland disaster fund.[483] Usually this money was awarded to the immediate dependents of men lost at sea. If the wife remarried, the financial support could be made available to the lost man's mother. Mrs. Frank Barron, of Placentia, appealed to King George V in November, 1922 for support in the name of her son Francis Barron. He had been lost in 1918 when the S.S. "Beverly" disappeared en route to Italy.

> I am a poor widow alone in the world absent from any means of support since my poor son was lost in the Mercantile Marine Service during the war . . . I have no means of support and I do not want to go on the charity of neighbours. If I could receive the pension it would be my support during the next few years I have to live as I am now an old woman. My husband also died 20 years ago.[484]

Unfortunately, there is no record to show how such appeals were greeted by the government or the King of England.

A South Coast woman, widowed in the 1940s, when her husband died in his fishing boat commented:

> Fortunately, he left me "square" (debtless); some men died without their accounts settled, and the widows were left with debts to pay off. The minister helped me get the disaster fund . . . [it] was $50 every six months for me and every child living at home. Besides that I got $30 a month widow allowance.[485]

In addition to this money, widows could receive $20 worth of food supplies per year from the dole. If she had two sons, over sixteen and able-bodied, widows received no allowance.[486] The patriarchal view of women being taken care of by men extended even to a widow and her sons. As we saw above, sons may not have been in a financial position to support their aged mothers as well as their own families.

Under the Mothers' Allowance Act of 1949, a widow could apply to the Mothers' Allowances Board for a monthly allowance to support her children. This act defined "widow" in an inclusive manner. It stipulated that a "widow" was any woman married to an incapacitated man, an inmate of a health or penal institution, or who was deemed to have been deserted, separated or divorced from a Newfoundland resident and could not obtain financial support from him.[487]

Since 1981, the Matrimonial Property Act has entitled the surviving spouse, widow or widower, to one-half of the couple's marital property. If a couple had attained a comfortable standard of living and been able to provide financially for their old age, a surviving widow might be relatively secure. This is undoubtedly an improvement for women who would face an impoverished old age without this legislation.

Pensions

The availability of old age pension plans for women is a fairly recent phenomenon. Historically, women were assumed to be supported by the male breadwinner in the family. In 1911, the Newfoundland government introduced An Act to provide for the Payment of Old Age Pensions.[488] This act provided $50 per year to men over the age of seventy-five years who had resided no less than twenty years in Newfoundland and who needed a pension in order to support himself. Women were not eligible for the pension under this act. Widows were not covered by the pension act until 1926 when the government introduced an amendment allowing widows aged sixty-five and over to claim a pension "until her death or remarriage."[489] With a further amendment in 1934, this section was retained. Additional amendments in 1942 and 1943 raised the annual old age pension to $60 and $72 per year respectively.[490]

The Canadian Pension Plan has been in place since 1966. Women and men initially did not receive equal treatment under the plan because of the traditional assumptions regarding male and female roles in the family and society. Men were assumed to be the earners of the family wages. Women only worked for "pin money." If women entered the labour market late in life, her lower wages (roughly 66 percent of men's wages) and her short time in a pension plan ensured her of low pension benefits.[491] Leah Cohen, writing about women and pensions, stated in 1984:

> As long as benefits depend on prior contributions and contributions are linked to earnings, women will suffer disproportionately until such time as there is full equality of participation in the workforce between men and women.[492]

Figures for 1979 show that only twenty percent of women aged sixty-five and over were receiving Canadian pensions. In contrast, seventy one percent of all men collected Canadian pensions.[493]

Benefits for surviving wives and husbands were not equalized until 1974. Women who had left marriages were not entitled to a widow's benefit if her estranged husband died. This could cause particular problems if the marriage had broken down later in a woman's life and she had never entered the workforce or built her own pension or savings.[494] Regrettably, in Canada today, being old, female and a widow is still the best combination to ensure an impoverished life.[495]

CONCLUSION

Between the seventeenth and twentieth centuries, tremendous social, economic and legal change has occurred in Newfoundland. The early years of settlement saw women contributing to the growth and development of families and communities, establishing the foundation for the Colony and Dominion of Newfoundland. The twentieth century saw the enfranchisement of women, the election of Lady Helena Squires as the first woman to sit in the Newfoundland House of Assembly, the opening up of the legal, medical and teaching professions to women and some increase in employment options for working- and middle-class women.

Confederation with Canada in 1949 brought about profound legal changes. Newfoundland joined with the other provinces under the umbrella of federal laws such as the Criminal Code of Canada, the Family Law Act and the Divorce Act. The Old Age Pension and Mothers' Allowance Act brought extra financial support for women after confederation. Increasingly, attitudes held by the public at large and the broader interpretation of law by judges at both the provincial and federal levels have encouraged the growth and development of new legal interpretations and precedents.

This progress did not come without cost and sustained effort. Women actively campaigned for legal changes which would make their position in society more equitable. They did not passively wait to be given the vote, they agitated and lobbied until their voice was heard. Women joined early unions like the Newfoundland Industrial Workers Association and struck for better working conditions and better wages. Female shopclerks, with their male colleagues, petitioned the government for the regulation of work hours, a move which resulted in the 1936 Shop Hours Act. Women demanded and received the right to vote.

Throughout the decades, women have demanded justice from the courts time and again, as they brought suit for maintenance allowances and release from marital violence, abuse and poverty. We usually have the court records or newspaper accounts to provide some documentation of these struggles. Yet the question arises as to the reality of women's lives under the law. Do the statements of judges or the court records or newspaper accounts accurately reflect women's experiences? How did the lawmakers and enforcers assist or obstruct women in seeking justice? How were the laws interpreted? If a judge awarded a specific maintenance payment to a woman, did she receive it? We have seen some implications of the difference between the court records and reality: a male name appearing in the court record under a suit for a woman's wages may not reflect the ultimate destination of the wage settlement; a will, bequeathing a share of a father's property to a daughter does not mean that she received it, or that her brothers did not contest its rightful ownership. The official records reflect only a small part of women's experience with the law.

When calling upon these records, we must be careful to take into consideration the patriarchal structure of society and its revered institutions. We must pursue each story as far as we can in order to glean a measure of the reality of women's lives and legal rights. This essay is only a beginning in the process of recovering women's experience of the law in Newfoundland and Labrador.

Change Within and Without 4

The Modern Women's Movement in Newfoundland and Labrador

Sharon Gray Pope and Jane Burnham[1]

INTRODUCTION

The early international women's movement was characterized by the formation of groups dedicated to fighting women's oppression. During the first part of the twentieth century, the suffrage movement, which focused on the fight for enfranchisement, brought issues of women's rights to public attention. A strong suffrage movement existed in Newfoundland, particularly in St. John's, and women in Newfoundland were granted the right to vote in 1925. However, throughout the rest of the century women continued to identify and protest their inferior legal, political and economic status, and to work to gain rights taken for granted by men. The efforts of these women led to the modern women's movement.

The modern women's movement, or the feminist movement, has become a loose network of individuals and women's groups bound together by a commitment to strive for equality. Feminist groups in the province formed at a grass-roots level and the effects of this formative process have been both negative and positive. Some negative aspects are evident in the fragmentation of the movement. Individual groups were formed by concerned women in particular areas and grew to meet the needs of women in those areas; however, such groups often had a narrower view of the provincial or national movement. Fragmentation within groups tended to occur as time and effort were expended on the group process. Most groups evolved through trial and error, but at the expense of alienating many committed women. Competition for information and for funds sometimes pitted groups and regions against one another and resulted in an element of distrust that contributed to the fragmentation. In addition, service oriented groups or groups that focused on specific issues often viewed the broader feminist movement as disruptive to their goals and they tended to keep a distance from radical activism.

The positive effects of the formation of feminist groups from the grass-roots level were many. Feminism in Newfoundland has truly relied on the belief that the personal is the political and this has been applied to helping women on all levels. In spite of fragmentation within groups and within the movement, women in the province who meet at gatherings such as provincial women's conferences were reminded of common goals and the shared truths about women's lives. They realized the need for representation that ensured the inclusion of their concerns in the political process, and they were in a position to identify the best ways to help women. When women's centres across the country were threatened with closure because of funding cuts, the strength of grass-roots feminism in Newfoundland and Labrador was powerful enough to initiate a block to the conservative political agenda. Women's groups are overwhelmed by the enormous task of dealing with evolving issues. As feminists work to include diversity of race, class, sexual orientation, age and ability, the problem becomes more complex. What is especially positive in this province is the willingness of women's groups to face problems and to work toward solutions.

This essay focuses on the history of women's groups in Newfoundland and Labrador and on their activities. Not all women's groups are discussed, and the achievements of groups, rather than of individuals, are highlighted.

The formation of feminist groups in this province, as in the rest of Canada, traces its roots to the impact of the 1970 Canadian Royal Commission on the Status of Women.[2] However, before exploring the rise of current feminism, it is important to briefly outline the history of a number of women's groups in the province that were active in the women's movement, but pre-date the Royal Commission.

WOMEN'S GROUPS BEFORE 1972

The first province-wide volunteer organization of women was founded in 1935 and was called the Jubilee Guilds. Its aim was to help people in outport communities improve the conditions of their lives and it relied on the Commission of Government for its funding. The board of directors of the Jubilee Guilds included men and women but directed its efforts toward rural women who were seen to be both interested and approachable; it was assumed that once men saw the value of the improvements to come they too would join in the effort.

During the Great Depression, members of the Jubilee Guilds focused on helping women learn how to make the best use of limited resources. Two other groups with similar purposes served as community connections for the Guilds. One of these, the Service League, existed on the South Coast of the island. Communities there had been devastated by a tidal wave in 1929 and volunteers from the Service League helped them to rebuild. By 1935, owing to the Depression, the economic and social problems of the area had become too much for the Service League to handle and the Jubilee Guilds took over its work. The second community connection for the Jubilee Guilds was the Women's Patriotic Association which had been formed during World War I to provide assistance to people at home and to men sent overseas.

The Jubilee Guilds grew during subsequent years. Its women field workers supplied materials and taught weaving, cooking and sewing, they encouraged social activities among women, and they helped outports organize themselves to deal with community issues. Guilds were patterned to meet the needs of the communities they served; at its peak period in the 1950s, there were 108 Jubilee Guilds with 3,457 outport members and 225 members in St. John's. As communities and needs changed, the Jubilee Guilds also changed; by the end of the 1950s, the work was beginning to move into the areas of outport organization, commercial production and a training school.[3]

An appeal to government for more funds in the early 1960s raised the issue of the significance of the craft producing industry. In 1964 the government saw it as advantageous to include the training component of the guilds in the Division of Vocational Education which would be cost-shared with the federal government. The justification given was that more money would then be available for training and standards could be set; however, the loss of craft field workers signalled a decline in membership in the Jubilee Guilds. Responsibility for supply and production was passed over to the Newfoundland Outport Nursing and Industrial Association (NONIA).[4] The guilds lost their field workers and membership fell to an all-time low with twenty-one guilds ceasing to operate in the year and a half following this move in 1964. A new organizational drive was undertaken, however, and membership slowly increased. The Jubilee Guilds' programme was now one of services in citizenship, education and home economics, a change in focus from crafts to education. In August 1968 the Jubilee Guilds changed its name to the Newfoundland and Labrador Women's Institutes; this association has a current membership of about fifteen hundred women.

It appears that the business and training work of the Jubilee Guilds grew beyond levels that could be managed without greater funding. This growth can be attributed to the commitment of the guilds to respond to community needs and, particularly, to its promotion of women's work. What is noteworthy is that women working in the guilds appear to have set the pattern later adopted by Memorial University and the Marine Institute for their extension services and the use of field workers. The guilds also contributed to what is now a thriving craft industry in the province and initiated craft training that has become incorporated in a number of institutions throughout the province.

While the guilds were in operation, other women were forming groups to meet their needs. In 1945 the St. John's Club of the Canadian Federation of University Women (CFUW) was founded, with the goals of stimulating the interest of women graduates in public affairs and promoting the higher education of women. At the second meeting of the new club in December 1945, author Margaret Duley spoke on the topic "We Think as Women." By 1950 study groups were established within the CFUW to discuss education, human rights and psychology. The study group topics changed over the years to include international affairs, penal reform, and the legal Status of Women. In 1957 another CFUW club was organized in Grand Falls. Teacher training in the province was of particular concern to the CFUW, and in a brief to the 1965 Royal Commission on Education and Youth its main recommendation was for emergency training of provincial teachers to upgrade them all to a minimum level of a grade ll certificate.

In October 1966 a Local Council of Women (LCW) formed in Newfoundland. It was affiliated with the National Council of Women, an organization dating back to 1893 and the first wave of the women's movement. LCW membership included representatives from other women's organizations such as the CFUW. During its decade of activities, the LCW researched housing conditions and presented a brief to government on the need for more and better housing for needy families and senior citizens. Members of the LCW also studied problems of aging and promoted programmes for dealing with the problem of drunken driving. A major project of the LCW was the publication of *Remarkable Women of Newfoundland and Labrador*.[5] Despite support from a variety of women's groups, including the feminist Newfoundland Status of Women Council, the LCW was unable to maintain membership and vitality; it folded in 1976.

Like those of many women in mainland Canada, the early efforts of women in Newfoundland and Labrador were directed toward improving the lives of women within families and communities. Women's struggle to achieve economic independence contributed to the later success of the Jubilee Guilds and the development of a provincial craft industry. Work by women in other groups identified social problems and indicated women's willingness to be part of the solution. However, women were not in positions of power so their influence was limited and frustrated. As in other parts of Canada, the Royal Commission on the Status of Women provided an outlet for Newfoundland women to voice their concerns.

THE ROYAL COMMISSION ON THE STATUS OF WOMEN

Women's groups and individual women in Newfoundland presented a total of six briefs to the Royal Commission on the Status of Women. The three women's groups that appeared before the Commission were the St. John's CFUW, the Association of Registered Nurses, and the Newfoundland Home Economics Association. In addition, three individuals presented briefs: Dorothy Wyatt, Ella Manuel and Doris Janes.

All the Newfoundland briefs addressed the problems of women and work, and most briefs identified areas of discrimination against women. The Newfoundland Home Economics Association's brief listed the difficulties married women experienced obtaining both day care and part-time work. The brief from the St. John's CFUW raised broad issues connected with working women. One such issue concerned a fair and equal minimum wage. "The biggest problem encountered by women in the labour force is exploitation," stated the CFUW in its brief.[6] The hourly minimum wage for women in Newfoundland and Labrador was fifty cents—twenty cents lower than the hourly minimum wage for men. The CFUW recommended a rise in minimum wage, with the same minimum wage for men and women. As the CFUW brief pointed out, long term welfare for a family of five provided $205 a month, but a man and a woman both working at minimum wage made only $192 per month so there was little incentive to avoid welfare. In addition, the CFUW brief addressed the status of domestic workers and recommended including domestic workers under the minimum wage law, regulating their hours of work, providing training programmes to domestics, and allowing working women an income tax deduction for wages paid to domestics they employed.

Another issue raised in the CFUW brief was discrimination against working women who were married. The brief pointed out that Memorial University's terms and conditions of employment stated: "Upon the marriage of a female teacher, her employment shall terminate"[7] (the university would employ married women but only on a temporary basis). This brief also identified the growing need for day care services and expressed concern over the fact Newfoundland had no regulations for licensing day care.

In addition, the CFUW brief recommended that in Section 97 of the Judicature Act of Newfoundland the word "person" be interpreted to mean a male or female person. Because of the wording, women at that time were barred from serving on juries.

In its brief, the Association of Registered Nurses of Newfoundland noted that married nurses experienced the same problems as other married women who worked. Many married nurses found it uneconomical to work because of expenses incurred for household help and because of income tax policies. To assist nurses with children, the association recommended that child care centres operate on a sixteen hour day, seven day week basis, and be subsidized by the Federal Government. The association recommended that income tax deductions for working mothers include expenses such as household help and child care; it also called for salaries commensurate with those of other similar professional disciplines.

In their briefs, individual presenters touched on problems experienced by many women in the province. Dorothy Wyatt, a registered nurse who later became mayor of St. John's, addressed the problem of discrimination towards married women who worked for their husbands. Wyatt's husband, a doctor, employed her as a registered nurse, but under the Canada Income Tax Act he was not permitted to deduct her salary from his gross income. Wyatt also pointed out that she was prevented from participating in the Canada Pension Plan because she worked for her husband.[8]

Doris Janes' brief to the Royal Commission called for retraining programmes for married women who wanted to re-enter the workforce. Janes, a Canadian Broadcasting Corporation (CBC) interviewer/broadcaster in Corner Brook, added that she deplored the "disinterest" in women's affairs shown by women in Western

Newfoundland: "They grumble about conditions, but do nothing about them."[9]

Ella Manuel, an early feminist/pacifist who was also a writer and one of the first recipients of the Persons Day Award, took a more traditional approach in her brief. She called for an education programme that would address the problems of rural Newfoundland women through centres that taught cooking, handicraft production, the use of modern home appliances, nutrition, child care and simple nursing techniques. She described the situation of women in Newfoundland as that of "inferior beings in a society of underprivileged citizens."[10]

All the briefs presented to the Royal Commission made recommendations to government in the hope, no doubt, that identifying women's issues would result in government better representing women. The Report of the Royal Commission on the Status of Women bore out the fact that many of the claims made by women's organizations across the country were similar, and concluded that women were suffering discrimination at every turn. Its strong recommendations had an impact on women in Newfoundland and Labrador, focusing energy into starting local Status of Women Councils to monitor government's responses to the report and to work to end the discrimination.

AFTER THE ROYAL COMMISSION

Following the Report of the Royal Commission, interest in issues relating to the Status of Women grew and, like women in the rest of Canada, Newfoundland women began to educate themselves on feminist issues through workshops and consciousness-raising groups. With awareness came action. The next major development in the women's movement in Newfoundland was the formation of formal feminist women's groups. It was an exciting time.

Initial efforts in St. John's were undertaken by women who were involved with the Social Action Committee of the Young Women's Christian Association (YWCA) and were particularly interested in learning more about the Status of Women. They invited a Toronto radical-feminist, Bonnie Kreps, to St. John's. Through public and private meetings, Kreps introduced women to the direction the women's movement was taking and to the idea of consciousness-raising groups.

Consciousness-raising groups, or CR groups, were an important step to organizing during the early years of the women's movement. They enabled women of different ages, backgrounds and experiences to come together and discuss issues and problems common to their lives as women. Typically a CR group would run once a week for several months, and the eight to twelve members were each given time to express their point of view on a structured series of topics starting with their early life and socialization as girls.

While CR groups proved popular among many of the women in St. John's, not everyone was equally interested in discussing their life experience. The groups appear to have had less interest for younger women. Anne Budgell, who went on to become a well known CBC broadcaster, recalled being bored in a CR group. She felt that the women's movement meant more for the older women involved at the time.[11] However, Fran Innes, an early participant in the Newfoundland feminist movement, viewed CR groups differently. She said: "In the women's movement, we were all at various stages of frustration and anger. We all had to find ways of talking to women and CR was very important. Women weren't used to speaking out, it was a struggle to make sure others had a chance to speak up."[12]

Organizing in St. John's

Women in St. John's were interested in learning about the movement and about each other, and they were anxious to see action taken on the one hundred and sixty-seven recommendations of the Report of the Royal Commission on the Status of Women. The impetus to form a Status of Women Council was growing and two gatherings in particular led to the eventual organization of the Newfoundland Status of Women Council in St. John's (NSWC). First, five women from Newfoundland, including Iris Kirby from the local Secretary of State office and Shirley Goundrey from the YWCA Social Action Committee, attended the April 1972 "Strategy for Change" conference in Toronto, which was held to discuss strategy for implementing the Royal Commission's recommendations. The second gathering occurred a month later when the St. John's Business and Professional Women's Club held a seminar with guest speaker Judge Doris Ogilvie, one of the commissioners on the Royal Commission on the Status of Women. These gatherings helped women recognize the need for a local group to monitor government's response to the report.

Over two hundred women attended the local gathering, and to ensure that the enthusiastic response was not lost, a meeting was quickly held to select an interim committee of women to organize a local Status of Women Council. One woman who became a stalwart member of the Status of Women group in St. John's was a middle-aged homemaker named Mary Walsh. She worked on the committee to organize the NSWC, and recalled with amusement how the organizing meeting marked her debut in the women's movement.

> I became a member of the Women's Movement because of a red, white and blue blazer. It may sound weird and bizarre, but it is the truth, so help me God. One evening after dinner I sat idly reading my horoscope, Gemini, the Sign of the Twins. It said "Go to a meeting to-night—it will change your whole life." I didn't have any meetings in mind for the evening but I picked up the daily paper and noticed an ad "Status of Women Meeting—Everyone Welcome." What the hell, I thought, it might be interesting so I put on my blue slacks and red, white and blue blazer with matched earrings, because I feel naked without earrings, and off I went to City Hall.
>
> I entered the room, soon realised I didn't know personally one single person, and happily anonymous, sat down. I listened politely to everything that was said, but being a compulsive talker it was just not in my nature to keep quiet the entire evening, so I had a couple of opinions to give and spoke up. When the time came for nominations for an interim committee and to get the organization started I didn't pay much attention and being slightly hard of hearing anyway, sat reading the paper I had been given. Someone said "I nominate the woman in the red, white and blue blazer," the secretary looked over at me and the woman next to me said "what's your name?" I gave it and she called it out. To my horror, my name was put on the list of nominations . . . .There I was, stuck on a committee with fourteen women whom I didn't know in an organization I knew nothing about . . . at least two months passed before I realised I was in the Feminist Movement.[13]

The local movement gained momentum. During the summer of 1972, while the groundwork was being laid for Newfoundland's first Status of Women council, a group of eight young women worked on a project funded under Opportunities for Youth. They wrote a booklet called *Women and the Law in Newfoundland*,[14] compiled a list of women's organizations in the province and began collecting materials for a feminist library. Also in July of that summer a women's collective called "Woman's Place" (later known as Women's Place) formed.

In September 1972 the interim committee to organize a local Status of Women Council called a general meeting and a nominating committee was chosen. In November the founding meeting of the Newfoundland Status of Women Council was held and an executive committee was elected for one year. The first members of the NSWC executive were Mary Lydon, Kathy Clark, Mary Walsh, Betty Richards, Susan Richter, Del Texmo and Sally Davis.

NSWC offered women the opportunity to promote issues from a women's perspective. When there was a move to merge the YWCA and YMCA, a group of women who felt women's issues would be lost in the merged organization and who preferred the direction of the NSWC joined the council. Jill Schooley, Anne Betz and Diane Siegel were among those women. Looking back, Diane Siegel commented, "I'm not really sure we knew what a monumental task we were taking on."[15]

The "monumental task" taken on by the NSWC was approached systematically by setting up "ginger" groups to deal with special areas of concern raised in the Royal Commission Report. Education, poverty, the family, and the economy were all targeted as areas for study and action. For example, in August 1972 a ginger group to address education was organized. Its first activity was to present a brief on sex education to the Provincial Task Force on Curriculum. The group suggested ways to present material on sex education to children, and stressed the need to educate teachers on how to present such material. A year later the education group presented a brief on sex-role stereotyping in school text books to the Committee on Teacher Education at Memorial University.

In the fall of 1972, the NSWC received a $500 seed grant from the Secretary of State's newly formed Women's Programme, and in February 1973 a further grant of $3,000 was received to set up a women's centre. Previously, NSWC had worked cooperatively to produce a newsletter with the Woman's Place collective. The $3,000 grant money received by the NSWC was turned over to the collective and they were given the autonomy to open and operate a centre called "The Woman's Place." A women's centre was set up in downtown St. John's at 144 Duckworth Street and moved to Water Street that winter.

A year later the collective and the council split apart as philosophical differences mounted. Sally Davis, a long-time member of NSWC and for many years editor of the council's newsletter, recalled that one problem arose because of structural differences that existed between the collective, which tried to operate on consensus, and the NSWC, which was a structured organization. The collective, she said, looked on the NSWC as middle class.[16] At one point members of the collective taped a sign over a back window of the Water Street NSWC that read "Workers of the World Unite." Davis said this was seen as idealistic and out of place because it was not in line with the thinking of the majority of women at the council. Helen Porter remembers that the Woman's Place (later called Women's Place) collective included more militant members of the women's movement: "They were a group that exemplified the word radical, as in the way they dressed. They were about as opposite to diplomatic as you could be."[17] Things came to a head when the NSWC wanted to hang curtains in the centre. This was viewed as bourgeois by the collective and has been recounted as the reason for the split; however, it was more likely representative of the problems between the two groups.[18]

Eventually the Women's Place collective changed its address and NSWC moved to another location and opened the Women's Centre. The Women's Place collective survived another year and produced the publication *Working Women in Newfoundland*.[19] Two members of the collective, Cathy Murphy and Liz Genge, went on to start the first crisis centre for women and operated it for a year despite lack of public support. Cathy Murphy eventually became a strong head of her local union; Liz Genge died of cancer.

The variety of lifestyles and philosophical approaches among early members of the feminist movement in Newfoundland made unity difficult, but these differences also encouraged lively discussion. Young women from the radical left were able to engage in stimulating talks with older women who belonged to the Conservative or Liberal parties; a mélange of clothing from army boots and ripped jeans to pumps and tailored suits mirrored inner differences that found common cause in redefining the role of women in Newfoundland society. To give voice to issues and debates and keep members informed, a newsletter was started; an early issue advertised consciousness raising groups for men:

> . . . inasmuch as men seem desirous of raising their consciousness, and as we wish to encourage this without jeopardizing the independence and ambience of our present groups, we would suggest that an all-male group be formed. Seasoned CR women would be available for advice and guidance.[20]

Some of the women working on early issues of the Woman's Place/NSWC newsletters were Jane Lewis, Ellen Antler, Del Texmo, Joan Mead, Janet Marshall, Vicky Hammond, Sharon Gray and Mary Lydon. These newsletters, which over the years strove to include news from other feminist groups throughout the province, provided a forum for philosophical questioning and often carried unsigned submissions in order to provide protection to budding feminist writers. An early article offered a feminist view of illness:

> The common cold aggravates not only the sinuses but our sex role behaviour as well. That is, women adopt the mother, caring-for role while men adopt the child cared-for role . . . . The male has learned that every so often he can afford to indulge himself and get sick,

for a female will be there to mother him, to take care of him, to deal with his helplessness.[21]

Early feminists embraced women's liberation and often endured public and private ridicule of their new views. In 1977 Pauline Bradbrook of NSWC wrote:

So what have I found since I left my "closet" and became publicly allied to the women's movement? The same thing I expect most of you have found before me. The universal question *"You're* not one of those women's libbers!" or "What do you *want* anyway?" And the inability to escape from being confronted on women's issues wherever I go. Of having to explain and defend our position, and above all to try and maintain a sense of humour, plus the capacity not to waste mental energies on those who confront while not really wanting to understand.[22]

The members of NSWC were very busy during their first few years of operation and the Women's Centre operated out of cold, inadequate locations. In the beginning, the executive held meetings the first Monday of each month, but by February 1974 meetings were held weekly and the number of issues addressed threatened to overwhelm the fledgling council. For example, representations were made at such events as Minimum Wage Board Hearings, an anti-poverty conference, and the Women and the Law Conference. In September 1973 a "Feminists Together" workshop was held by NSWC to exchange ideas on the theory and practice of the women's movement. In November 1973 the council presented a brief to the government on women's involvement in and appointments to the civil service. The first International Women's Day activities were held in St. John's in March 1973, and featured tapes on the socialization of women. For International Women's Day in 1974, a two-day feminist symposium was held to challenge sex discrimination and help women enter the labour force. In addition, letters were sent to politicians and newspapers to protest sexist remarks and outline the council's position on various issues.

Organizing in Rural Areas

Women in rural areas were also interested in the developing women's movement, though many were suspicious of what they saw as St. John's "come-from-away" feminists.[23] It took several years and considerable effort before effective alliances were built between avowedly feminist and more traditional women's groups. Many rural women who were concerned about Status of Women issues in the early 1970s became active in existing women's groups, such as Women's Institutes or church women's groups. Sheilah Mackinnon

Drover served as president of the Women's Institutes (WI) during those years, and said that many concerned women in rural areas joined Women's Institutes because it was in the community and "you could be a feminist within WI and not be seen as a threat."[24] Wendy Williams, a nurse who had worked in rural Newfoundland and who became a staunch feminist and member of NSWC, added that WI groups in rural areas were more radical than those in the city.

Mackinnon Drover indicated that initially there was reluctance on the part of some members of Women's Institutes to be involved with the new Status of Women group in St. John's: "By calling itself the Newfoundland Status of Women Council, they assumed that what was right for them was right for everyone. But what is right for St. John's is not necessarily right for rural areas. The Status of Women groups and Women's Institutes do have common goals, but the public perception of what the two groups stand for is really quite different."[25] Wendy Williams added that NSWC membership consisted of a number of women who were not from Newfoundland; because they did not have family connections in the province they were able to be more radical.[26]

Although feminist philosophy (or "women's lib" as it was commonly called at the time) did not appeal to all women, pockets of feminist organization began to spring up throughout the province in the early 1970s. By the end of 1974, women in Corner Brook, Labrador City and Grand Falls were organizing groups to fight for women's rights; this activity planted the seeds for the mushrooming of feminist women's groups and services that would emerge in the next decade.

THE MOVEMENT GROWS

Before 1975 the women's movement in the province was a long way from being firmly established. Paying workers to promote women's rights was a dream, and raising money to keep the Women's Centre in St. John's open was a constant battle. A measure of change came in 1975 with International Women's Year. Government used this year as a form of public acknowledgement of its support of women's issues and, as a result, federal funding was made available for special projects. Under a Local Initiatives Project, nine people were employed part-time at the St. John's Women's Centre. A speakers' bureau was set up, leaflets were printed and sent to all community organizations and schools, and numerous courses were offered on topics as diverse as issues in the women's movement and auto maintenance.

The St. John's Local Council of Women produced a book of historical biographies titled *Remarkable Women of Newfoundland and Labrador.*[27] The Women's Institutes undertook a programme called "Animation of Rural Women" which featured seminars designed to animate women to think about the laws concerning their lives and to protect rights belonging to them. The Women's Institutes co-operated with the Canadian Federation of University Women on a fall provincial conference for women on the theme "Women—Creative Leadership."

Activities spread to the arts community and to native women's groups. The Art Association of Newfoundland and Labrador mounted an exhibition of women's paintings. The St. John's based Femfest Committee staged a number of events. Two plays presented were Ibsen's *The Doll's House,* and *What Glorious Times They Had,* a play that told the story of Nellie McClung and her struggle for the women's vote in Manitoba. The committee also sponsored a week of women in the movies. Three Newfoundland writers, Helen Porter, Geraldine Rubia and Bernice Morgan, worked together during 1975 to publish the writings and poetry of women in the province titled *From This Place.*[28] Further north, the native women of Nainemuit Women's Group in Labrador obtained funding to visit Igloolik in the Northwest Territories to exchange ideas, discuss problems, and learn about programmes and crafts.

Some women felt that International Women's Year would raise public awareness to such an extent that discrimination against women would come to an end. Wendy Williams, chair of NSWC during International Women's Year, believed such discrimination would soon be a thing of the past.

> I was full of naiveté about how easy it was going to be. I really did believe that this was all common sense and of course it would all be settled in time. That really was my belief and I didn't change that belief for a very long time, when I read a book called *Women in Western Political Thought* by Susan Moller Okin.[29] Some of the older women may have had a better idea of how systemic the discrimination was.[30]

A comment by Lillian Bouzanne, one of the founders of the first Status of Women council in Newfoundland, sums up the heady feeling of women in 1975 during the United Nations International Year for Women: "We all felt in 1975 that by 1985 the world would belong to women."[31]

However, it became evident that this was not so and women in the province became increasingly involved in fighting for women's rights through organized groups. The decade from 1975–1985 saw the women's movement establish new groups on two levels in the province: on a grass-roots level, and on a bureaucratic level. On a grass-roots level, many new groups that adopted the name "Status of Women" grew independently, inspired by the national women's movement and responding to local needs. Women's centres were opened by volunteers and gradually obtained regular funding, largely through the federal government's Department of the Secretary of State. Native women also formed groups. All the groups lobbied to raise public awareness of issues significant to women, and worked together to provide services for women in crisis, and training for women in need.

In addition, on a grass-roots level, the women's movement became an important part of the labour movement. The growth of the women's movement in Newfoundland and Labrador in the 1970s and 1980s was accompanied by a dramatic growth of women in the labour force and from 1976 to 1986 the number of women in the provincial labour force increased by 56.9 percent, from 58,000 to 91,000.[32] As a result, many issues addressed by other women in the province, as well as women in the labour movement, were workplace issues and included: equal pay for work of equal value, child care, sexual harassment, pension benefits, affirmative action and the effects of microtechnology.

On a bureaucratic level, a feminist presence became incorporated as part of the provincial government. Reflecting what was happening elsewhere in the country, feminists, mainly from the middle class, lobbied for change within the political system and joined the run for elected seats. Through women's efforts, the province established a Provincial Advisory Council on the Status of Women and a Women's Policy Office to advise on women's issues.

During the summer of 1988, Sharon Gray Pope had the opportunity to visit some of the women's groups in the province and discuss the feminist movement with those involved. The following brief histories offer an impression of the growth and activities of the women's movement during the 1970s and 1980s, and a sense of where those groups were heading in 1988.

Status of Women Councils

Corner Brook: A Status of Women council was established in Corner Brook following a meeting in Toronto in 1973 on "Women for Political Action" attended by eighteen women from the province, including Marie Newhook of Corner Brook. She recalled that following the meeting in Toronto, a small group of women in Corner Brook began to meet regularly to discuss issues and enlist new members.[33] In November 1974 about fifty women in Corner Brook attended a luncheon featuring guest speaker Kay Armstrong, President of the National Council of Women. The idea of joining the National Council of Women was discussed; however, Corner Brook women decided to remain autonomous and form a Status of Women council based on the St. John's model. The following month an election of officers was held and Marie Newhook became interim president. Other members of the executive were Gladys Costella, Lynn Verge, Denise Turner and Mary MacIsaac.

The Corner Brook Council provided services to women in the community. In March 1975 the council rented space for a Women's Centre staffed by volunteers, who offered support and referrals within the philosophy of helping women help themselves. The centre gave courses in areas such as assertiveness training and operated a lending library containing research material on women's issues. In addition, the council planned and organized the founding meeting of a local branch of the Human Rights Association in April 1975; in January 1976 a Family Planning Association was formed at a meeting at the Corner Brook Women's Centre. Marie Newhook said that while council members had autonomy to do their own thing, "we all came together on a common desire to improve the lot of women."[34]

Newhook was the first president of the Corner Brook Status of Women Council and looked back at the early years of the council in a 1985 newsletter article:

> What a serious, sober lot we were in those days—pointing out the insidious dangers of sex-role stereotyping in children's text books; constantly complaining about sexist advertising in the electronic media; deploring the presence of pornographic publications . . . on local newsstands; expressing ever-increasing dissatisfaction with the small representations of women on provincial and federal boards and commissions and in government; engaging in numerous "letters to the editor" campaigns on everything from the patronizing aspects of local "beauty contests" to our perception of the social justice dimension of the Gospel![35]

In January 1976 the Corner Brook Council achieved provincial notoriety in a controversy that developed over its opposition to the local Miss Winter Carnival Contest. A press release by the council described the competition as "degrading to women" and said it "promotes inequality between the sexes."[36] The Mayor of Corner Brook, Noel Murphy, proclaimed it was not a beauty contest and wrote to the St. John's *Evening Telegram* attacking the new Status of Women council.

Opinions differed about the effect on the council of the ensuing publicity. Ann Bell felt that reactions of people like the mayor painted a public picture of the group "which was difficult to overcome."[37] As a result of that experience, she advised other women's groups to start with a good public image to ensure that initial efforts were positive. Marie Newhook, however, felt that the furore surrounding the beauty contest protest was "our best vehicle for publicity at the time."[38] The Corner Brook Status of Women Council's objection to the contest succeeded in having the name changed to the Winter Carnival Ambassador Contest, open to both boys and girls.

Ann Bell also recounted that when the local Kinettes club tried to sponsor a "Little Miss Winter Carnival" contest, the Corner Brook Council was able to stop it. This was partly credited to its enlisting the help of a young male psychologist who, when interviewed, related the negative impact such a contest would have on children.[39]

The Corner Brook Council hosted the first provincial Status of Women Conference in 1978, beginning a tradition that annually brings women in the province together. Marilee Pittman remembered the effect of attending the conference and connecting with women around the province:

> My God, it's good to be a woman! That was how I felt after the first women's conference I attended. The women I met were tremendous. They were bright, articulate, energetic and committed. Collectively they were awesome. I was truly impressed and very proud to be included in their ranks. Out the window went a lot of stereotyped notions I had harboured about women.[40]

The Corner Brook Council successfully initiated a number of special services for women in the area. The council worked to improve employment for women and a Single Moms Centre was begun in August 1984 to provide information to single mothers and assist them towards economic independence and self-reliance. Overall, the Corner Brook Status of Women Council has been a focus for social change and the improvement of women's services in the community.

Labrador West: In Labrador City, in 1974, a small group of women became interested in discussing women's issues following a meeting sponsored by the United Church women where Iris Kirby from the Secretary of State Office spoke. Dorothy Robbins, one of the founding members of the group who later worked for the Provincial

Advisory Council on the Status of Women and who is now director of the provincial Women's Policy Office, remembered: "It was a catalyst for me. A group of us started meeting every couple of weeks in each other's homes to discuss issues."[41]

The group continued meeting informally until early 1977 when Marion Atkinson and Barbara Doran, members of the Canada Employment Centre's Pro Femina team from St. John's, visited Labrador City and Wabush to talk about starting a women's centre. Women who attended the meeting committed themselves to establishing their own centre. By March of that year the Labrador West Status of Women Council was officially formed with Heather Duggan as president and Dorothy Robbins as vice-president.

The council tackled a number of local and national issues. It maintained a public profile through action on pornography, articles in the local newspaper, dinner meetings, International Women's Day Celebrations, and a Take Back the Night march. In the fall of 1980 the Labrador West Council followed up its commitment to establish a women's centre; a temporary location was found and after several moves a women's centre was permanently located in 1985 at the city's new community centre.

The Women's Centre provided programmes to meet the needs of women in the area. As a single-industry northern town, Labrador City offers few jobs to women outside the home. In her master's thesis *Passing the Time: The Lives of Women in a Northern Industrial Town*, Linda Ann Parsons examined the experiences of women in Labrador City and found that depression was a common problem: "Constrained by the physical exigencies of life in Labrador City and a tightly circumscribed social role, women have few avenues for self-fulfilment."[42] The programmes at the Women's Centre helped open some avenues and relieve pressure. Two successful programmes were a Wednesday morning "crafts, conversation and coffee" and a Friday morning "creative play for little people." The centre also featured assertiveness training and a support group to help mothers cope with child-raising.

Central Newfoundland: In Grand Falls, the nucleus for the Central Newfoundland Status of Women Council began during International Women's Year. Liz Batstone, one of the founders of the group and its first president, said there was a "great reluctance" on the part of many women in Grand Falls to get involved in a formal Status of Women council.[43]

Batstone felt that early efforts of the council were frustrating and painful because Grand Falls was a small community and "you were easily labelled." But despite the difficulties, the group persisted and one issue they tackled was domestic violence. "As members of this council we were constantly getting what I would call covert phone calls from women in great distress. We did not have the ability to deal with that. The community pretty well refused to accept that this was a problem so what we did was open up the issue and force the community to know about it."[44]

In 1979 the council hosted the second provincial Status of Women Councils conference. When members of the community saw that other women in the province shared the same concerns, the Grand Falls Council's public image seemed to improve. At the conference, delegates from the Corner Brook, Labrador West, Central Newfoundland and St. John's councils were joined by four women from Goose Bay who were organizing their own Status of Women council. The conference theme was "Education: Key to the Eighties," and one issue highlighted was "sex role stereotyping in the classroom." Provincial Education Minister Lynn Verge spoke on the difficulties of being a politician and a feminist, and of initiatives within her department to introduce women's issues into the curriculum.

In July 1984 the Grand Falls Council began operating the Demasduit Centre, a women's centre named after one of the last of the Beothuk Indians. But two years later the council became inactive when the small group of women who kept it going ran out of energy and failed to attract new members. Founding member Gwen Tremblett says they had a "rather rough road" and that in retrospect the Grand Falls Status of Women Council was made up of a small core group "fighting an uphill battle all the way." In conservative Grand Falls, "anything controversial didn't wash."[45]

Growth and Tension within the St. John's Council

While new Status of Women councils were being established in Corner Brook, Labrador City and Grand Falls, the St. John's-based Newfoundland Status of Women Council struggled to operate a women's centre. For years the Women's Centre moved about the city from one inadequate location to another. Finally some members decided that the best solution was to purchase a house; in 1977 NSWC member Diane Duggan persuaded twenty council members to loan $100 each for a down payment on a dilapidated three-storey downtown rowhouse at 83 Military Road. Renovations were undertaken with help from a Canada Works grant and the permanent Women's Centre opened in June 1978.[46] The following month St.

John's City Hall granted $1,000 to the centre and a Rape Crisis 24-hour Hot Line opened.

The opening of the Women's Centre in St. John's, 1978, provided a permanent home for the local women's movement. This gathering included Frances Innes, left, and Shirley Goundrey, front.

Credit: St. John's Status of Women Council.

It was a tense year with much energy focused on obtaining and renovating the house. Some council members felt the NSWC was failing to reach out to the membership and to attract active support. A period of disharmony followed and a resolution was made to devote time to examining the council. This occurred during a series of six meetings between February and March of 1978, and the recommendation from these meetings was that the council concentrate on increasing its active, feminist membership. An open day of discussion was held May 27, 1978, to work through the conflicts and difficulties that had arisen. This day ended positively, with a commitment and enthusiasm to working out overall aims and goals; one goal was to ensure that women contacting the centre encounter feminists who would encourage them to join the orientation programme for new members. "What was striking (about the day of discussion) was the willingness of members to afford each other the respect of listening. That is the element that makes us different from many groups and affords us hope that sisterhood can work," reported Dorothy Inglis.[47]

Ann Bell and Wendy Williams at the opening of the Women's Centre in St. John's, 1978.

Credit: St. John's Status of Women's Council.

Internal problems were not the only concern; a thorny issue arose during the 1979 provincial conference in Grand Falls when the new Status of Women councils objected to the St. John's group using the name "Newfoundland" Status of Women Council. The other councils felt the name NSWC implied a province-wide status and urged its members to change its name to reflect geographic location. This proposal was strongly resisted for many years by

NSWC members: some felt the group had a historic right to the name; others did not want to be the St. John's Status of Women Council and wanted a name (one suggestion was the Feminist Union of Newfoundland) that would clearly indicate a philosophical and political position. But even in 1979 some NSWC members were willing to compromise with other councils in the province. On May 1, 1980, Wendy Williams wrote to the four other councils, reviewing their concerns over funding and the issue of abortion. Williams acknowledged the group's name could permit NSWC to receive government grants and information which should be dispersed among all four councils; she also acknowledged that positions taken by NSWC, particularly on abortion, were assumed to be the positions of other councils. Her letter called for solidarity and co-operation: "We must find a way for this name-change to be a positive step."[48] Finally, four years later, in May 1984, the membership of the Newfoundland Status of Women Council narrowly voted to change its name to the St. John's Status of Women Council.

Through these difficulties, time was devoted to larger problems. For example, women's health issues concerned women's groups in the province and during the summer of 1978 the Newfoundland and Corner Brook Status of Women Councils carried out research in St. John's and Corner Brook on the abuse of alcohol and other drugs by women in Newfoundland. The results of the research indicated that thirty percent of women surveyed abused alcohol. These findings prompted members of the then-Newfoundland Status of Women Council to approach Health and Welfare Canada and obtain funding in 1980 for a long-term project. Health and Welfare suggested that the St. John's women join with rural groups on this project; as a result, a co-operative proposal was worked out with the Women's Institutes for a three-year Women's Health Education Project (WHEP). This landmark project built important bridges between urban and rural women, uniting groups around the common cause of women's health.

The WHEP project started in 1981; the first task was to develop a questionnaire for rural women. Coordinator Frances Ennis (who had previously worked for the Women's Institutes and provided an important link between WI and the Status of Women Councils) remembers that a great deal of thought went into questions because organizers did not want "the kind of thing where there was any suggestion of what might be a health problem."[49] She said the questionnaire was successful because it ensured the project was firmly based on issues identified by rural women. These issues included things such as water and sewage facilities which were not immediately apparent as health issues. Rural women linked health concerns closely to their family and community situations; to them, alcohol abuse, poor nutrition or emotional problems were symptoms of difficult living conditions. As a result of questionnaire findings, the project was organized around five different themes: medical and community services, nutrition and eating habits, mental health, alcohol and drug abuse, and reproductive health.

Workshops on the themes were developed and made available to about sixty communities. The workshops did not rely on experts to provide advice, but allowed women to explore problems and come up with their own solutions. As part of the evaluation of WHEP, Linda Dale said the success of the project provided important guidelines to other health educators regarding the value of the participatory process: "Using this method the Project was able to involve women that general campaigns have not been able to reach. From people's comments it was evident that a small-scale programme tailored to participants' needs was more effective and efficient as an educational tool than a large information dissemination approach."[50]

Further benefit from the project was gleaned when the network established by WHEP was used for another health education project sponsored by NSWC with the guidance of geneticist Dr. Penny Allderdice, called "Ask Your Family Tree." This project was designed to help people spot hereditary tendencies in their families in order to facilitate early detection of disease.

Mokami Status of Women Council: In 1979, in Happy Valley-Goose Bay, women concerned about problems of wife abuse formed a group to explore ways to establish a transition house. Application to the Department of the Secretary of State provided a sustaining grant for a women's centre rather than a transition house. With this grant the women started the Mokami Status of Women Council, rented a trailer and hired a coordinator. To raise funds, the council opened a thrift shop. Barb Maidment remembered attending meetings of the new Status of Women group and "falling in love" with the energy and enthusiasm of the group.[51]

In April 1982 the Mokami Status of Women Council hosted the annual provincial conference for Status of Women Councils at North West River. The theme "Breaking down the Barriers" proved most appropriate when poor weather kept women from Nain, Davis Inlet and Hopedale from arriving until Saturday evening. Despite weather problems, over one hundred women from Labrador and the island gathered to learn and share. Jean Lestage of Labrador City wrote in an April 1982 newsletter:

> What impressed me about the women I met was the tremendous wealth of experience and talents these women at the conference possessed. I met for the first time women from the coast of Labrador. One lady came by an eight hour skidoo ride to the conference, others came by small planes and helicopters. I heard two older Inuit women sing in their native language.[52]

Marilee Pittman of the Corner Brook Council was also impressed with the conference and wrote in the council's newsletter that barriers came down between native women and their sisters in a "learning and sharing weekend, one that exemplified the best of the women's movement—the collective effort and the joys of sister-hood."[53]

Dorothy King worked as coordinator of that conference. She recalled that feminists in Happy Valley/Goose Bay did not have the same support structures as in a larger centre like St. John's: "My feeling is that we are quite isolated in some ways. We've spent a lot of time talking to different organizations and individuals to let them know what we are about."[54] Isolation was a common theme with Newfoundland women's groups and its effects were felt even more in Labrador because of the physical division of the province.

Gander: In Gander a handful of women were interested in forming a Status of Women council, so they met several times with Secretary of State representative Iris Kirby to discuss plans. In May 1983 a dinner meeting, featuring Ann Bell as guest speaker, drew about sixty women and fourteen volunteered to serve on a founding steering committee.

The steering committee was co-chaired by Marie Matheson and Pat Kennedy. Initial efforts of the Gander Status of Women Council were reflective of many women's groups as members worked to increase their knowledge of women's issues before taking on an active public role. Matheson remembered that the first year was spent building up the group's focus and knowledge: "To some members the whole idea of feminism was new. We were at different steps along the road to a real understanding of feminism."[55] Gerry Devereaux was involved in the new council and recalled that activities during that year included: "group education, haggling over philosophy and grass-roots learning."[56]

By its second year the Gander Council recognized the need for a Women's Centre which would be accessible to people in the community. The centre, staffed by volunteers, opened in February

1984. Crystal Eagan recalled "begging, borrowing and stealing" enough furniture to make the centre presentable in time for its official opening.[57]

The Gander Status of Women Council was going full steam ahead, and a month later, at the 1984 provincial conference of Status of Women Councils held in Labrador City, the fledgling council volunteered to host the 1985 conference. The Gander conference, organized on a health care theme, helped the new Gander Council because it attracted new members, provided public visibility in the community, and garnered respect from other councils for the excellent organization. The Gander Council has maintained a lively public presence through its Women's Centre, weekly articles in the local newspaper, Take Back the Night events, and International Women's Day celebrations.

The Provincial Women's Conference in Gander, February, 1989, focused on 'Women in Politics.' Left to right: Joyce Hancock, Bernice Hancock and Agnes Richard.

Credit: Provincial Advisory Council on the Status of Women, St. John's, Newfoundland.

Gateway Status of Women Council: The Gateway Status of Women Council in Port aux Basques was founded in October 1982 at a meeting attended by about forty women. As an initial step, the council opened a Women's Centre which was run for two years by volunteers before funding was obtained for a coordinator. The centre provides a number of services including: self-help and support groups, information on women's issues and seminars on child abuse, women's health, single parents, women and the law, teenage sexuality, and family violence. The Gateway Council publicizes women's issues through a weekly section in the local newspaper titled *From a Woman's Point of View*. In April 1988 the council hosted the annual provincial conference of Status of Women Councils on the theme "Women and Progress."

Bay St. George: As relative newcomers to the women's movement, the women of Stephenville and the Bay St. George area lost no time making their presence felt. In February 1985 a meeting of women in the area chose a steering committee to develop a Status of Women Council. In April the first newsletter of the Bay St. George Status of Women Council publicized the wide variety of issues that concerned the council and that summer a survey of women in the area confirmed the need for women's rights advocacy and information.

Peace and nuclear disarmament have been particularly important issues to this group; in August 1986 they organized a March For Peace which drew over two hundred participants. This event was repeated in August 1987 as part of a women's day of activities sponsored by the council: women from the Port au Port Peninsula and Corner Brook were among the three hundred and fifty people on the peace march.

Joyce Hancock, first president of the Bay St. George Council, said the council struggled to work in a non-hierarchical fashion: "If we're not really careful about the way we have meetings, to include all women and give voice to women, we will create another structure like the male structures that are there, that people just flow away from."[58]

The Stephenville Women's Centre opened in June 1986 with Hancock as coordinator. Featuring a large living room and kitchen as well as a playroom for children, the centre buzzed with activity as events were organized and carried off successfully on issues such as family law, day care and the problems of single parenting. In March 1988 the Bay St. George Council held four days of activities for International Women's Day, including a day devoted to the concerns of native women in the area. Another day was devoted to young feminists and several high school classes toured the Women's Centre and participated in a discussion about the need for a women's movement.

Participants at the Provincial Women's Conference in Gander, 1989, included active supporters of the 52% Solution. Clockwise: Ann Bell, Sheilah Mackinnon Drover, Linda Sue Chambers and Sheila Curran.

Credit: Provincial Advisory Council on the Status of Women, St. John's, Newfoundland.

Loosely grouped under the name "Status of Women," feminist organizations grew throughout Newfoundland and Labrador during the 1970s and 1980s. Not all groups gained public support and in many ways feminism did not appeal to Newfoundland women. As we have seen, the Central Newfoundland Status of Women Council was not able to gain enough support in Grand Falls to continue operation. Similarly, in the tiny community of Main Brook on the Great Northern Peninsula, a handful of women struggled for six years to keep the Great Northern Peninsula Status of Women Council going. Ella Pilgrim was a founding member and past president, and said the group of ten to twelve women were never able to gain the support of the community.[59] Lack of external support was one problem for Status of Women councils, another problem was evident in lack of support for certain feminist issues such as freedom of choice for abortion, which even failed to gain support within some avowedly feminist groups.

But through heroic volunteer efforts and the limited financial support available from the federal government's Secretary of State Women's Programme, women's centres were established in many communities. Opening a women's centre was an immediate goal of most Status of Women councils. Women's centres served many purposes, but mainly provided a place for women to visit and find help with personal problems. The Gateway Women's Centre in Port aux Basques, for example, defined its goal as providing "a relaxed place where women may turn for friendship, support and a source of information."[60]

Through daily contacts with a variety of women and their concerns, women's centres provided the opportunity to recognize the needs of women in the province and to work toward solutions. Special needs were met through support groups at women's centres for single parents and victims of family violence. In addition, about a third of the calls made to most women's centres in the province were for assistance and included crisis calls from battered women and victims of incest, requests for housing, and calls requesting help with financial and marital problems. Members of the St. John's Status of Women Council started a Rape Crisis Centre in response to the many calls received at that women's centre from victims of sexual assault.

Over the years the staffs of women's centres have listened to women, provided them with support, acted as advocates, increased awareness about legal rights, and referred women to professionals. Feminist counselling at women's centres has treated individual women as competent people with the ability to make decisions about their own lives. Women's centres have assisted students and others researching feminist issues and acquired libraries and clippings on issues of concern to women.

Status of Women councils have encouraged women interested in developing feminist ideas, and Status of Women conferences have stimulated women to share ideas and experiences as well as to learn to present a united front on issues. (See Appendix D for a list of conferences from 1975 to 1988.)

Though they included both men and women, two other significant groups that formed in the province were the Planned Parenthood Association and the Canadian Abortion Rights Action League (CARAL). These groups are not discussed in this document, but their work provided information and services necessary for living independent, healthy lives. Many other women's groups in the province were formed in the 1970s and 1980s to deal with specific groups of women or with specific concerns. The following discussion provides information on those groups.

Related Women's Groups

Memorial University Women's Resource Centre: The Council of the Students' Union at Memorial University of Newfoundland responded to the need for services for female students and in November 1981 opened the Women's Resource Centre. It was established to provide information to female students on such topics as birth control, venereal diseases, rape, pregnancy, alcoholism, drugs, depression, career planning and education. One of the first issues taken up by the Women's Resource Centre was better lighting on campus so female students would not be afraid to walk there in the evening.

Programmes offered at the Women's Resource Centre included, at various times, self-defence courses, a speaker's series, special events such as "Sexual Harassment Awareness Week" and International Women's Day Celebrations. The long term goal of the Women's Resource Centre is to form a strong feminist community on Memorial University's campus and to participate in more community activities.

Testimony to the university's commitment to women's issues was the development of a Women's Studies Programme. The programme grew to offer an interdisciplinary minor in women's studies. Research, lectures and discussions sponsored by this programme give women who participate the opportunity to analyze feminism and learn to be more focused in their approach to feminism.

Native Women's Groups: The lack of information in this section is a reflection of two factors. First, until 1990 and the Oka experience, native women's issues were not effectively incorporated with the mainstream women's movement. This was partly because of government programmes and policies that dealt with native women's issues separately under Secretary of State's Native Women's Programme, and until recently the women's movement did not clearly recognize what actions could be taken to support native women. Secondly, native women's groups in Newfoundland were centred in Labrador and there has always been a problem, in provincial organizations of any type, with effectively including Labrador groups. This has been attributed to distance and cost; as an example, the research for this document was constricted by these factors. However, the following is in recognition of native women's groups and presented in the hope that further research will do them justice.

Native women in the province first got together in 1978 at the Nain Northern Labrador Women's Conference. Native women were concerned about women's role in their society, where disruptive elements such as alcohol and crime were destroying traditional family life. Delegates pinpointed the need for more information to be provided in the two native languages, Inuktitut and Muchuau Innu, as well as in English, and for new programmes, services and facilities to address their problems. They decided to establish local community women's groups to deal with the concerns raised at the conference and to improve life in their communities.

Native women's groups developed in many small Labrador communities. They raised money for local projects and publicized community concerns. The Nain Women's Group identified the need for services such as family planning, a community health council and a day care centre in the community. Day care was particularly important in the summer months when many women worked in the fish plant. The Nain group opened a day care centre funded primarily by provincial Social Services, and a thrift shop where residents could buy inexpensive used clothing. The group worked towards establishing a Nain Refuge Centre for battered women.

The Sheshatshit Women's Group opened its doors in August 1982 on the top floor of an old craft store. A full-time coordinator was hired to get the office into operation, network with other feminist and native groups, and provide referrals and counselling to women in the area. In Hopedale a women's group formed in March 1984 and became active in community events, raised money to help pay a pre-school teacher's salary and gave gifts to children in the community at Christmas. The North West River "Women of the Land" group, the Inuatsuk Women's Group of Happy Valley, the Women's Group at Makkovik and the Native women's group at Port Hope Simpson also served their communities. Native women's groups ran thrift shops and raised money for community events through darts, card games and bingo.

The Labrador Native Women's Association formed as an umbrella group for the women of Northern and Central Labrador communities. Member groups included representatives from the communities of Nain, Davis Inlet, Hopedale, Makkovik, Postville, Rigolet, North West River, Sheshatshit and Happy Valley. Women from Innu, Inuit and Metis native cultures were represented in this association, and non-native women could participate through associate membership.

During a meeting with two provincial cabinet ministers, in March 1986, native women gave voice to a variety of issues. The Hopedale Women's Group protested the application for a liquor licence in that community and the Nain Women's Group lobbied for funds for its day care centre and for a proposed refuge centre for battered women and children. The Davis Inlet Innu Women's Group brought forward its need for a public bathhouse because of the lack of water and sewage facilities to individual homes. The Sheshatshit Innu Women's Group requested a full-time interpreter at the Melville Hospital and for visits related to health care services such as those of an eye specialist. The Postville Women's Group voiced its concerns about teenage pregnancy, and the Rigolet Women's Group stressed the need for specialized medical services in coastal communities.

The Conne River MicMac Indian Band does not have a women's group, but at the November 1984 conference in St. John's on "Women and the Constitution," Marilyn John spoke about her fight for the rights of her band. While not identifying herself with the women's movement, John's activities as a tireless fighter for her people's rights earn her a place in any discussion of outstanding women in the province. What was significant about her presentation at the conference was that it presented the opportunity for women in the women's movement to recognize the need to include native women's issues when addressing issues within the local movement.

Provincial Farm Women's Association: A Provincial Farm Women's Association of Newfoundland was formed at a conference in April 1987. Five regional farm women's groups exist in Newfoundland, which were organized to educate members and the public on agricultural issues and to lobby governments. The Avalon Farm Women's Association in the St. John's area represents mainly dairy farmers, and the Cape Shore Farm Women's Association on the Southern Avalon Peninsula represents fox and sheep farmers. The Central Farm Women's Association, the Humber Valley Farm Women, and the Goose Head Farm Women's Association on the east coast of the province represent farmers who produce a wide range of commodities.

Farm women's groups have organized Farmers' Field Days and held a number of workshops on topics such as building a better organization, public speaking, the media, lobbying and parliamentary procedure. These workshops proved effective, especially when the Goose Head Farm Women's Association undertook a study in 1987 to assess agriculture's contribution to the economy of the Lethbridge-Musgravetown area. In addition, farm women have lobbied government on many issues. For example, when the provincial government proposed development of the large Sprung Greenhouse in the St. John's area, members of the Goose Head Association attended a public forum in the area and questioned the Minister of Agriculture on thirty-two concerns. They took the opportunity to address the lack of an agricultural agreement between Newfoundland and Ottawa, and the effects of high freight costs on agriculture.

Francophone Women: By the summer of 1988, there were francophone associations in many areas of the province and a move was under way to establish a provincial association of francophone women. Francophone associations in St. John's, Labrador City, Cape St. George, Mainland, Black Duck and Stephenville helped to serve the needs of women in these communities. According to Melin Foley of Cape St. George, efforts to organize a francophone women's group in her community were unsuccessful.[61]

Women in Unions

Women do not have a long history of active involvement in the province's unions. During the mid-1970s, however, more women took leadership roles and encouraged others to become involved in union activities through special women's committees.

The Newfoundland Association of Public Employees (NAPE) formed a constitutionally guaranteed women's committee in 1976. As part of the concerted effort to involve more women in the union, the NAPE Women's Committee held regional women's conferences on a regular basis beginning in 1977. Sessions at women's conferences included assertiveness training, union structure, collective bargaining and affirmative action. Sandra Perry, who has been actively involved with NAPE since 1974, said the regional women's conferences were very popular, "we just don't have enough room for everyone who wants to go."[62] She felt the conferences effectively encouraged women to become more involved in union activities.

One of the best known trade unionists in the province and the country, Nancy Riche, played a key role in motivating NAPE's female workers to become actively involved in union affairs. She spearheaded the NAPE Women's Committee and in 1981 became NAPE's director of Education, Research and Communications. In May 1984 she was elected secretary/treasurer of the National Union of Provincial Government Employees and in April 1986 became an executive vice-president of the Canadian Labour Congress. Ruby Piercey, a past chair of the NAPE Women's Committee, related from personal experience just how effective Nancy Riche and women's conferences were:

> I went to an assertiveness training workshop in 1983 and heard Nancy Riche say things that I always felt I was being selfish even thinking about. It drew me out. Right from the time I was small I always thought a woman's place was in the home, looking after her family. If I wanted anything for myself I always thought I was being selfish. I even thought I was being selfish getting involved in the union because it took up so much time.[63]

By 1988 the membership of NAPE included over seven thousand three hundred female workers which is half of the total membership. Through the commitment and effort of women in the union, NAPE developed position papers on women and pensions, day care, affirmative action and microtechnology. The union advocated free, quality day care for all who want or need it, affirmative action legislation at the provincial level to make it mandatory for employers to negotiate programmes with unions, adequate pensions for all and security within work places where jobs are threatened by technological change.

The Newfoundland and Labrador Federation of Labour formally recognized the growing importance of the women in its membership by holding a special women's conference in April 1984 called "We Are Organized Women." Workshops were held on technological change, assertiveness, sexual harassment and parliamentary procedure. Women at the conference called on all affiliates of the federation to establish women's committees and to develop affirmative action measures and programmes to eliminate barriers to women's employment in the labour movement. Conference delegates also called on the Federation of Labour to expand its executive council by two seats specifically reserved for women.

The women's committee called on the Federation of Labour to take up the issue of part-time work as a priority and pointed out that one out of every four women who worked was employed part-time. It recommended that the federation lobby government to amend labour standards legislation to improve the situation for part-time workers. It called for benefits to part-time workers such as seniority, vacation and sick leave, medical and disability insurance, and pro-rated pensions. The women's committee urged the Federation of Labour to encourage its affiliates to organize part-time workers and to assist this organizing effort financially.

Women in the Newfoundland Fishermen, Food and Allied Workers Union (NFFAWU) formed a special women's committee in 1984 to bring forward concerns of the 30 percent female membership in this union.[64] At the 1984 NFFAWU convention, women publicized their presence with buttons bearing the slogan "30 percent women, 100 percent committed." Convention workshops concerning day care and sexual harassment were held, and three women were elected to the union's executive board.

Women involved in union activities found themselves developing a "hard-nosed attitude," according to Judy Vanta, a past president of the St. John's and District Labour Council.[65] She was involved in one set of negotiations in which a representative from government's classification and pay division said that women do not want higher-paying jobs and that they are not physically capable of the same work as men. Vanta said that after that meeting she became a believer in women's issues. "When you see that sort of attitude you discover that you have to take a hard-nosed attitude in order to get what we need to reach."[66]

Within the Newfoundland Teachers Association (NTA), the Special Interest Council on Women's Issues in Education worked to involve teachers in improving the position of women in education. Fifty-three percent of teachers in Newfoundland were female, yet women were not equally represented at leadership levels. For example, only fourteen percent of senior high principals were female, and at the elementary level only twenty-three percent of the principals were women.[67] In October 1978 the first provincial conference on the Status of Women for teachers was held in Gander, and efforts were made to promote equality of the sexes at all levels in the education field through newsletters and meetings of the council.

In 1988 a major struggle was successfully undertaken on the issue of equal pay for work of equal value, and in June 1988 agreement was reached between NAPE and the provincial government on pay equity for public employees. This was the first time in

Canada a negotiated agreement was reached on pay equity with a provincial government.

Union women in the province fought hard on issues that ultimately benefited all women. While little overlap existed in the membership of union women's committees and Status of Women's councils, there was a feeling of support and conviction that the same battles were being fought on different fronts as women tackled issues important to them.

TACKLING SOCIAL ISSUES

The 1970 report of the Royal Commission on the Status of Women confirmed that women suffer systemic social injustice because of their sex. Status of Women's councils formed to ensure the application of recommendations from the report which were aimed at improving the situation for women. As has been pointed out in this essay, that was a "monumental task." Part of tackling that monumental task was to educate women about the feminist movement and to raise their consciousness. Through this process, women in the province identified common social problems and efforts were made to deal with the social injustices women suffered. To deal with social injustices, women put issues significant to them on both the public and political agendas. This section will address direct actions women in Newfoundland took to provide public services to women and to raise public awareness of women's issues. This will be followed by a section on direct actions women took to include women in the formal political process and to influence government policies that regulate women's lives.

Providing Services

"The trend appears to be towards action rather than discussion; women are working to make changes in the issues that affect women in their communities," wrote Susan McConnell, Newfoundland's National Action Committee representative, in her January 1987 report.[68] She noted that women's groups in the province were actively involved in providing such services as assertiveness training, shelter and counselling for battered women, employment counselling, job training and job creation, second-hand clothing stores and day care centres.

Women working with women through women's centres, Status of Women councils and other women's groups became acutely aware of the need for services for women. In particular, they recognized the need for transition houses and employment opportunities for women. This recognition led to an extension of services offered through women's centres, by councils and by specific groups.

Transition Houses: Desperate calls from abused women seeking refuge made the issue of family violence and the need for shelters, or transition houses, a priority with many women's groups. The objective of providing this service was to offer a violence-free refuge for a maximum of six weeks with non-judgmental counselling where abused women could be given space and time to make decisions about their own and their children's lives.

The Newfoundland Status of Women Council was the first to put a proposal to the provincial government for a transition house. It was presented in 1975 and turned down. In 1979, the council defined its priority issue for the year as the establishment of a transition house. Five years of lobbying on this issue were rewarded in December 1980 when the province announced support for a transition house with funding from the Department of Social Services. A five-bedroom house in downtown St. John's was purchased and renovated. The province's first transition house opened in June 1981 and immediately received applicants. Services at the house expanded to offer counselling and support for children of battered women through a children's services worker.

An experiment to provide longer-term shelter was undertaken in the St. John's area and a second stage house for victims of family violence was opened in November 1983. It was named Kirby House in memory of Iris Kirby, formerly of Secretary of State, who had been instrumental in organizing Status of Women councils throughout the province. This long-term shelter operated for several years and provided accommodation for women and their children who could not find affordable housing when they left Transition House. It proved impossible to keep the two houses going and in May 1987 Transition House moved into the Kirby House premises and adopted the name "Iris Kirby House." The original Transition House building became the administrative offices for Iris Kirby House.

Women's centres throughout the province were swamped with calls from battered women who had no place to turn. In Corner Brook, the Committee on Family Violence worked for four years to establish a transition house. In November 1983 the opening of an accommodation for twenty-four women and children was made possible through a combination of fund-raising in the community and government funding, and served as the only shelter for battered women in Western Newfoundland. In March 1986 in Happy Valley/ Goose Bay a shelter called Libra House was established through the efforts of the Mokami Status of Women Council. Hyra Skoglund remembers it was "a dream come true" when Libra House finally opened.[69]

Drinking and wife-beating were serious problems in the Labrador City community. In 1982 a "Safe House" programme was started on a volunteer basis, but was forced to close two years later because of loss of volunteers. In September 1984 two members of the Labrador West Council attended a two-day workshop in Corner Brook held by the Committee Against Family Violence, and came up with the idea of changing the name of the programme to suit the community. Toward the end of November, a steering committee formed and set up the Labrador City Family Crisis Shelter. The Labrador West Status of Women Council, however, continues to work towards improved services for battered women and hopes to see a funded transition house for the area. Together with the three transition houses, the Family Crisis Shelter offered some help to abused women in the province.

The province's facilities for battered women were still far from adequate. The Women's Centre run by the Gander Status of Women Council received many crisis calls from women in abusive situations and directed energy towards establishing a transition house. Long waiting lists were common in areas where transition houses existed, and many women travelled distances to find a shelter. While women's groups in St. John's, Corner Brook and Happy Valley struggled to maintain existing services, lobbying to increase the number of shelters in the province continued.

In addition to the need for more shelters, major areas of concern identified by the women's movement and associated with family violence were the lack of charges being laid by the police intervening in wife battering situations, the lack of good quality, affordable housing to offer women as a permanent alternative to leave battering situations, and the need for public education and prevention in the area of family violence. Women worked hard to address these problems.

Employment: Transition houses offered a step to independence for a number of women, but without the opportunities for employment many other women were vulnerable. Union women's committees worked to improve the situation for women in the work force. Women's groups lobbied government to change tax regulations that discriminate against working mothers, and women's groups identified the need to help women enter the work force. In response to the identification of these needs, Canada Employment funded programmes directed at women. The first Career Exploration for Women course was offered in St. John's in 1977 and, during the next four years, over twenty such courses were held in six Newfoundland communities. Career Exploration for Women offered a six-week course for mature women wishing to move into the paid labour force. The programme involved women in career education and worked to develop interpersonal skills.

A Sole Support Mothers' Project was also sponsored by the Canadian Employment and Immigration Commission (CEIC) and conducted by the Division of Adult and Continuing Education of the provincial government. The target group was mothers with dependent children who wanted to take training or find paid employment. It was an eight week project where fifteen women explored both their personal characteristics and the world of work to help them choose training courses. The object was to develop skills related to applying for, and successfully completing, training courses. A need to provide programmes to help women re-enter the workforce was identified as a target by the Women Interested in Successful Employment (WISE) programme, which had been started in St. John's in the spring of 1988.

In June 1979 the Corner Brook Women's Centre was able to open on a daily basis due to a grant for "The Feminist Service Training Programme." In November 1980 it started a Women's Employment Counselling Project designed to improve the employability of women. The service was set up to help women make career choices, explore training courses, develop job search skills as well as to provide information on needed services such as day care, financial counselling and personal counselling. The project successfully helped many women gain the confidence and insight needed to enter or re-enter the workforce.

Women's groups were able to provide some direct employment for women and to subsidize their own operations through government-funded employment projects. As they developed expertise, the Corner Brook Status of Women Council was frequently approached by funding bodies to develop and administer projects offering employment to women. From 1983 to 1986, the council employed fifty women in short-term projects of sixteen to twenty-three weeks' duration, with budgets ranging from $15,000 to $67,000. These projects included developing bed and breakfast facilities in the Corner Brook area, training women as homemaker assistants, clearing the Marble Mountain ski slope and training women as bus drivers. Many other councils served as a channel for women's employment projects funded by CEIC.

Other women's groups did what they could to encourage govern-ment to improve training in their communities. To counteract the serious lack of employment opportunities for women, the Labrador West Council recommended government consider establishing a trades training facility in the area. The Mokami Status of Women Council, on the other hand, worked with the Department of Social Services to sponsor make-work projects for women in that area.

One women's group was formed specifically to assess the em-ployment situation of women in their area. Because women in the Upper Trinity South area constantly telephoned the Upper Trinity South Development Association looking for information on employ-ment, a public meeting was held on November 17, 1982 to identify job opportunities. About two hundred women gathered and identi-fied seventy opportunities. Eleven women, representing twelve communities from Heart's Desire to Blaketown, volunteered to sit on an Upper Trinity South Development Association committee called the Women's Involvement Committee (WIN) to investigate and follow-up on these opportunities.

The committee compiled and distributed a questionnaire to every woman over the age of sixteen who lived in the represented communities. Wendy Murdoch, the first president of WIN, remem-bered the objectives of the questionnaire: "We wanted to get an idea of where women were and what their needs were."[70] Results of the questionnaire, published in June 1985, showed that eighty-three percent of the women were unemployed despite the fact that seventy -two percent wanted work. In addition, most women who completed the questionnaire were willing to travel from five to twenty miles per day in order to find paid employment.

The WIN committee was concerned about the effect of fish plant closures on women and they organized a one-day forum on May 10, 1983, in South Dildo called "Women and Fish Plant Labour." Again, about two hundred women attended. A report on the forum, *Trinity Bay South Women on the Move—Women Working for Women*, high-lighted the issues discussed.[71] These included quality control, work sharing, trucking out of fish, and developing new products and markets. Discussions on training and equal opportunities were also highlighted. Women at the forum stressed the need to access train-ing in traditionally male-dominated areas such as filleting, cutting and trucking fish. A year later, the WIN committee administered a follow-up survey on issues raised in the forum and found women still concerned about the same issues, especially access to higher-paying "male" jobs in the fish plants.

In September 1983 the WIN committee submitted a hard-hitting brief to the MacDonald Royal Commission on the Economy. It stated the problems women in the area faced:

> When we are fortunate enough to find employment, we are discrimi-
> nated against by our male counterparts, just for being women.
> What we mean in regards to discrimination is, when it comes to
> hiring women, we are the last hired and the first to be laid off. .
> Besides the hiring practices, there exists a second problem for the
> women of Trinity. It is the unfair practice of paying women less for
> work of equal value . . . .[72]

WIN defined the problems facing women from the Upper Trinity South area, but was limited in ways to solve them. Part of the solution was achieved through project grants, which enabled the committee to hire women to build a small building, a community wharf and storage sheds for fishing gear.

It became apparent there were other issues to address, so WIN set up an office which served as a drop-in centre for women in the area to acquire information and discuss their concerns. "We began to expand our ideals and our ideas about the things we wanted to achieve, but it didn't quite fit in with the Rural Development Association's line of thinking, so in 1983 we separated," said Wendy Murdoch. She added that: "During the separation, we lost a lot of the women who had been members, and now we have just six women on the executive. We run meetings collectively now instead of Robert's Rules of Order."[73]

The new independent WIN committee looked at the whole socio-economic picture and its effect on women. "If women were being oppressed in the home it was unfair to expect them to become viable in the workplace. We got into the whole area of family violence," said Murdoch.[74] In June 1988, WIN opened a Women's Centre in Green's Harbour, and a sub-committee of WIN worked on setting up a transition house for the area. The group started with a focus on basic economic concerns and changed to meet the needs of the local communities.

Women advocated for and assisted each other in many ways. For example, in 1978 the Corner Brook Council played an effective role by helping women who worked in the squid fishery on the Twillingate Islands to organize. Traditionally, women in the area, and in the rest of the province, have been involved in the seasonal work of this fishery, usually by working on their husbands' boats or by drying squid on shore. This work, however, did not entitle women to unemployment insurance benefits, since only independent, self-employed squid-jiggers qualified. In 1978 the squid were unusually abundant, and women jigged, cleaned, dried and sold squid as a processed product, and they paid unemployment insurance premiums from their earnings. When these women applied for UIC benefits in the fall, only two of the two hundred and fifty women claimants received benefits and their first names happened to be Georgie and Frankie. The other women became suspicious and they told their story. Because the Corner Brook Status of Women Council helped the squid-jiggers organize, and through meetings held in Ottawa, the women's claims were recognized and processed.

Raising Public Awareness

Ann Bell, former president of the Provincial Advisory Council on the Status of Women, said the major accomplishment of the women's movement has been to put issues on the public agenda and have them debated: "It's not telling women you should do this or you should do that, but making women think, making men think, making our society think about what life has been like for women and what life is still like for some women."[75]

Only two Status of Women Councils, St. John's and Bay St. George, as well as the Provincial Advisory Council on the Status of Women, officially adopted a public pro-choice stand on abortion. In her history of the early years of the Newfoundland Status of Women Council, Shirley Goundrey wrote:

> A petition to repeal the abortion law was circulated at the May 1972 meeting and gave rise to much emotionalism and hostility, and in many instances, the petition was taken to mean pro-abortion. This one issue alienated many women from the whole movement, which was unfortunate because many of these women were aware of and concerned about other issues of concern to women.[76]

Wendy Williams recalled that, during discussion of the abortion issue, some NSWC members were concerned about alienating members of the women's community who either saw pro-choice as pro-abortion, or were concerned about being perceived by the public as going against the church. Their decision to support the repeal of the abortion law was made because of NSWC's commitment to support the recommendations of the Royal Commission, including removal of abortion from the criminal code. In 1975 the council joined the Canadian Association for the Repeal of the Abortion Law (CARAL).[77]

The decision to adopt a public pro-choice stand was not as easy for women living in small communities who were more susceptible to pressures from family, church and community than were women in the larger centre of St. John's. The Gander Status of Women Council chose to avoid a public stand on the abortion issue because it was too controversial. "For some of our members this was disillusioning, to them abortion was feminism," said Marie Matheson.[78] The Corner Brook Status of Women Council also discussed the abortion issue early in its history, but members held various views on the matter so they decided to agree to disagree, and the council never took a public position on the issue. This issue caused hard feelings between councils: for example, some felt it was not right for feminists to be judgemental of those who did not want to adopt a pro-choice stand, yet others found it difficult to accept a situation in which feminists denied women the right to choose.

Other issues were not so divisive. For example, the campaign against child sexual abuse produced unity. The case of Dr. Stephen Collins, who was convicted on eleven counts of child sexual assault and initially sentenced to five years in prison, brought this issue into clear focus and women in the province presented a united approach. When the Court of Appeal announced that Collins' five year sentence would be reduced to two years plus three years' probation and compulsory medical treatment, there was a massive outcry from individuals and groups across the province. Diane Duggan of the St. John's Rape Crisis Centre spoke for many women when she commented on CBC Radio on July 7, 1986:

> Now the "old boys' network" is closing in to protect their friend; they feel that he should not be punished for his crime but deserves our sympathy. Where is the sympathy for his victims and their families? If only the old boys' network had been there to protect the children he violated.[79]

Dorothy Inglis, in her weekly "Bread and Roses" column in the *St. John's Evening Telegram*, wrote:

> We want our society to take the crime that Dr. Collins committed seriously. Until recently, the sexual abuse of children was a hidden problem . . . . There was little attention to the trauma inflicted on the child victim; courts often took the attitude that if no overt violence occurred, no really lasting damage had been done.[80]

For Inglis, and other feminists, the issue was not revenge on Dr. Collins, but justice for his victims. Increasing public awareness about the causes and effects of sexual abuse on children continues to be a priority for women's groups.

Further efforts to increase public awareness on issues important to women occurred when most women's groups in the province participated in openly angry public protests during annual Take Back the Night Marches. The St. John's Rape Crisis Centre started organizing marches as a way for women to show the public their feeling on issues of violence against women and children: "Women are saying we're bloody angry and we're screaming and yelling in the streets. We're not going to send a polite letter any more, we're going to keep screaming and yelling until we get what we want," said Diane Duggan of the Rape Crisis Centre.[81]

A 'Take Back the Night' march in St. John's. The annual September march protests the lack of safety for women on the streets, particularly after dark.

Credit: St. John's Status of Women Council.

Concern about violence against women and children was reflected in concern over the growing problem of pornography. To raise public awareness, a forum on pornography was held in September 1983, sponsored by the Provincial Advisory Council on the Status of Women. Maude Barlow, president of the Canadian Coalition Against Media Pornography, spoke to about seventy-five people; her presentation included excerpts from the Playboy Channel and some home video tapes. The impact of this presentation was described by Roberta Buchanan in an article in the Newfoundland Status of Women newsletter:

The woman is victimized, tortured, raped, degraded by a stronger and more powerful man. It is a message of sexual politics. It has nothing to do with eroticism, everything to do with power. Sex is presented in terms of male domination over female.[82]

This analysis of pornography has been adopted by a variety of women's groups in the province. For example, in their 1984 brief to the federal government's special committee on pornography and prostitution, the Newfoundland Teachers Association said that pornography mitigates against mutual respect and equality among people by lying about human relations and sexuality. "It [pornography] suggests that the sexual life of women ought to be sub- ordinate and devoted to the service of men. It depicts women as being acceptable objects of violence by the mere fact of being women."[83]

A Coalition of Citizens Against Pornography was formed in November 1983 as a follow-up to the forum. The coalition organized public protest marches, developed a "porn free" campaign for store owners, and provided an awareness and action kit on the issue. Dorothy Inglis suggested that a provincial regulatory board with public accountability would help the province regulate materials entering the province.[84] The coalition lobbied successfully for legislation that enabled municipalities to regulate the way pornographic magazines and video material were displayed in stores. They continue to work to increase local community awareness of the need to control pornographic materials.

Action against pornography was not restricted to St. John's, but was supported by women around the province, especially in Labrador City and Bay St. George. A dinner meeting of the Bay St. George Status of Women Council in April 1986 drew over one hundred people who signed a petition requesting the town of Stephenville to enact its legislated right to regulate the display of pornographic material for sale or rental, and regulate access by children to shops where such material is available.

Women also worked to raise public awareness through researching and publicizing issues. In 1985, a Committee on Young Women's Issues was formed to research the career choices of young women in the province. The resulting report, *Growing Up Female: A Study of Adolescent Women in Newfoundland and Labrador*, demonstrated that young women were making career decisions from a narrow range of choices and, in general, were unaware of the fact they would likely be part of the paid labour force all their lives and could end up with sole responsibility for raising a family.[85] As a result of the findings of this study, the Committee made ten recommendations including improved career guidance in the school system directed toward girls. This report contributed to keeping feminist concerns in the public eye by demonstrating that discrimination against women was a major social problem.

Raising public awareness has proved to be a long, slow process. Over the years, it has been accompanied by much work to change political policies that affect women and to influence government decisions that regulate women's lives.

POLITICAL ACTION

Political action by women in the province has taken three forms. One has been the direct participation of feminists in the political process and as candidates in elections. The second has sought to entrench feminism within the existing government bureaucracy, and the third has been the lobbying of governments to influence policies that regulate women's lives.

Feminists and the Political Process

By the early 1970s, many feminists were aware of the need to encourage women to participate in the political process. First steps in this direction were taken by one of the ginger groups set up by the Newfoundland Status of Women Council in 1972, the "Women in Public Life Group." Jury duty was an issue of particular importance to this group. The Jury Duty Reform Act of June 1972 enabled women to serve on juries; however, it specified that women could opt out if they chose. Faced with negative public opinion because women were choosing to opt out of jury duty, the Jury Duty Reform group worked towards making women liable for jury duty on the same terms as men. Public education on the issue was carried out through such activities as a one-day workshop in March 1973 at the Provincial Citizen Rights and Freedoms Conference. (See also the essay in this volume by Linda Cullum and Maeve Baird.)

Along with the push to involve women in the political process, there was a concerted effort by many feminists to enable women to actually run for political office. Two members of the "Women in Public Life Group," Fran Innes and Barbara Walsh, ran in the 1973 St. John's municipal election. Both joined a reform slate called "Five for Change" and, while neither woman was successful in that election, this effort laid the groundwork for Fran Innes to gain a council seat in the next municipal election. Two other members of the group ran unsuccessfully for political office. Lillian Bouzanne stood for the Liberal seat in the St. John's West riding during a

federal election, and Helen Porter ran twice in Mount Pearl as a
provincial candidate for the New Democratic Party (NDP).

In June 1979 Lynn Verge, a past president of the Corner Brook
Status of Women Council, ran for the Progressive Conservatives and
won the House of Assembly seat for Corner Brook East. She went
on to become one of two female cabinet ministers in the Peckford
cabinet.[86] and, as minister of education, established a Ministerial
Advisory Committee on Women's Issues in Education (MACOWIE).
Women in general, however, and feminists in particular, tended to
be divided along philosophical and partisan lines so that feminists
running for elected positions often did not have the support of a
united feminist vote. This, no doubt, limited the number of successful feminist candidates in political elections.

Many women felt political change could only occur if women
participated equally in political institutions. A number of Newfoundland women became inspired by the Iceland Women's Alliance which
was a political force in that country. As a result, these Newfoundland
women formed a group called the 52% Solution: Women for Equality,
Justice and Peace. The group took its name from the fact that women
make up fifty-two percent of the population and it adopted the policy
statement of the Iceland Women's Alliance which reads:

> We want women's collective experiences and value judgements to
> be evaluated as equal to the experiences and value judgements of
> men as a policy forming force in society. We want human values to
> take absolute precedence when decisions are made in national
> affairs. We want a society where everybody, women, men and
> children, are equally respected and have equal rights. We want a
> revolutionary change in people's way of thinking.[87]

Members of the 52% Solution participated in a province-wide
action in August 1987 when about thirty members travelled the
island in a yellow school bus to promote the need for more women
in government and other decision-making bodies. The minister of
justice, Lynn Verge, joined the bus tour for the stretch between
Corner Brook and Stephenville. In Gander, Corner Brook, Stephenville and Dildo, additional workshops were conducted by members
of the bus tour to help women in those areas explore a number of
topics, including: government decisions that affect women, women
and family violence, women and the paid workforce and women and
male-dominated institutions.

Efforts to include women in the political process were also part
of political action and extended to developing specific government
agencies and departments to assist women, to provide advice to

government, and to influence political decisions from within the bureaucracy. The following describes this work.

Promoting the need for more women in government and other decision-making bodies was the focus of the 52% Solution bus tour in August, 1987. Thirty members travelled the island in a yellow school bus which left from the Confederation Building in St. John's.

Credit: Provincial Advisory Council on the Status of Women, St. John's, Newfoundland.

Provincial Advisory Council on the Status of Women: In the fall of 1978, representatives from several women's organizations held a series of meetings to discuss the structure and role of a provincial advisory council on the Status of Women. The group was convened by Gertrude Keough, the provincial human rights commissioner, and included representatives from the Newfoundland Status of Women Council, the Women's Institutes, the Canadian Federation of University Women and the Federal Advisory Council on the Status of Women. The group developed a proposal for an advisory council, but no action was taken by government. In 1979 NSWC presented a further proposal to Premier Brian Peckford, and the Corner Brook Status of Women Council actively lobbied for an advisory council.

Draft legislation for a Provincial Advisory Council on the Status of Women was drawn up by government in 1980, and Ann Bell was asked to review it. She was not pleased with the draft: "When I saw the draft I couldn't believe it. It was exactly what we had not recommended, it was modelled on the Nova Scotia legislation which had no public mandate. I felt the council should have a public as well as an advisory role and be able to make things public without the Minister's approval."[88]

The draft legislation was changed, and an act to form an advisory council was introduced in the House of Assembly. During debate on the bill, women kept watch from the galleries, and about fifty women appeared in the galleries on June 5, 1980 to give support to second reading of the bill. They represented the Newfoundland Teachers Association, the Newfoundland Association of Public Employees, the Association of Registered Nurses, Planned Parenthood, the Early Childhood Development Association, the Rape Crisis Centre, the Women's Institutes, the five Status of Women Councils, the Canadian Advisory Council on the Status of Women, the Canadian Federation of University Women, the MUN Faculty Association and the Women's Association of MUN.

On June 6, 1980 the act was passed. The Provincial Advisory Council on the Status of Women was established Friday, November 21, 1980, with Ann Bell of Corner Brook as president, Barbara Doran of St. John's as vice-president and the following members: Sheilah Mackinnon Drover from Springdale, Clara Michelin from Happy Valley, Gwen Tremblett from Grand Falls, Ann Power from the Port au Port Peninsula, William Collins from St. John's, Nancy Riche from Seal Cove, Alice Collins from Corner Brook, Becky Roome from St. John's and Margaret Martin from Labrador City.

The advisory council was not wholly embraced by the women's community, nor by its members. Barbara Doran resigned as vice-president after one year because she felt the advisory council fed information to the bureaucracy. According to Doran: "It institution-alizes the movement and takes away a lot of energy and anger." In addition, Doran said she did not have the energy after a year on the council to continue to debate the issues "from scratch."[89]

Despite initial scepticism, the advisory council maintains a lively public presence and never hesitates to speak out on issues. The council has contributed to public education through a variety of booklets and information kits on topics such as pornography, sexuality, violence against women, single parents, and family law. An important part of the advisory council's work was to nurture new women's groups in the province and to offer support and expertise as requested.

Women's Policy Office: There still remained a need for a coordinated effort within government so women's issues would not get lost in the system. Luanne Leamon recalled that, because of her position as social policy adviser to Premier Brian Peckford in the early 1980s, and because of a personal interest in women's issues, she took on responsibility for ensuring issues of concern to women were directed to the appropriate people in government. It became clear to her that Newfoundland was one of the few provinces without a bureaucratic mechanism to deal with women's issues and that there was a need to have provincial representation on the national scene. She brought this to the premier's attention. Leamon was committed to increasing awareness of women's issues within government and with the public and to coordinating the efforts within government toward women's issues.[90]

In September 1985 the Women's Policy Office was established by the provincial government. Leamon said the establishment of the office within government came about because it was "the right place, the right time and the right people."[91] Leamon was appointed assistant deputy minister of the new office and Dorothy Robbins, formerly administrator at the Provincial Advisory Council on the Status of Women, joined as director. A former co-ordinator of the St. John's Women's Centre, Beth Lacey, is researcher for the office.

The office was set up to work within government and be responsible for co-ordinating efforts to address women's issues within government, to liaise with and complement work of other government departments and to liaise with similar offices in other provinces. In addition, the office published a series of fact sheets, a manual for the victims of wife abuse and reports on non-traditional employment and on women and work. By the summer of 1988, it had sponsored two public conferences, one for young women and the other on women's involvement in public policy.

Political Lobbying

Individual women around the province became involved in the political process and exercised political influence by actively lobbying government. In Newfoundland and Labrador, as a result of a strong lobby by women's groups, the Matrimonial Property Act came into force in July 1980. Lobbying for this reform was not easy and met with unsympathetic attitudes from politicians. Barbara Doran, of the Newfoundland Status of Women Council, remembered lobbying for matrimonial property law reform in 1975:

> We went to see one cabinet minister as part of the lobby. After we finished reading a synopsis of our brief, he pushed back in his chair and said, "Now, just let me get this straight. You're asking me to speak in the House in favour of this bill that if it was to be accepted that my wife, on divorce, would get fifty percent of the house . . .is that what you're saying?" And I said "Yes, Mr. Minister." To which he replied, "My wife! My wife who sits home on her big fat ass all day long looking at television and drinking Pepsi! Get out of my office, I haven't got time for this nonsense."[92]

Lobbying that minister was "like talking to a brick wall," said Doran. She added that this was because of the attitude "that we were trying to give women an easy role by taking half of the property away from the man they lived with."[93] The Church posed another barrier. "We were seen as home wreckers, matrimony was seen as a sacred state, not something that had to be divided up."[94]

The reform came about because women's groups persisted and lobbied the public as well as politicians. For its part, the Labrador West Status of Women Council circulated questionnaires on matrimonial property rights to people in their area. These questionnaires were presented to the minister of justice, the Honourable Alex Hickman, at a meeting in St. John's on March 8, 1978, where representatives from Status of Women Councils from Corner Brook, Grand Falls and St. John's were in attendance. To continue these efforts, the Labrador West Council met with the Liberal caucus and held various press conferences on the issue. The Grand Falls group actively lobbied for matrimonial property rights even though many women in the community opposed the efforts of the council "and yet they ended up benefitting."[95]

The adoption of the Matrimonial Property Act was a strong victory for women in the province, but a review of the act conducted by the Department of Justice three years later brought to light weaknesses in the legislation. Further recommendations were made by the Provincial Advisory Council and Status of Women Councils to include business assets as part of property division. They also asked that the joint tenancy section be strengthened to ensure sole ownership of the matrimonial home by the surviving spouse, and that pension credits be divided and remain as credits rather than used as lump sum trade-offs. Unfortunately, these recommendations did not result in changes to the act.

One of the best examples of collective lobbying action by women took place in November 1981, when women's groups across the country learned that the new Canadian constitution would include a resolution that would cause certain rights and freedoms guaranteed in the constitution to be subject to an "override" provision. This meant that Clause 28, which provided equality of the sexes, could be overridden by provincial legislatures.

Women's groups in the province reacted quickly. Petitions were circulated and lobbies organized. In Labrador West women sent telegrams and made telephone calls protesting the move. "It is good to know that we here in Labrador West were able to play a part, if only a small one," wrote Grace Stapleton in the January 1982 newsletter.[96] In St. John's the Provincial Advisory Council on the Status of Women organized an ad hoc committee on the constitution with representatives from various women's groups and labour groups. A demonstration was held at Confederation Building where two hundred women made their concerns known to Premier Brian Peckford. Women's Centre co-ordinator Gerry Rogers exchanged angry words with the premier, and the demonstration featured a new version of "O Canada," written by Bonnie James:

> O Canada
> Our White, male-governed land
> True Patriarchal Love in all the sons command
> With shattered hopes, we see them rise
> The false north, we're not free!
> We stand on guard, but Canada
> Won't stand on guard for me
> O Canada, I must be free
> Clause 28 will stand on guard for me.
> Clause 28 will stand on guard for me![97]

Even though Premier Peckford announced that Clause 28 was not intended to be subject to the override, women in Newfoundland worked with women in mainland Canada and continued lobbying other Canadian premiers. Lobbying was successful; the constitutional bill was passed in the House of Commons with Clause 28 intact.

A reflection of the growing political maturity of the women's movement in the province emerged clearly in the November 1984 conference in St. John's on "Women and the Constitution," which featured the first official provincial women's lobby. Veteran women's rights activists Bonnie James and Dorothy Inglis organized the conference, along with lawyer Eve Roberts, provincial representative for the national Legal Education Action Fund (LEAF). The conference focused on the new Canadian Constitution and Charter of Rights and Freedoms. Keynote speaker, Professor Christine Boyle of Dalhousie Law School, warned conference delegates that women could not rely on Section 15, the equality rights section of the Charter, to be forceful if women did not make demands. "The position remains as it always has been. Change will come if women organize and demand change. Now we have Section 15 as a weapon. We can at least say 'we have been promised equality—what are you doing to keep that promise?'"[98] Because of careful preparation in the form of teleconferencing and preparation of background papers, the conference was a success and fifteen women's groups stood prepared to directly participate in the official lobby.

Twelve questions were posed to MHAs during the lobby. The questions were developed through detailed research and study into major issues concerning women in the province. The Labrador West Status of Women Council, for example, addressed equality of education and the elimination of sex-role stereotyping. The Central Newfoundland Status of Women Council presented a resolution on the need for transition houses and follow-up support services for battered women. The Labrador Native Women's Association focused on alcohol problems and the problems caused by isolation, seasonal jobs, economic disparity, unreliable and costly travel, the lack of perishable food supplies and the lack of water and sewage facilities. Other resolutions dealt with divorce, the need to train child care workers and the housing needs of single parent families.

This lobby left women's groups determined to keep the pressure on politicians. Each group took responsibility to follow up on their resolution. The second women's lobby took place March 23, 1987. Once again, teleconferencing and position papers helped refine issues and determine priorities. As in the previous year, lobby questions reflected a diversity of issues. Again, from coastal Labrador, concerns were brought forward on freezing sewer lines, inadequate housing and alcohol problems. The need for pension rights for part-time workers and the problem of illiteracy were also presented at the lobby, as well as the old, but unresolved, issue of including domestics within the minimum wage system.

Newfoundland and Labrador women's groups united in their concern over child sexual abuse. Many women felt that sentences for child sexual assault offenders were not severe enough, and on appeal these sentences were consistently reduced. Politicians were told that "sentencing has not reflected the severity of the crime, nor has it recognized the long-term emotional trauma resulting from sexual assault against children."[99] At the 1987 lobby, child sexual assault was a significant issue and women called for a minimum appropriate sentence for abusers.

The women's movement is dedicated to eliminating discrimination against women and working for legal and social change to help women achieve equality. However, within the women's movement nationally and internationally, the issue of lesbian rights has been divisive, and lesbians have experienced discrimination from other feminists, as well as from people outside the movement. Opinions about discrimination against lesbians in the province differed. Barbara Doran said that lesbianism never actually became an issue with the St. John's Council. "The development and acceptance of lesbian women came through a very slow, quiet process that was almost an internal thing. Both sides knew there wasn't going to be any public attention drawn to it, and somehow both sides lived with that."[100] Yet Diane Duggan recalled that, when she moved back to Newfoundland in 1976 from Waterloo, Ontario and became involved in the St. John's Women's Centre, lesbian rights were not taken up as an issue. "It's a very scary issue for a lot of women's centres, they're afraid of scaring people away. But the issue of lesbianism has to be incorporated into our work . . . or we are doing our own oppressing."[101]

An attempt to include lesbian issues occurred at the 1981 annual provincial conference of women's groups which was held in St. John's on the theme "Our Sexual Beings." During the conference, a discussion on lesbianism was held, and the St. John's Status of Women Council lobbied government for the inclusion of sexual orientation in Section 15 of the Canadian Charter of Rights and Freedoms.

Most lesbians involved with the St. John's Council said they felt comfortable working within the council. For lesbians living outside St. John's, public recognition of their sexual orientation was difficult, if not impossible. Many lesbians avoided involvement with the women's movement out of fear of public recognition. Those who were involved were often reluctant to publicize their sexual orientation, and felt that the women's movement in Newfoundland and Labrador was not prepared to endorse lesbian rights. The women's movement formally recognized the issue of lesbian rights again during the second provincial women's lobby in March 1987, when they urged the provincial government to include sexual orientation as grounds for non-discrimination in the provincial Human Rights Code.

The women's lobby gave many women a chance to get involved, often for the first time, in influencing the political process, and it provided a regular forum for women's groups to make their concerns known. The lobby made the women's movement visible and showed politicians that it was not based solely in St. John's.

Another issue that benefitted from lobby efforts was child care services. The provincial regulations in the 1975 Day Care and Homemaker Services Act were minimal. As the number of children in need of day care services grew, parents found themselves increasingly frustrated in trying to obtain adequate services. Lobbying groups advocated government provision of universal day care throughout the province to all who require it.

The Provincial Advisory Council on the Status of Women undertook a research project on day care in 1982, and, based on the results of a report by researcher Joanne Dunne Glassman, the council adopted a position paper on day care in May 1982.[102] In February 1983 the Advisory Council held a public meeting in St. John's to bring together people interested in accessible, quality day care services. Sixteen of the eighty people at the meeting volunteered to serve on a steering committee to form a community group for day care advocacy.

The day care issue embroiled one cabinet minister in controversy with women's groups. In June 1987 the minister of social services, Charlie Brett, was questioned about his government's commitment to increase its involvement in day care services. In response he said "that the province needed more conscientious mothers to sacrifice their careers and stay home to take care of their children" rather than more day care. He further commented that if "conscientious mothers stayed home to raise their children there may be fewer (juveniles) in correction institutions."[103] Status of Women Councils were deluged with calls and, consequently, wrote the premier calling for Brett's resignation. Jeanette Andrews, president of the nurses' union, demanded he either support his opinions with facts or apologize to the working mothers of the province.

In September 1986 an important development in child care services saw the establishment of a two-year Early Childhood Education programme at the Cabot Institute, a programme that had been lobbied for by women's groups. However, a number of areas such as insufficient licensed spaces, lack of licensed care for children under two years of age, lack of extended hours for care of children whose parents work shifts, and insufficient licensed care for children outside school hours still needed attention. Above all, funding for day care continued to be primarily based on fees, which made it inaccessible to many who needed it most.

Women again lobbied and organized around constitutional issues over the Meech Lake Accord. In September 1987 an ad hoc group representing a coalition of thirteen groups presented a brief to the premier outlining their objections to Clause 7, which allowed provinces to opt out of cost-shared programmes such as education, childcare, healthcare and welfare. The coalition's concern was that women rely on these programmes and, therefore, stood to lose the most if these programmes were not protected.

CONCLUSION

The women's movement in Newfoundland and Labrador grew to encompass Status of Women Councils, union women's groups, native women's groups and rural women's organizations. Feminists are found in the church, in business and in politics. No one organization speaks for all women in the province, yet women come together on many issues. Annual political lobbies and regular provincial women's conferences have become established unifying events. Together, participants in the women's movement have raised public awareness of issues significant to women and have improved services to women.

The story of the women's movement in Newfoundland and Labrador is the story of women working to understand and improve not only their own lives, but the lives of all. Countless hours of work go into preparing briefs, staffing volunteer women's centres, lobbying on issues, attending meetings and discussing issues and problems with other women. At times it is a story of frustration, at other times a story of celebration as victories and a sense of common purpose are achieved. Above all, it is a story of dedication to the concept of a society in which women receive equal treatment and equal benefits, and can live free from violence.

This was especially evident during 1990 when the federal government withdrew funding for women's centres across the country. Newfoundland women refused to accept this decision and drew together in protest. Initial protest took the form of women writing to Prime Minister Brian Mulroney, Finance Minister Michael Wilson and the Secretary of State Gerry Weiner. Appeals were also made to the public to bring pressure on these officials. Demonstrations were held and written and verbal appeals to local government officials were made. It became evident that the federal government was not interested in listening to these forms of protest. After many meetings to develop a strategy, women in Newfoundland made a decision to occupy local Secretary of State offices on March 26, 1990.

The occupation was both frustrating and exhilarating. The causes of frustration were many. Days into the occupation, while watching the national news, women were stunned at the realization that the CBC was not reporting the occupation and their efforts were being ignored. Initial calls to the National Action Committee on the

Status of Women (NAC) for support were also ignored. Women in Newfoundland were frustrated by the feelings of isolation, but isolation is a way of life in Newfoundland and, undaunted, women continued the occupation. Further frustration followed and the sense of isolation was increased when Secretary of State staff disconnected fax and telephone communications to the office. On the third day Noel Kinsella, an assistant to Weiner, arrived to meet with the occupants. The results of this meeting heightened frustration and increased the determination of women not to back down. Theresa Mackenzie's report of the meeting confirmed that government "wanted to exert control over what we do."[104] Kinsella was not in a position to reinstate core funding, yet one of the conditions of the meeting was that the women were only interested in speaking with someone who held that authority. Kinsella's efforts to focus the meeting on project funding, which would result in unacceptable control over the work of women's centres, resulted in talks coming to an impasse at the end of one hour. During the following days of the occupation, the move by Nova Scotia and British Columbia women to occupy the Secretary of State offices in their provinces proved encouraging, but Newfoundland women were still frustrated that a national movement was not afoot.

The exhilarating aspects of the occupation gave women courage to stand their ground. Fax and telephone messages from around the province and around the country were displayed throughout the offices, and these encouraged the occupants. Local restaurants and individuals donated food, time, and supplies. Daily support was evident in the number of men, women and children who participated in the occupation; some for hours, and some for days and nights. Women at the Women's Centre, and Marion Hopkins in particular, maintained contact between other organizations and the occupants, and worked hard to keep everyone informed of the situation. Two other women who were instrumental in developing strategies and in carrying out the work of the occupation were Evelyn Riggs and Camille Fouillard. They covered many angles: Riggs and her guitar filled many nights and demonstrations with music, while Fouillard, with her knowledge of French, was able to connect the occupants with women in Quebec and to translate when federal officials at the local Secretary of State offices spoke French to carry on closed discussions.

However, on March 30 members of the Newfoundland Constabulary notified the occupants that charges would be laid if they did not leave the offices. The occupation ended and additional demonstrations followed. Throughout the month of April protestors walked and chanted, up and down the street in front of the Secretary of State offices. Protestors were encouraged by the support people voiced passing on the side walk, and the support people honked from their cars and trucks. NAC's support became evident and women's groups across the country joined the protest. "Weiner roasts" became a popular form of protest. However, there was still no indication that government would change its decision.

Theresa Mackenzie of the St. John's Status of Women speaks with Gordon Slade, Chairman of the Atlantic Canada Opportunities Agency, Monday after being told that a letter to Elmer McKay, the minister responsible for ACOA and a member of the federal Planning and Priorities Committee, had been received by the minister. The letter, denouncing the elimination of the operational funding for women's centres, was sent to all members of the committee (*Evening Telegram*, 24 April 1990, p. 3).
Photo: The *Evening Telegram*.

The next step in Newfoundland came when protestors returned to the Secretary of State offices to deliver a letter to Gerry Weiner and await his reply. Twenty-three women and two men stayed in the office waiting area in anticipation of Weiner's reply. They were removed and arrested by the Newfoundland Constabulary and charges were laid against each of them.

On May 4 funding was reinstated. The protest was a success, but charges against the group arrested in April were not withdrawn by Secretary of State and remained on file for almost a year, until they were dropped by the crown prosecutor.

What was most exhilarating about the whole protest was the strong sense of community support both within the women's community and with the community in general. This one incident brought women in Newfoundland, and particularly in St. John's, together. Participation in the protest and occupation crossed political, economic and social barriers. It grew to represent a national effort by women and men to support equality and justice for women. No one person can take credit for the success.

The women's movement has grown and matured; many women have become more radical, and many have turned their attention to promoting women for positions of power in order to bring about change. Concerns and issues facing women in the 1970s and 1980s remain the same in the 1990s: to end violence against women, to better career education for young women, and to win financial equality in the workplace. The first two years of the 1990s have seen victories and defeats. Gander women celebrated the opening of a long awaited transition house. The relative ease surrounding the opening of a Morgentaler Clinic in St. John's served to confirm public support for pro-choice options.

Nevertheless, many feminists have grave concerns with the Free Trade Agreement between Canada and the United States, which they feel eliminated many jobs held by women in Canada. As well, women in the province suffered defeats when the current provincial government under Clyde Wells legislated a wage freeze and struck down a pay equity agreement previously negotiated by the union.

In 1990 and 1991 there were great pressures on the movement in the province. Enormous energy was expended on the occupation of Secretary of State offices and the months of insecurity that followed. Early government support of women's issues is viewed with scepticism. Dependence on government grants and government control, in the form of funding for specific projects that meet government objectives, continues to affect the direction and energy of the movement.

Publicity surrounding the Oka experience in 1990, however, encouraged women in Newfoundland to open discussion with native women to discover what role native women want women in the feminist community to play. The 1990 provincial Status of Women conference, appropriately called "Gathering Our Strength," featured Marilyn Kane from Kanasatake as guest speaker and offered a workshop on native women and their issues as a step toward incorporating native women's issues with the provincial movement.

Women gather at the Women's Centre in St. John's, November, 1989, to celebrate the seventeenth anniversary of the centre. Left to right facing the camera: Helen Porter, Sally Davis, Frances Innes and Evelyn Riggs.

Credit: St. John's Status of Women Council.

The lobby at the 1990 conference continued to address lesbian women through a workshop on homophobia. Extensive work in the women's community in St. John's is focused on this problem, and women are engaged in open discussion to identify how non-lesbian women can better include lesbian women in the community so they feel safe and respected.

Despite financial problems, the women's movement in the province continues to evolve, striving to meet new needs. A quarterly newspaper, *Waterlily*, for a time provided a feminist voice in the province, symbolizing the success of women in finding their own voice. The newsletter of the Provincial Advisory Council, *Tapestry*, reaches a wide audience and helps to keep women aware of current issues. No matter what the issues facing women in the 1990s may be, the women's movement in Newfoundland and Labrador has a history of solid achievement and a feminist base has been firmly established for future action.

Appendix A

Documents: Women's Suffrage

Compiled by Margot Duley

Methodist College Literary Institute Debate, February 1895

"Should Women have Equal Rights with Men?"

The speakers for the affirmative (W. Burt, G. Ayre and W. Peters) argued that:

> . . ."No taxation without representation" was a principle underlying constitutional government, and as she pays as much indirectly as man the right of franchise should be conferred upon her. Her ability was not inconsiderable in the case of the wives of Mr. Gladstone and the Earl of Beaconsfield, to whom these great men attributed much of their success. The success of women in the pursuit of art and science, in religious movements, and in the field of literature, eminently qualified her for any position in life. Her exemplary uprightness and honesty fitted her to move in every sphere of life and where she is employed as cashier, stenographer, leader in temperance movements, or on the farm, she fills her position with honor and ability. "The hand that rocks the cradle rules the world."

Negative speakers (Noseworthy, W. Rideout and J. Mesher) argued that:

> This was not a question of her ability to serve, but one as to the expediency of her serving. There are avocations in life where she shows superior ability to man. The medical profession is one in

which she has been successful where her influence has a mollifying effect. She has also been successful in the legal profession. Whilst she may have equal rights in these two professions, it was contended that she should not have such in the political arena, not because she lacks executive ability—her ruling power is universal—but because she risks the burning of the bread in the oven while she is attending to matters political. In order words we lose the *mother* in the female politician. When they become politicians they cease to be true mothers.

That modern bone of contention—female suffrage is another sphere in which women should have no part. The influence of want of education, instanced in the lewdness of thousands in such cities as London, would cause more moral destruction than an army of moral reformers could repair in a life time. Feminine characteristics are such as do not adapt women to equal rights with men.

The vote passed in the negative by 33 to 10.

Source: *Daily News*, February 21, 1895.

The Suffragette's Creed.

1. I believe that woman is in every respect the equal of man.

I believe that the man who allows a woman to stand in a car should forfeit his vote.

2. I believe that woman should receive equal pay with men.

I believe that women should have shorter hours than men.

3. I believe that there should be no head to the family, the authority to be equally divided.

I believe that the man who fails to support his family is beneath contempt.

4. I believe in the vote for women, though it must be obtained through shedding of blood.

I believe that if women had the vote the inhuman practice of vivisection would be abolished.

Finally, I believe in the total emancipation of woman, and the complete subjugation of man. I believe—I believe that's a mouse! Oh, Jack, come quick.

Smart Set. Reprinted *Daily News*, October 26, 1910.

Armine Gosling Defends the Suffragettes

"It is just as important to convince the public that women are angry, as it is to convince them that women are right."

Women suffragists learned that in politics it is always the strong who receive attention. To be out of sight is to be out of mind. The needs of a voteless contingent will be neglected in the natural course of things, because it has no means of redress, but no interest with votes behind it can safely be ignored for long. They learned that the only measures politicians understand and respect are violent ones. And they are the ones by which men have time and again won their political rights.

I am not here to defend all the actions of the militant suffragists. Throwing stones, ("concrete messages," Punch calls them), has always seemed to me a singularly unconvincing form of argument. But let it be clearly understood that these tactics which men so loudly condemn in women, are the very ones they have used and approved themselves, on many occasions. A distinguished member of the Labour Party, Mr. T.D. Benson, wrote recently of the riots which preceded the Reform Bill, in 1831:

> Of course, when men wanted the franchise, they did not behave in the unruly manner of our feminine friends. They were perfectly constitutional in their agitation. In Bristol, I find they only burnt the Mansion House, the Custom House, the Bishop's Palace, the Excise Office, three prisons, four toll houses, and forty-two private dwelling and warehouses, and all in a perfectly constitutional and respectable manner. Numerous constitutional fires took place in the neighbourhoods of Bedford, Cambridge, Canterbury and Devizes. Four men were respectably hanged in Bristol and three in Nottingham. The Bishop of Lichfield was nearly killed, and the Archbishop of Canterbury was insulted, spat upon, and with great difficulty rescued from amidst the yells and execrations of a violent and angry mob.

And adds:

> I think we are well qualified to advise the Suffragettes to follow our example, to be respectable and peaceful in their methods as we were, and then they will have our sympathy and support.

From: Armine N. Gosling, "Woman Suffrage." A Paper Read at the Ladies' Reading Room. St. John's, Newfoundland, January 15, 1912.

Some Arguments in Favour of Votes for Women by Armine Gosling

May I now present for your consideration a few arguments in favour of Woman Suffrage. Women should have the vote—*Because*—most laws affect them as much as they do men, and some laws affect them more, and they are now framed without consulting the persons they are intended to benefit.

Because—people who have to obey laws should have a voice in making them. This is the foundation of all liberty.

Because—laws dealing with the welfare of children should be regarded from the women's point of view as well as the man's. Questions concerning the home are now continually being legislated upon, and women have knowledge and experience which could be brought to bear helpfully on domestic legislation.

Because—men no matter how well-meaning they may be, never have made, and never can make suitable and just laws for women. No law concerning women has ever passed the House of Commons, that has not borne the unmistakable stamp of sex-legislation.

Because—no class, or race, or sex, can have its interests properly attended to in the legislation of a country, unless it is represented by direct suffrage. Women workers, for example, have learned that unless you have political power you cannot get industrial justice. And, lastly, women should have the vote.

Because—a very large number of representative women all over the world are asking for it.

The laws dealing with women are notoriously unfair and badly administered. Very few women of the better class, living what we call a sheltered life, have any idea whatever of their legal position. It would probably surprise them very much to learn that as mothers they have no legal existence, and no more rights over their children than their own nursemaid has. The father is the only parent recognized by law, and his is the sole control over his children. He can take them away from their mother when they are infants, can direct their education and occupations, and regulate their lives generally, quite regardless of the mother's wishes. The only case in which, by English law, a mother has a right to control her children, is when they are illegitimate. The unmarried mother is rewarded by being given the full custody of her child. She becomes the sole parent. But let us not delude ourselves into thinking that this is done by way of concession to women. It is merely for the purpose of shielding the father from the penalty of his misdeeds.

Similarly, in marriage, according to English Common Law, the wife ceases to be a person. For purposes of legislation husband and wife are regarded as one, and needless to say the husband i that one. Further, no promise made by a man before marriage can deprive him of his rights over wife and children. He may make a hundred promises before marriage, and break them after it, and the law will sanction his conduct. Fortunately for us, men are seldom as bad as the laws they make, the position of women would be intolerable if men acted up to their legal rights. Only twenty years ago a married woman couldn't call a penny her own. When she married, her husband, in theory and with the assistance of our archaic Marriage Service endowed her with all his worldly goods. In fact, however, he absorbed her property and herself. He could, and did, possess himself of her earnings, and squander them in riotous living. Since the Married Woman's Property Act passed in 1883, women have been graciously allowed to keep what belongs to them. But, even now, if a man refuses to give his wife a suitable allowance or a reasonable share of his income, she has no redress. A well-to-do man can legally starve his wife for years, and dying, can cut her off without a penny and still be within the rights the law gives him.

If he die intestate, his wife gets one-third only of his real estate, but if a woman dies intestate her husband inherits her entire property, real and personal. This is an appalling injustice, and bears very heavily on the average housewife possessing no qualifications for earning her own living. John Stewart Mill [sic] said, 'If marriage were all it might be, looking to the laws alone, a woman's life would be hell upon earth.

From: Armine N. Gosling, "Woman Suffrage." A Paper Read at the Ladies' Reading Room, St. John's, Newfoundland, January 15, 1912.

"The Thing is Hopeless . . ."

We are also told that they have the vote in Australia and Canada but that is no reason why they should have it here. I do not believe in the theory of following the crowd.

I believe that the members of Parliament in England allowed the measure go through because they were actually intimidated into doing so and as soon as they got the women in the House they saw the folly of ever having permitted it.

Another argument that is put forward in support of the contention that women should have their vote is that of their war record but I do not see how people can allow their minds to become so warped. A woman who would make an excellent Red Cross nurse might be hopeless as a politician. Now, I wish to say that I intend to oppose this Bill at every stage and especially when it comes into committee. It is not that I think women are not good enough for the vote, it is rather that I think the vote is not good enough for women. When we come to equal rights for women, I believe that the women themselves would be the very first to object to the principle when they realized what it really meant. Equal rights would mean that one would no longer need an introduction to a lady to address her because one does not need an introduction to a man if he gets on board a train and wishes to enter into conversation with him. He simply drops down beside him and starts talking and if the same thing applied to women, all a man need do would be to sit down and start talking to the first pretty girl he saw, regardless of whether he knew her or not. The same way a man would no longer give a lady his seat in a tram if it happened to be filled because I am sure I would not give my seat in a car to any hon. member of this House; nor should I raise my hat to him if I met him on the street but I do take off my hat to ladies of my acquaintance. The thing is hopeless and I know the women themselves would be long sorry to see it work out to that extreme.

Source: James R. McDonnell (Liberal, St. George's), House of Assembly Proceedings, 1921

". . . One Enormous Opposition, Always Bickering"

[I support] giving the women the vote and not the right to representation in the House. That is what I think, Mr. President, because to my mind it would cause more troubles than we have now, in that a great body of women would naturally look towards legislation affecting themselves and their interests, and they would then become one enormous opposition, always bickering and always finding fault.

Source: Hon. Mr. A.W. Mews, Legislative Council Proceedings, May 9, 1921

". . .A Traitor to Her Sex"

The woman who is opposed to Woman Suffrage is a traitor to her sex. Woman Suffrage is the root of every Reform Social Service— Girl Guides (why teach girls to be good citizens when by the law of Newfoundland they are classed with imbeciles and criminals), Child Welfare, etc., etc., are all branches of the Woman Franchise Movement. We are told, "A Woman's place is in the home," by women who are never in their homes. The thousand and one societies and clubs in this town all have their women's auxiliaries.

What for? To raise funds. There is never any objection raised to a woman's being out of her home all day as long as she is working for these Societies. Women work hard, cook and brew and make a lot of money but they are not asked how it shall be spent. The men take it and spend it as they think fit. How many women are there on the various school and church boards, and how many churches and schools would survive without the Women's auxiliaries?

An interest in politics goes hand in hand with the welfare of the home.

Source: "Suffragist," May 18, 1923. *Daily News*, May 19, 1923.

". . . A Vote for the Home"

Suffragists as well as anti-suffragists agree that the place of woman is the Home. However much women may go out into the world and engage in work outside the home, it will still remain true that the great majority of women will always be first and foremost the home-makers and that the bringing up of the children will always be entrusted to the women. This is in fact the most important reason women should be given the vote. It would be a vote for the home, just as the working-man's vote is a vote for business. No woman nowadays can be an efficient home-maker unless she understands the relation between her home and the government. The home nowadays cannot be limited to the four walls that enclose the dwelling and the efficient home-maker cannot limit her intelligence and her activities to what goes on within those four walls. The duty of the wife and mother includes the spreading of the family income, and the purchase of all those needful things which in olden times were largely produced within the household—clothing, food, furnishings, utensils and adornments. To perform this duty it is necessary to have a proper understanding of the dollar, and to perform it fully, a woman ought also (to have) some control over those government activities which can so greatly influence this purchasing power.

Source: "Votes for Women." *Daily News*, January 20, 1925.

". . . Against War"

It is not alone a personal struggle, nor a struggle of one sex, but a dream of a better humanity that women are fighting for, and this dream can be realized by man and woman working shoulder to shoulder.

Women pay the first cost of life. They are the bearers of the race, they know the value of life as men cannot know it. In the long run this instinct, if given a chance to voice itself will eventually throw its influence against the sacrifice of life.

Source: "Votes for Women." *Daily News*, February 8, 1925.

"The Radicals of Today are the Conservatives of Tomorrow"

The objections to the political woman and to the educated woman present some instructive analogies. Not so long ago, it was seriously believed that knowing the classics would ruin her morals, philosophy her religion, and mathematics her health. In general a college education would take away the desire to be a good wife and mother. To protect a being so frail the colleges were carefully closed against her.

This merely shows that human nature is conservative. The persons who take a strong interest in any reform are generally few and they are habitually regarded with disfavour by most of those whom the proposed reform is to benefit. On the one hand we condemn every new expression of thought while on the other hand we are forced to acknowledge that many of the heroes of the past to whom we do honour are those who dare to stand out against the current standards and ideals and had ideas ahead of their time. It is a continuous performance, this struggle between the old and the new. The radicals of today are the conservatives of tomorrow, yet seemingly we shall never realize this enough to give freedom of expression and individual initiative their right. Each age has struggled to crush the oncoming generation of thought and progress.

Source: "Votes for Women." *Daily News*, January 21, 1925

Appendix B

Documents: Women and Law

Compiled by Linda Cullum and Cynthia Penney

Evening Herald, 4 February 1890 "Police Court" column

[Prowse is hearing an assault case of a man who stole a horse belonging to another man]

> Judge Prowse said he did not know of anything more aggravating than running away with a man's horse; he believed it was next to taking away a man's wife. He fined the defendent twenty-five cents and costs. (p. 4 unmarked)

Evening Herald, 10 April 1890 "In and Around the City"

> Judge Prowse is to be commended for his efforts in trying to get cases of trouble between husband and wife settled outside of court, instead of scandalously making public every little grievance between man and wife. (p. 4 unmarked)

Evening Herald, 26 April 1890 "Police Court" column

> Two employees of the Ropewalk were heard respecting trouble arising from disagreements from time to time between their wives, the result of which was an altercation between the two husbands, one of whom, as alleged by the complainant, threatened his life. The case was dismissed, as the judge said, since the days of the

Ten Years War in the time of Pliny, to the days of the racket at the Ropewalk, women were the cause of every trouble. He dismissed the case, and warned the women that in the future they should conduct themselves in such a manner as to prevent a breach of the peace, if not, they would be seriously punished. (p. 4 unmarked)

Evening Herald, 28 September 1895 "Police Court Jottings"

Judge Prowse says he is going to stop the disgraceful conduct of women who abuse and vilify one another. As a proof of what he said, his Honor this morning, fined Susannah King $15, or in default, 30 days. Every other day women of middle age, most of them married, present themselves in the police court, the language used, in most cases, is very revolting and obscene, and, unless such garrulous parties bridle their too flippant tongues and avoid the police court, they may expect to be taught a salutary lesson by the Judge.

Evening Herald, 22 October 1895 "Events and Echoes"

Last night a neatly dressed woman called at the residence of a well-known professional gentleman in this city, and left a parcel for the proprietor. On being opened it was found to contain the body of a still-born infant, and there is a big sensation accordingly.

QUEEN v. TRAVERS
1860, January. By The Court.

Criminal Law—Concealment of birth—Evidence necessary to sustain indictment.

In an indictment charging concealment of birth, in order to sustain the indictment evidence of the disposal of the body, with a view of concealing, must be clearly established.

The defendant was indicted for endeavoring to conceal the birth of her infant child by placing the body of said child between her bed and the lacing thereof. The prisoner is a single woman, and served one William Walsh as a fishery servant on the Labrador during the past summer. In the month of June she was confined, and was delivered of the child—no one being present. The fact of her pregnancy was known to her fellow-servants; she had not stated it to them; a woman had been sent for to attend her. There was no direct evidence of her having placed the body of the child between the bed and the lacing, merely that she had denied its birth; when asked for the body of the child she took it, as was thought by the principal witness, from between the bed and the lacing of the bed

—but this witness would not positively swear whether it was so or not; no clothes were prepared or other provision made. The counsel for the prisoner moved for her discharge, there being no evidence of the disposal of the dead body of the child, or any endeavor by prisoner to conceal the birth thereof, as laid in the indictment.

The court then took the matter into consideration, and decided that the charge as laid in the indictment had not been proved or sustained by evidence, and ordered the prisoner to be discharged.

Attorney General for the crown.
Mr. J.P. Little for defendant.

Queen v. Travers, [1860], Newfoundland Law Reports 521 (Newfoundland Supreme Court)

EX-WIFE CAN'T CLAIM HER SHARE

JUDGE SAYS LAWS SHOULD BE CHANGED

A Newfoundland Supreme Court judge has called upon the government to enact laws which would give the courts power, in suitable cases, to order property settlements for partners of a broken marriage who have contributed financially to the marriage but yet, do not legally have rights to the property.

Mr. Justice Noel Goodridge made the statement in a written judgment concerning an action in which a city woman who is divorced from her husband asked the court to rule she is entitled to a one-half beneficial interest in the home she and her husband had occupied.

When she and her husband separated she received nothing. After the divorce her husband remarried and is living in the house with his second wife and their child.

The couple married Dec. 11, 1961, and separated on Feb. 1, 1970.

Judge Goodridge dismissed the action because the law states that unless a woman's name is on the title deed of the house (which was not the case in this action) she and her husband lived in, or unless she can show a common intention of herself and her husband that she had an interest in the house (which is difficult to prove), she has no interest in the property.

However, in dismissing the action, the judge called for legislation to overcome such situations.

"It all underlines the need for legislation to empower a court to create property interest in one spouse in property vested in the name of the other in appropriate circumstances," he said. "Few married couples enjoying the first warmth of their marriage foresee the darker days ahead for some of them when 'unhappy differences' will divide them but not their matrimonial wealth."

ONLY A PROMISE

The wife in most cases sacrifices her economic value on the labor market but will provide economic value to the husband even if it consists only of housekeeping; in other cases she will work and contribute her earnings to the marriage. Unless she can establish a trust—a difficult task—she is turned out at the end of the marriage wiser perhaps, but penniless. This situation will prevail until the jurisdiction of the court is enlarged to order property settlements."

Evidence indicated the woman, on several occasions, was promised an interest in the home where she and her husband lived. However, the promises of the husband were never legally acted upon.

She had worked for more than five years during the nine-year marriage, postponed having a child during those five years while construction on their home continued, and contributed her wages to monthly household expenses. She didn't waste any of the money she earned.

There was also evidence she helped to the best of her ability with construction of the home, landscaping, ordering materials, obtaining discounts on materials through her place of employment and had her parents provide labor and materials.

In summary, she worked until construction on the house was completed and paid toward the household expenses which allowed her husband to pay building expenses and pay on a house mortgage loan.

After that, she raised the child born in the marriage and maintained the home while her husband worked.

LAWYER AGREES

David Day, the lawyer who represented the woman, agreed with Mr. Justice Goodridge's comments about the need for proper legislation to cover such cases.

In a number of other cases, Day explained, women have told him they were certain they had joint interest with their husbands in the family's home because they had signed papers.

"On checking, I discovered they had signed papers alright; papers under which they guaranteed payment of large mortgages on the family house, but they had no legal interest in the home," the

St. John's lawyer said. "If the legislature acts on the comments of Mr. Justice Goodridge, I believe that, as he suggests, authority should be given to order property settlements."

Day pointed out that in some parts of the world laws have been passed which give a wife the right to a portion of the husband's property, simply because she married him. There are cases, he said, in which this would bring hardship and unfairness against a husband, especially if the wife has made no contribution to the marriage in money or services or, in the case of a very short marriage.

However, he said that if the court had the authority in suitable cases, as Judge Goodridge suggested, perhaps the woman in the present case would have come out of a marriage to which she contributed with some financial benefit to assist in her future support and as compensation for the years she invested in a partnership which produced certain material assets.

Joe Walsh, *Evening Telegram*, 12 September 1977, p. 3.

CAP. XVI.

An Act to amend Chapter 54 of the Consolidated Statutes, (Second Series), entitled "Of the Law Society, Barristers and Solicitors." [PASSED MARCH 22ND, 1910.]

SECTION 1. Respecting the right of Women to practice law.

WHEREAS it is desirable that women should not be excluded from practising at the Bar nor from being enrolled as Solicitors of any Court in this Colony.

Be it therefore enacted by the Governor, the Legislative Council and the House of Assembly, in Legislative Session convened, as follows:

1. Wherever in chapter 54 of the Consolidated Statutes, (2nd Series), entitled "Of the Law Society, Barristers and Solicitors," the word "person" occurs, such word shall be held to extend to and to include a female person so as to confer upon all women the right to be entered as clerks, admitted as law students, enrolled as Solicitors, and called to the Bar, and to exercise fully all the rights and to impose upon them all the obligations which are conferred and imposed upon men under the provisions of the said chapter.

Acts of the General Assembly of Newfoundland, 1910, C. 16, s. 1.

Authority of the Father

Excerpt of Letter: To Mr. L. Crummey, Secretary, Department of Public Health and Welfare, from the Right Reverend George F. Bartlett, D.P., P.P. of St Michael's Presbytery, Bell Island, Newfoundland, October 15, 1947, page 2.

It must be taken into consideration that Bell Island is primarily a mining town and much that we hear and read concerning mining towns of our day must be applied to any law affecting its people. Most fathers of Bell Island's families live for ten long hours each day in the mud, muck and confinement of a mine. It is expecting a great deal to find in very many of our homes that same culture which we expect in homes of people performing easier and brighter tasks. Frequently also, although it is our prayer and wish that it were otherwise, many fathers leave their homes in the evening seeking the comradeship they have missed during the day. Since it is largely the father's authority which rules and governs most homes, in his absence the children must be less rigourously reared.

Provincial Archives of Newfoundland and Labrador, Gn 13/2/a, Box 51, File #1, Pieces #142-143.

Outport girls come direct to us for good places; bring references from your clergy or some reliable person and you are always sure of a situation when you apply at the Newfoundland Employment Agency.

Mrs. George Walsh, 235 Theatre Hill.

14 girls now wanted for St. John's—2 nursemaids, another girl kept, washing out; 4 housemaids wages $4 to $6; 5 plain cooks, $5.00 to $7.00; 2 general girls; 1 general girl, family two; 2 more girls wanted this week for Bell Island, one for a family of three; 1 for Carbonear, $5 to $7, passages paid; 1 girl to go by this "Rosalind," wages $12; a dining room girl to go to Shelburne. also, 3 other girls for Shelburne, and 6 girls for different parts of Nova Scotia.

The Newfoundland Employment Agency. Mrs. George Walsh, 235 Theatre Hill.

Evening Herald, 3 May 1905, P. 1.

Appendix C

Chronology of Laws and Important Legal Changes

1275   Statute of Westminster

1633   An Act to Prevent the Destroying and Murdering of Bastard Children (first English Infanticide Law)

1803   Infanticide Law amended to drop presumption of guilt

1820   Whipping Act (prohibited whipping of women)

1828   Offences Against the Person Act (amended to include married women)

1834   An Act to Afford Relief to Wives and Children, Deserted by Husbands and Parents

1836   An Act for the Encouragement of Education in this Colony

1837   An Act to Extend the Criminal Laws of England to this Colony under Certain Modifications

1840   An Act to Defray Certain Charges that have Arisen for the Support of Aged and Infant Paupers up to the First of February, 1840.

1844   An Act to Provide for the Establishment of an Academy in Saint John's

1857   Matrimonial Causes Act

1858   Amendment to the Act of 1834 included the attaching of wages of deserting husband or father

1865   Repeal and Amendment of Act of 1858

1867   Canadian Confederation/Canadian Criminal Legislation

1870   Married Women's Property Act, Britain

1872   Infant Life Protection Act

1876   Married Women's Property Act, Newfoundland

1886   An Act to Punish Seduction and Like Offences and Make Further Provision for the Protection of Women and Girls.

1892   Criminal Code of Canada Trial by Jury

1906   An Act Restricting the Immigration of Chinese

1908   Mines Regulation Act

1911   Amendment to the Law Society Act

1914   British Naturalization Act

1920   An Act Concerning the Registration of Midwives

1921   Women Granted the Municipal Vote in Newfoundland

1922   English Infanticide Act

1925   Women Granted the Vote in Newfoundland

1926   An Act to Secure Better Training of Midwives and to Regulate their Practice

1929   Newfoundland's First Female Lawyer—Louise Saunders
       First Woman Elected to House of Assembly of Newfoundland—Lady Helena Squires

1930   Divorce Jurisdiction Act

1931   Health and Public Welfare Act

1934   Commission of Government in Newfoundland

1936   Shop Closing Act
       Act to Govern the Practice of Midwifery

1942   School Attendance Act

1944   Welfare of Children Act

1947   Civil Service Act

1947   Citizenship Act

1948   First application for Judicial Separation in Newfoundland

1949   Confederation with Canada

Divorce now requires Private member's Bill in Canadian House of Commons

Mother's Allowance Act

Memorial University Act

1952   The Shop Act

The Shop Act, St.John's

The Maintenance Act

1955   Criminal Code of Canada

1963   Hours of Work Act

Sale and Disposal of Property by Women Allowed

1968   The Divorce Act

1975   Criminal Law Amendment Act

(Women's testimony in rape cases no longer requires corroboration;
Women's sexual history no longer considered pertinent in rape cases)

1977   Labour Standards Act

(minimum wage established; domestics assigned "special" lower minimum wage)

1978   Bill C-52

1979   Matrimonial Property Act

Civil Service Act Repealed

1982   Criminal Code Amendment

(husband can now be charged with rape of wife)

1985   New Divorce Act

1989   Family Law Act

1991   Minimum Wage Regulations Revised

(special minimum wage for domestics eliminated from Labour Standard's Regulations; minimum wage raised to $4.75 per hour for all employees over sixteen years of age)

Appendix D

List of Women's Conferences 1975–1988

Oct. 1975 The Canadian Federation of University Women and the Women's Institutes held a joint provincial conference in Gander on the topic "Women: Creative Leadership."

Oct. 1978 The first provincial conference of Status of Women Councils held in Corner Brook with representatives from Corner Brook, Labrador City, St. John's and Grand Falls.

Nov. 1978 The Nain Northern Labrador Women's Conference brought native women together for the first time.

March 1980 The second provincial conference of Status of Women Councils held in Grand Falls on the topic "Education: Key to the Eighties."

Feb. 1981 The third provincial conference of Status of Women Councils held in St. John's on the topic "Our Sexual Beings."

April 1982 Fourth provincial conference of Status of Women Councils held at North West River on the topic "Breaking Down the Barriers."

March 1983 Corner Brook hosted the fifth provincial conference of Status of Women Councils on the topic "Women and Work: Yesterday, Today . . . Tomorrow?"

March 1984 The sixth provincial conference of Status of Women Councils held in Labrador City on the topic "Balancing the Scales."

Nov. 1984 A special conference on "Women and the Constitution" held in St. John's and the first provincial women's lobby took place on Nov. 19, 1984.

May 1985 The first Newfoundland and Labrador Women's Peace Conference held at the Rotary Sunshine Camp near St. John's brought together representatives of 38 organizations from women's, peace and social action groups.

Sept. 1985 An international conference on "Women and the Offshore" held in St. John's.

Oct. 1985 The seventh provincial conference of Status of Women Councils held in Gander on the topic "R/Evolution in Women's Health Care."

Nov. 1986 The eighth provincial conference of Status of Women Councils held in St. John's on the topic "Women and Our Work: Philosophy, Issues."

March 1987 The second Women's Annual Provincial Lobby held in St. John's.

April 1988 The ninth provincial conference of Status of Women Councils held at Port-aux-Basques on the topic "Women and Progress."

Appendix E

Highlights of the Women's Movement in Newfoundland and Labrador 1972–1988

April 1972 Five women from Newfoundland attended the "Strategy for Change" conference in Toronto to discuss implementation of the recommendations in the Report of the Royal Commission on the Status of Women.

May 1972 More than 200 women attended a meeting in St. John's to hear guest speaker Judge Doris Ogilvie of the Royal Commission on the Status of Women.

May 1972 Ten women selected at a public meeting in St. John's to work on a constitution for a local status of women group.

May 1971 Planned Parenthood Newfoundland and Labrador established at a public meeting in St. John's.

June 1972 The Jury Duty Reform Act was passed, enabling women to sit on juries.

Summer 1972 Eight young women received an Opportunities for Youth grant to research and publish *Women and the Law in Newfoundland.*

July 1972 First newsletter published by the Newfoundland Status of Women Council/Women's Place Collective.

Sept. 1972 General meeting held to establish a Status of Women group in St. John's.

Nov. 1972 Founding meeting held for the Newfoundland Status of Women Council. Committee elected for one year.

Feb. 1973 A grant of $3,000 was received from Secretary of State to set up a women's centre in St. John's. The money was turned over by the NSWC to an autonomous collective which opened "The Women's Place."

March 1973 The Jury Duty Reform group of NSWC held a one-day workshop at the Provincial Citizen Rights and Freedoms Conference.

March 1973 International Women's Day celebrations held in St. John's for the first time.

June 1973 Eighteen women from Newfoundland attended a "Women for Political Action" meeting in Toronto. Women from Corner Brook who attended began meeting regularly and formed the Corner Brook Status of Women Council.

Sept. 1973 "Feminists Together" workshop held in St. John's to exchange ideas on the theory and practice of the women's movement.

Nov. 1973 Two members of the NSWC's "Women in Public Life" group, Fran Innes and Barbara Walsh, run unsuccessfully in the St. John's municipal election. Dorothy Wyatt was elected the first female mayor of St. John's.

March 1974 For International Women's Day, NSWC held a two-day feminist symposium on the themes of challenging sex discrimination and helping women enter the labour force.

July 1974 NSWC member Lillian Bouzanne ran as the only woman candidate in the St. John's area for the July 8 federal election.

Dec. 1974 The province's Human Rights Commission was established, headed by Gertrude Keough. Improvements in the Human Rights Code added sex and marital status to the list of illegal grounds for discrimination along with race, religion, religious creed, political opinion, colour or ethnic, national or social origin.

Jan. 1975 At its January meeting, the NSWC collected money to join the Canadian Association for the Repeal of the Abortion Law.

March 1975 Corner Brook Women's Centre opened.

June 1975 The first regulations governing daycare in the province were established with the passage of the "Daycare and Homemakers Act."

Oct. 1975 The Canadian Federation of University Women and Women's Institutes held a joint conference in Gander on the topic "Women: Creative Leadership."

Dec. 1976 Representatives from Grand Falls, Corner Brook and St. John's Status of Women Councils presented a brief to government on matrimonial property rights.

March 1977 Labrador West Status of Women Council established.

May 1977 A joint conference between NSWC and the Women's Institutes entitled "Women—Where Are We in Community Action?" was held in St. John's, followed by a lobby of Premier Frank Moores.

Sept. 1977 The first "Career Exploration for Women" course for mature women was offered in St. John's by the Canada Employment Office.

May-June 1978 NSWC and the Corner Brook Status of Women Council sponsored a study on "The Abuse of Alcohol and Other Drugs by Women in Newfoundland."

June 1978 The Women's Centre on Military Road in St. John's was officially opened.

July 1978 The Rape Crisis 24-hour Hot Line, operating out of the St. John's Women's Centre, was officially opened.

Oct. 1978 The first provincial conference of Status of Women Councils was held in Corner Brook.

Oct. 1978 The Nain Northern Labrador Women's Conference brought native women together for the first time and delegates decided to establish local community women's groups to deal with issues raised at the conference.

Summer 1979 NSWC started a project to document the need for housing for battered women.

June 1979 Lynn Verge won the seat of Corner Brook East for the Progressive Conservative Party.

March 1980 The second provincial conference of Status of Women Councils was held in Grand Falls on the topic "Education: Key to the Eighties."

June 1980 An act was passed to provide for the Provincial Advisory Council on the Status of Women. The Council was established Nov. 21, 1980.

July 1980 The Matrimonial Property Act came into effect.

Sept. 1980 Labrador West Status of Women Council opened a Women's Centre.

Oct. 1980 The federal government's "Persons Award" was awarded to Ella Manuel of Bonne Bay.

Nov. 1980 The Women's Employment Counselling Project was started by the Corner Brook Status of Women Council.

Jan. 1981 NSWC purchased a house in St. John's for use as a transition house for battered women.

Feb. 1981 The third annual provincial conference of Status of Women Councils was held in St. John's on the topic "Our Sexual Beings."

Feb. 1981 Doris Anderson resigned as president of the Canadian Advisory Council on the Status of Women. Council member Liz Batstone of Grand Falls resigned in support.

June 1981 Official shower and opening of Transition House, the first shelter for battered women in Newfoundland and Labrador.

Nov. 1981 The Women's Resource Centre opened at Memorial University.

Feb. 1982 The Women's Network in St. John's began with a dinner meeting featuring speaker Judy Erola, federal minister responsible for the Status of Women.

April 1982 The provincial conference of Status of Women Councils was held at North West River, hosted by the Mokami Status of Women Council on the topic "Breaking Down the Barriers."

Oct. 1982 Gateway Status of Women organized at Channel, Port aux Basques.

Nov. 1982 Two hundred women from communities in the Upper Trinity South area gathered to discuss ways to create employment in their area. A Women's Involvement (WIN) committee was formed.

Jan. 1983 Women's Studies Programme began at Memorial University.

Jan. 1983 Iris Kirby died. The transition house in St. John's carries her name in honour of her memory because she was a constant source of encouragement and support to women in the province.

Feb. 1983 Day Care Advocates group formed at a public meeting in St. John's.

March 1983 The annual provincial conference of Status of Women Councils was held at Corner Brook on the topic "Women and Work: Yesterday, Today . . . Tomorrow?"

May 1983 Founding steering committee selected for the Gander Status of Women Council.

Sept. 1983 The Provincial Advisory Council on the Status of Women sponsored a one-day forum on pornography, with keynote speech by Maude Barlow, president of the Canadian Coalition Against Media Pornography. The Coalition of Citizens Against Pornography was formed at a follow-up meeting in October.

Nov. 1983 A transition house opened in Corner Brook.

Nov. 1983 Kirby House, a second stage house for victims of family violence, opened in St. John's.

Jan. 1984 A public march was held in St. John's as part of a national protest against pornography.

Feb. 1984 Gander Women's Centre opened.

March 1984 The annual conference of Status of Women Councils was held in Labrador City on the topic "Balancing the Scales."

March 1984 Dorothy Inglis of St. John's was elected as one of three vice-presidents of the National Action Committee on the Status of Women.

March 1984 A three-day women's festival was held in St. John's, sponsored by the NSWC.

April 1984 The first women's conference of the Newfoundland and Labrador Federation of Labour, "We are Organized Women," was held in St. John's.

May 1984 The Newfoundland Status of Women Council changed its name to the St. John's Status of Women Council.

Aug. 1984 Single Moms Centre started in Corner Brook.

Sept. 1984 First "Take Back the Night" march was held in St. John's.

Nov. 1984 Demasduit Women's Centre officially opened in Grand Falls.

Nov. 1984 "Women and the Constitution" provincial conference held in St. John's with first women's lobby of provincial MHA's.

Feb. 1985 In Stephenville a steering committee was selected to develop the Bay St. George Status of Women Council.

March 1985 Sarabande, a St. John's-based all-women's singing group, made its debut at an International Women's Day concert.

May 1985 A Women's Peace Conference was held at the Rotary Sunshine Camp near St. John's.

Sept. 1985 An international conference on "Women and the Offshore" was held in St. John's.

Sept. 1985 The Women's Policy Office was established within the provincial government to coordinate the development and communication of programs and policies for women in Newfoundland and Labrador.

Oct. 1985 The Gander Status of Women Council hosted the annual provincial conference of Status of Women Councils on the topic "R/Evolution in Women's Health Care."

April 1986 Nancy Riche was elected executive vice-president of the Canadian Labour Congress.

June 1986 The Bay St. George Status of Women Council opened a Women's Centre in Stephenville.

Aug. 1986 A march for peace in Stephenville, organized by the Bay St. George Status of Women Council, drew over 200 people.

Sept. 1986 "Take Back the Night" marches held in St. John's and Labrador City.

Sept. 1986 A two-year early childhood education program was established at the Cabot Institute in St. John's.

Oct. 1986 Delegates from battered women's shelters in Newfoundland and Labrador held their first teleconference as members of a provincial association on family violence.

Oct. 1986 The Provincial Advisory Council sponsored a workshop on political action and strategies to overcome obstacles faced by women in politics. Key speakers were Gudrun Agnarsdottir, a member of the Iceland National Assembly, and NAC president Louise Dulude.

Nov. 1986 A children's services consultation, sponsored by Transition House, was held in St. John's. This was the first conference in Canada to focus entirely on services to children in shelters.

Nov. 1986 Provincial Conference of the Status of Women Councils held in St. John's on the topic "Women and Our Work."

March 1987 Second Women's Lobby of the provincial government.

April 1987 The Farm Women's Association of Newfoundland was formed.

Aug. 1987 The 52% Solution bus tour crossed Newfoundland to organize women's involvement in politics.

Sept. 1987 The women's committee of the St. John's Board of Trade held a two-day conference on "Success Strategies for Women."

Oct. 1987 Frances Laracy of Conception Harbour received the federal government's "Persons Award."

April 1988 Annual provincial conference of Status of Women Councils held at Port-aux-Basques on the topic "Women and Progress."

June 1988 The Women's Involvement Committee opened a Women's Centre in Green's Harbour, Trinity Bay.

June 1988 Single Mothers Against Poverty (SMAP) held its first annual conference in Gander.

Appendix F

Documents: The Modern Women's Movement

WOMEN MADE IT HAPPEN

During the 1960s pressure on the federal government by women's groups grew steadily, until it was impossible for the politicians to ignore any longer the inequalities faced by women in Canadian society. In 1970 the government established a Royal Commission on the Status of Women, chaired by Florence Bird (now a senator).*

The report bore out many of the claims that women's organizations had been making. It concluded that women were suffering discrimination at every turn and made a set of strong recommendations for government action.

The women's groups who had been responsible for the establishment of the commission were well aware of the time-honoured Canadian strategy of setting up commissions to get governments off the hook. The commissions hold a lot of public hearings, report their findings, and make their recommendations, all with maximum publicity, and the general public assumes somehow that government has acted. Women's groups were aware of the danger that the report on the Status of Women could join all the others on dusty House of Commons shelves. They knew that nothing was going to happen unless they made it happen.

*The Royal Commission was appointed in 1967 and reported in 1970.

ACTION COMMITTEE

Preliminary meetings were held that led to the formation of the National Action Committee on the Status of Women, with delegates from various women's groups. They were some of the strangest meetings I have ever attended. It was still a time when upper-middle-class women felt it important to wear white gloves and fancy hats but it was also a time when young people were experimenting with a whole range of styles. It was not unusual to see a cluster of women involved in intense discussion, some of whom were wearing mink and silk and others bib overalls and work-boots. Women from the working class mingled with professionals. Business women talked to artists and writers. Housewives listened and contributed as trade union women explained difficulties at the workplace.

These were women who would normally never be in the same room together, let alone talking to one another. I used to go home from meetings shaking my head in wonderment, believing that if we women could cross so many barriers and stay friends then we could go on to accomplish almost anything. "They're not just talking at each other," I would say to my neighbour. "They are honestly listening to one another. They really want to understand the other's viewpoint." We all knew why we were there. We wanted to insure women's dignity and equality and that common bond drew us together.

ITS OWN STYLE

There was a lot to talk about. We were just starting to examine the many discriminatory practices affecting women in every phase of life. Research was undertaken. Briefs were composed. Information was shared. We were doing all the things that are usually done when an organization is forming. What we did not realize at the time was that we were also doing something else of great importance—we were working out our own ways of getting things done. The women's movement had developed its own style of democracy.

One of the first things to go was the head table that traditionally separates the "important" people from the rank and file at dinners and banquets. Our executive members, guests and speakers all sit at tables with ordinary delegates, until it is their turn to go to the podium. It gives them a chance to meet others and indulge in real conversation.

Wherever possible, feminist meetings take place at round tables. We shun the old fashioned male model of the long "Board of Directors" table with the authoritative chairman sitting at the head.

Instead of using gavels and complicated rules of order to shut off debate, chairpersons go to great lengths to encourage discussion, often to the point of tedium. We try to reach consensus rather than push for arbitrary majority vote.

We encourage rotation so that more women can contribute, gain experience, and develop confidence. We don't want "stars" to emerge, we want more women to be empowered. (If there is one word that characterized the women's movement it is that word, "empowerment.")

FEMINIZATION OF POWER

We try to share not only burdens, but also the experience and the rewards. We scorn back-room decision making and we make it easy for our representatives to be accountable to us. We are developing in fact, a whole new style that is much closer to real democracy. And this "feminization of power," as it has been called, may well be more threatening to the boys in authority than any of our specific demands.

Our society has been based on patriarchy, a system of values that teaches us that men are valuable and that women are not. We are determined to change that system, but the process by which we bring about change is as important to feminists as is the final goal.
. . .

Dorothy Inglis, "Bread and Roses," *Evening Telegram*, 10 January 1987, p. A4.

WOMEN TAKE BACK THE NIGHT

A demonstration organized by women for women

- to stand together as women, refusing to be silent about the violence done to us by men.
- to state our refusal to take responsibility for sexual harassment, sexual assault, battering and incest.
- to celebrate the steps we are taking to support each other and to create change. To live without being dependent on the protection of men.
- to remind each other that as individuals we have strength and together we are even stronger.
- to shout out our desire to live freely, without the threat of violence.

Women taking to the streets at night to protest against the violent attacks, was started by our American sisters. In 1981, the third Friday in September was adopted by the Canadian Association of Sexual Assault Centres as "Take Back the Night" day. Demonstrations now take place throughout North America and Europe. Take Back the Night is an action created to enable large numbers of women to publicly express our anger and rage at the reality of the violence we are subjected to daily. We will be silenced no longer! Not all of us have been brutally raped in a back alley, but *all* of us, because we are women, live with that fear. We march at night, but we are also afraid during the day, in public places, at our workplaces, at our schools and in our homes.

From *WEB*, Newsletter of the St. John's Status of Women Council, September 1987, p. 13.

WOMEN MARCH INTO FEDERAL OFFICES TO STATE CASE FOR RETAINING CENTRES

The battle for reinstatement of operational funding for women's centres in the province continued Monday as a delegation from the women's centre in St. John's, and their supporters carried their case straight to a number of federal officials in the city.

Do you support the reinstatement of funding to women's centres?

That question was posed to the 21 ministers who make up the Planning and Priorities Committee of the federal cabinet, which, according to secretary of State Gerry Weiner, is responsible for any decisions or changes with respect to cuts in funding.

Operational funding for women's centres across Canada was eliminated in the recent federal budget. Since then, an ongoing battle has been waged in a bid to have Ottawa alter its decision and reinstate funding. Besides the St. John's centre, six other facilities in Newfoundland and Labrador are affected.

The women's centre in St. John's is hoping to gain support from the ministers who make up the committee by faxing letters and requesting a response by Wednesday on their positions on reinstatement of funding.

Of the committee members, 14 have offices in St. John's.

The delegation visited each office Monday, presenting the letter to an office representative who then faxed it to the appropriate minister.

Among the offices visited were those of International Trade Minister John Crosbie, deputy prime minister Don Mazankowski and Energy Minister Jake Epp.

Theresa Mackenzie, spokesman for the St. John's Status of Women said, "the worst thing about it is the minister responsible for the status of women, Mary Collins, is not even on the committee."

Ms. Mackenzie lead the delegation in and out of the 14 offices around the city, presented the letters and then waited for a confirmation that the letter had in fact been faxed to the federal ministers.

"It's a hard way to talk to ministers but it's the only way we have," Ms. Mackenzie said.

The delegation formed about 10:30 a.m. at the St. John's centre with the first stop being at Mr. Crosbie's office in the Cabot Building. Ms. Mackenzie said the group finished delivering the letters around 1:30 p.m.

"Most of the letters were confirmed and for those that weren't, we will call the offices tomorrow for confirmation. We will also call the offices in Ottawa to see if they have the letter," she said.

Asked how she might react should the federal response be negative, Ms. Mackenzie said, "I think it would be politically not very bright. I think you will see a lot of public activity and demonstrations, but I'm hoping that is not going to be the case."

On the other hand, she said, if the ministers all state their support to reinstate funding, "it would be great and then they can all go to work on Mr. Weiner."

Evening Telegram, 24 April 1990, p. 3.

STATUS OF WOMEN CORNER BROOK AND WEST COAST OF NEW-FOUNDLAND

I. Laws and practices under federal jurisdiction concerning the political rights of women.

The majority of women in this region of Newfoundland have no idea of questioning the laws and practices concerning the political rights of women.

There is a great apathy as far as politics are concerned; to the average woman, politics belong to men, and any woman brave enough to take any part in any election, be it federal, provincial, or municipal, is subject to a certain amount of suspicion.

2. Present and potential role of women in the Canadian labour force, including the special problems of married women in employment,

and measures that might be taken under federal jurisdiction to help meeting them.

The present role of married women in this district, as far as employment is concerned, is more or less on a part time basis.

There has been some criticism from young women just joining the labour force, that married women are taking jobs that could be done by them. a check with employers brought out the point that they preferred married women, they were more reliable, valued the work more, and were not just putting in time until they married, as many young girls seemed to do. there is certainly a need for educational facilities to help in the retraining of married women who wish to reenter professional or skilled employment. . .

The disinterest shown by most women in this part of canada, in the affairs of women as a whole, is to be deplored.

They grumble about conditions, but do nothing about them. what great cause, or grave injustice, can rouse them from their apathy is a matter for conjecture.

The answer is education . . . and education is very much in the limelight in newfoundland at this time.

The next generation of women, will be better fitted to take their part in the affairs of their country, and to bring the status of women to a higher plane in years to come.

Excerpt from a Brief to the Royal Commission on the Status of Women, by Doris Janes, Corner Brook and West Coast of Newfoundland, 1968. Courtesy of the Centre for Newfoundland Studies, Memorial University of Newfoundland.

INTRODUCTION

A provincial women's conference was held in St. John's Nov. 16 to 19, 1984. A total of 129 delegates, 55 from outside the city, attended this conference.

The purpose of the weekend conference was two-fold. On Friday evening (Nov. 16) and all day Saturday (Nov. 17) the focus was "Women and the Constitution." Through speakers, panels, and discussion, women in Newfoundland and Labrador learned about the effects of the new Canadian Constitution and Charter of Rights and Freedoms.

The second part of the conference concentrated on a political lobby. On Sunday (Nov. 18), delegates from groups involved in organizing this conference spent a hard-working day in plenary workshops. The end result was eleven resolutions based on background briefs that had been prepared by different groups. Based on the consensus arrived at during Sunday's sessions, these resolutions were prepared and rehearsed for presentation to each of the three provincial political parties. The actual presentation took place Monday (Nov. 19) in three separate hour-long sessions.

For everyone concerned, the conference was a tremendous success. Women learned about the new Canadian Charter, and had a chance to press their concerns on a political level. . . .

INEQUALITY—THE SILENCE OF THE LAW

I would like to begin by saying how delighted I am to be here in St. John's. I met some of you in Labrador some months ago and was very pleased to be invited back. So I just jumped at the chance to come.

I decided to use the word "inequality" in the title of my remarks because it refers to the reality that the women of Canada experience. I think it is important to focus on the real problems faced by the women of Newfoundland, Labrador and of Canada generally.

An emphasis on the opposite, equality, is an emphasis on an ideal, a goal, a dream of a different world. Equality is what we have been promised in the Canadian Charter of Rights and Freedoms. This promise will be of little significance if it is not an assistance in tackling the real problems of our lives.

The Charter promises us equality in Section 15. Sex is a prohibited grounds of discrimination. Section 28 emphatically promises equality between the sexes with respect to all other Charter rights.

Section 28 is important in that it probably prevents judges and legislators putting limits on equality as they otherwise could under Sections 1 and 33. It also, I think, stresses the importance which ought to be attached to sexual equality in Canadian society.

It is clear that what we are thinking about here is an ideal, not reality. The Charter may or may not help us achieve the reality of sexual equality. Whether it does or not will depend on political will. The political will of legislators who have a responsibility to bring the law into conformity with the Charter. The political will of the judges who will have to decide whether something offends the Charter. What is most important is our political will—we must keep saying—we have been promised equality . . . where is it? . . .

Keynote Address by Prof. Christine Boyle, Dalhousie Law School, Final Report of "Women and the Constitution Conference," 16–19 November 1984.
Bay St. George Status of Women Council
P.O. Box 501, Stephenville, Nfld., A2N 3B4

The Bay St. George Status of Women Council was formed in February of 1985. Since that time, we have been quite active. Our first task was to make ourselves known in the area; and through several meetings since February, we feel that a good start has been made.

Some of the activities and services we have provided to our membership thus far include:
- newsletters
- medium to address women and issues in the local area.
- public meetings (see below)
- literature on women's issues.

Listed below are the specific details and dates of the activities pursued:

FEBRUARY 4—Initial meeting and appointment of Steering Committee

FEBRUARY 19—Public meeting on "Day Care." A group of approximately 20 met at the Community College. Guest speaker for the meeting was Dorothy Robbins, Advocates Committee. The meeting was very informative.

MARCH 25—"MEET YOUR CANDIDATE NIGHT." A very successful event. Approximately 200 voters attended to ask questions and meet their candidates. Questions were addressed regarding unemployment, day care, hydro rates, labour legislation, etc. The meeting was received well by all.

APRIL 19—"CITIZEN OF THE YEAR." Early in April we nominated a woman in the Stephenville area, "Mary Ennis," and on April 19, 1985 she was pronounced "Citizen of the Year." Mary was nominated for her involvement with the Correctional Centre, Allied Youth, the Addiction Resource Centre, Elizabeth Fry Steering Committee, and the Stephenville Marathon. We are very proud of Mary.

MAY 2—Public meetings on "Family Law." A very informative evening for all those who attended. Guest speaker for the evening was Beverly Marks, L.L.B., who spoke on separations, divorce, maintenance act, custody, etc. The attendance for this meeting was approximately 50. It proved to be a very good topic, as many questions were asked.

MAY 10–13—Two delegates (Karen Decker, Chairperson and Rowena Park, Secretary) attended the NAC Conference in Ottawa.

MAY 17–19—Two delegates (Joyce Hancock and Peg Jones, Committee Members) attended the Women's Peace Conference held in St. John's.

JUNE 24—We have been successful in obtaining a grant for a summer project. We have hired two students who will commence work on June 24th. The aim of the project is to survey the Bay St. George area to see what the concerns of the local women are. Also, through this project we hope to promote our organization and become more widely known. We are quite anxious to see the outcome of these surveys.

These have been our activities to date. We are quite pleased with our progress thus far and look forward to even more participation and involvement in our community.

Karen Decker
Chairperson

From Conference Booklet, Gander Status of Women Council, *R/Evolution in Women's Health Care. It's happening now!* 18–20 October 1985.

Bibliographic Notes

Chapter 1

1. See for example, Linda Kealey, (ed.), *A Not Unreasonable Claim: Women and Reform in Canada, 1880s–1920s*, Toronto: Canadian Women's Educational Press, 1979.

2. Gail Campbell, "Canadian Women's History: A View From Atlantic Canada," *Acadiensis*, XX(1):184–99 (Autumn 1990).

3. Ruth Roach Pierson, *"They're Still Women After All": The Second World War and Canadian Womanhood*, Toronto: McClelland and Stewart, 1986; Veronica Strong-Boag, *The New Day Recalled: Lives of Girls and Women in English Canada, 1919–1939*, Toronto: Copp Clark Pitman, 1988; Alison Prentice, *et al.*, *Canadian Women: A History*, Toronto: Harcourt Brace Jovanovich, 1988.

4. Campbell, "Canadian Women's History," p. 186.

5. Hilda Chaulk Murray, *More Than Fifty Percent: Woman's Life in a Newfoundland Outport, 1900–50*, St. John's: Breakwater Books, 1979; Dona Lee Davis, *Blood and Nerves: An Ethnographic Focus on Menopause*, St. John's: Institute of Social and Economic Research, Memorial University of Newfoundland, 1983. In particular, Davis takes issue with Ellen Antler's, "Women's Work in Newfoundland Fishing Families," *Atlantis*, 2(2):106–114 Part II (Spring 1977).

6. Marilyn Porter, "'Women and Old Boats': The Sexual Division of Labour in a Newfoundland Outport," in Eva Gamarnikow, *et al.*, (eds.), *The*

Public and the Private, London: Heinemann, 1983, pp. 91–105; "'She Was Skipper of the Shore Crew': Notes on the History of the Sexual Division of Labour in Newfoundland," *Labour/Le Travail*, 15:105–23 (Spring 1985); "Mothers and Daughters: Linking Women's Life Histories in Grand Bank, Newfoundland, Canada," in Veronica Strong-Boag and Anita Clair Fellman, (eds.), *Rethinking Canada: The Promise of Women's History*, 2nd edition, Toronto: Copp Clark Pitman Ltd., 1991, pp. 396–414; see also Marilyn Porter and Sandy Pottle, *Women and the Economy in Newfoundland*, St. John's: Women's Policy Office, Government of Newfoundland and Labrador, 1987.

7. Jane Nadel-Klein and Dona Lee Davis, (eds.), *To Work and to Weep: Women in Fishing Economies*, St. John's: Memorial University of Newfoundland, Institute for Social and Economic Research, 1988.

8. Elizabeth Goudie, *Woman of Labrador*, Agincourt: The Book Society of Canada, 1983 [1973]. See also Mrs. Leonidas Hubbard, Junior, *A Woman's Way Through Unknown Labrador*, New York: McClure, 1908; Millicent Blake Loder, *Daughter of Labrador*, St. Johns: Harry Cuff Publications, 1989; and Lydia Campbell, *Sketches of Labrador Life*, Happy Valley, Labrador: Them Days, 1980. Campbell's daughter also published an autobiography: Margaret Baikie, *Labrador Memories: Reflections at Mulligan*, Happy Valley: Them Days, 1983. For more on Labrador women's autobiographies, see Roberta Buchanan, "Auto biography as History: The Autobiographies of Three Labrador Women —Lydia Campbell, Margaret Baikie and Elizabeth Goudie," in Shannon Ryan, (ed.), *Newfoundland History 1986: Proceedings of the First Newfoundland History Society Conference*, St. John's: Newfoundland Historical Society, 1986, pp. 73–85, and her "'Country Ways and Fashions': Lydia Campbell's *Sketches of Labrador Life*—A Study in Folklore and Literature," in Gerald Thomas and John Widdowson, (eds.), *Studies in Newfoundland Folklore: Community and Process*, St. John's: Breakwater Books, 1991, pp. 289–308.

9. Margaret Giovannini, *Outport Nurse*, St. John's: Faculty of Medicine, Memorial University of Newfoundland, 1988, Occasional Papers in the History of Medicine, No. 7, edited with an introduction by Janet McNaughton. See also the following autobiographies of nurses: Bessie Jane Banfill, *Labrador Nurse*, London: Robert Hale, 1954; Dora Elizabeth Burchill, *Labrador Memories* (2nd ed. Shepparton, Victoria, Printed by "The Shepparton News Pub. Co., 1947); Leslie Diack, *Labrador Nurse*, London: V. Gollancz, 1963; Dorothy Jupp, *A Journey of Wonder and Other Writings*, New York: Vantage Press [1971]; refugee doctor, Ilka Dickman, was employed as an outport nurse during WWII; see her *Appointment to Newfoundland*, Manhattan, Kansas: Sunflower University Press, 1981.

10. Janet E. McNaughton, "The Role of the Newfoundland Midwife in Traditional Health Care, 1900–70," PhD thesis, Department of Folklore, Memorial University of Newfoundland, 1989; Cecilia Benoit,

Midwives in Passage: The Modernisation of Maternity Care, St. John's: Memorial University of Newfoundland, Institute of Social and Economic Research, 1991.

11. Benoit, *Midwives*, p. 49.

12. Marilyn Porter, "'The Tangly Bunch': Outport Women of the Avalon Peninsula," *Newfoundland Studies*, 1(1):77–90 (Spring 1985); see also Janice Reid, "Changing With the Times: Women, Household Economy and Confederation," BA Honours thesis, Department of History, Memorial University of Newfoundland, 1991. On the need for a broader definition of women's politics, see Linda Kealey and Joan Sangster, (eds.), *Beyond the Vote: Canadian Women and Politics*, Toronto: University of Toronto Press, 1989.

13. See for example, S.J.R. Noel, *Politics in Newfoundland*, Toronto: University of Toronto Press, 1971, p. 180 and Frederick W. Rowe, *A History of Newfoundland and Labrador*, Toronto: McGraw-Hill Ryerson, Ltd., 1980, p. 382.

14. Joyce Nevitt, *White Caps, Black Bands: Nursing in Newfoundland to 1934*, St. John's: Jesperson Press, 1978; Linda White, "The General Hospital School of Nursing 1903–30," MA thesis, Department of History, Memorial University of Newfoundland, 1992.

15. Alison Prentice and Marjorie R. Theobald, (eds.), *Women Who Taught: Perspectives on the History of Women and Teaching*, Toronto: University of Toronto Press, 1991.

16. Sister M.J. Dinn, *Foundation of the Presentation Congregation in Newfoundland* [s.l.: s.n.] 1975; Sister Williamina Hogan, *Pathways of Mercy in Newfoundland, 1842–1984*, St. John's: Harry Cuff Publications, 1986.

17. Phillip McCann, "Class, Gender and Religion in Newfoundland, 1836–1901," *Historical Studies in Education*, 1(2):179–200 (1989).

18. Nancy Forestell, "Women's Paid Labour in St. John's between the Two World Wars," MA thesis, Department of History, Memorial University of Newfoundland, 1987; see also her "Times Were Hard: The Pattern of Women's Paid Labour in St. John's Between the Two World Wars," *Labour/Le Travail*, 24:147–66 (Fall 1989).

19. Sean Cadigan, "Economic and Social Relations of Production on the Northeast-Coast of Newfoundland, with Special References to Conception Bay, 1785–1855," PhD thesis, Department of History, Memorial University of Newfoundland, 1991.

20. Marjorie Cohen, *Women's Work, Markets, and Economic Development in Nineteenth-Century Ontario*, Toronto: University of Toronto Press, 1988.

21. Peter Pope, "The South Avalon Planters, 1630–1700: Residence, Labour, Demand and Exchange in Seventeenth-Century Newfoundland,"

Ph.D. thesis, Department of History, Memorial University of New-foundland, 1992.

22. On the Jubilee Guilds and Women's Institutes, see Agnes M. Richard, *Threads of Gold: Newfoundland and Labrador Jubilee Guilds, Women's Institutes*, St. John's: Creative Publishers, 1989 which is based on her Master's thesis.

Chapter Two

1. S.J.R. Noel, *Politics in Newfoundland,* Toronto and Buffalo: University of Toronto Press, 1971, p. 180; and Frederick W. Rowe, *A History of Newfoundland and Labrador,* Toronto: McGraw-Hill Ryerson Limited, 1980, p. 382.

2. The undergraduate papers are Terry Bishop, "Newfoundland's Strug-gle for the Women's Franchise," paper submitted to Professor J. Hiller, December 10, 1982; Janice O'Brien, "Woman's Suffrage in Newfound-land: A Determined Goal," paper submitted to Professor Linda Kealey, April 7, 1982; and Gaynor Rowe, "The Woman Suffrage Movement in Newfoundland," paper submitted to Professor K. Matthews, December 1973. All are available at the Centre for Newfoundland Studies, Memorial University of Newfoundland. One short published account appears in the pioneering study of Catherine L. Cleverdon, *The Woman Suffrage Movement in Canada,* Toronto and Buffalo: University of Toronto Press, 1950, pp. 208–13; the Newfoundland section was added hastily as the book went to press, and Cleverdon did not have access to many sources.

3. *Evening Telegram,* April 20, 1893 and June 13, 1893.

4. *Daily News,* Feb. 21, 1895.

5. Letter to the editor by "Bay Isles," *Daily News,* April 13, 1910. "Bay Isles" was Myra Campbell's pen name. The name of the club was not identified but in all likelihood it was the Methodist College Literary Institute.

6. [Agnes Ayre], "Current Events Club," in J.R. Smallwood, (ed.), *Book of Newfoundland,* Vol. 1, St. John's: Newfoundland Book Publishers, 1937, p. 199; this article dates the delivery of information as 1898 but that is likely a printing error. Agnes Ayre links the supplying of the information with the formation of the Ladies' Reading Room.

7. Armine N. Gosling, "Woman Suffrage." a paper read at the Ladies' Reading Room, St. John's, Newfoundland, Jan. 15th, 1912. St. John's: Herald Printers, 1912. No copy survives in Newfoundland archives. I discovered it among the papers of Armine Gosling's sister, Adelaide Nutting, at Columbia University.

8. A.N. G[osling], *William Gilbert Gosling: A Tribute,* New York: The Guild Press, 1935, p. 17.

9. Helen E. Marshall, *Mary Adelaide Nutting: Pioneer of Modern Nursing*, Baltimore, Maryland: The John's Hopkins University Press, 1972, especially Chs. 1 and 2.

10. Adelaide Nutting to Vespasian Nutting, March 6, 1892 and October 9, 1893 (Nutting Collection, Columbia University).

11. See Cathedral Restoration Records, Archives of the Anglican Cathedral, St. John's.

12. A.N.G., *William Gilbert Gosling*, p. 47.

13. *Daily News*, November 30, 1904 and Armine Gosling to Adelaide Nutting, January 21, 1941 (Nutting Collection).

14. Adelaide Nutting to Armine Gosling, January 12, 1905 (Nutting Collection). Also, Teresa E. Christy, "Portrait of a Leader: Lavinia Lloyd Dock," *Nursing Outlook*, June 1969, 58–61: and Vern Bullough *et al. American Nursing: A Biographical Dictionary*, "Lavinia Lloyd Dock, 1858–1956," pp. 91–94, New York and London: Garland Publishing Company, 1988.

15. Adelaide Nutting to Armine Gosling, August 1, 1909 (Nutting Collection).

16. Gosling, "Woman Suffrage," p. 6.

17. Gosling, "Woman Suffrage," pp. 9 and 11.

18. Gosling, "Woman Suffrage," p. 3.

19. Quotes from Myra J. Campbell, "Woman's Wrongs," *Daily News*, June 15, 1920.

20. Myra J. McCormick and Christopher Campbell. Her children were William (1900–1985) civil engineer; Christopher (1902–), electrical engineer; Janet Marjorie (1904–1949), registered nurse and mother of Dr. Myra McCormick, orthopaedic surgeon; Catherine (1906–1952), artist; and Margaret (1908–1985), medical technologist. John and Myra Campbell moved to Brantford, Ontario, upon his retirement in 1925. A grandniece, Lynn Verge MHA, is a lawyer and a former minister of justice for the Province of Newfoundland.

21. Biographical details from personal correspondence with Christopher F. Campbell (son); Myra J. McCormick (granddaughter), September-November, 1987; and Presbyterian Women's Missionary Society records, St. Andrew's Presbyterian Church, St. John's.

22. *Daily News*, June 11, 1920.

23. *Daily News*, June 12, 1920.

24. *Daily News*, June 15, 1920.

25. *Daily News*, June 15, 1920.

26. *Daily News*, June 11, 1920.

27. *Daily News*, June 15, 1920.

28. *Daily News*, December 10, 1909.

29. P.J.K., "The Gentle Suffragette," *Daily News*, April 18(?), 1913 (undated press clipping in Nutting Collection); see also A.N. Gosling, "A Suffragist on Suffragettes," *Daily News*, April 16, 1913.

30. "A Beautiful Sermon," *Daily News*, June 16, 1913.

31. *British Dominions Woman Suffrage Union. Report of First Conference and First Year of Work*, London, 1914.

32. *The Distaff: In Aid of Red Cross Branch, Newfoundland, W[omen's] P[atriotic] S[ociety]*, 1916, St. John's, Newfoundland, pp. 17–18.

33. The daughter of H.W. LeMessurier, who was editor of the *Evening Telegram*, 1889–92, Registrar of Shipping and Deputy Minister of Customs. In 1917 Mabel LeMessurier married Llewellyn A. Feild-Jones, son of Llewellyn Jones, Anglican Bishop of Newfoundland, 1878–1917. She spent much of the rest of her life in Kenya where her husband was in the Colonial Civil Service. Personal correspondence, Lt. Col. Hugh S. LeMessurier, October 20, 1987.

34. *The Distaff*, 1916, p.1.

35. *The Distaff*, 1916, p. 10. For other patriotic poems that stress the importance of women's work see Mrs. T.J. Duley, "A Pair of Grey Socks: Facts and Fancies." Verses by Margaret Duley. St. John's, circa 1916. Pamphlet at Centre for Newfoundland Studies, Memorial University of Newfoundland, and Eunice T. Holbrook Ruel, "Queen Mary's Needlework Guild," *Newfoundland Quarterly*, XV(1) (July, 1915).

36. "Our Walking Tour," *The Distaff* (1917), p. 14.

37. *The Book of Newfoundland*, Vol. 1, mentions only fourteen Newfoundland nurses and VADs who served overseas. My own research has uncovered forty-three; there may well be more.

38. "Unveiling of the Dickinson Monument," *Newfoundland Quarterly*, XX(3):8 (Dec. 1920); and picture and brief biography, *Newfoundland Quarterly* XVIII(3):15 (Dec. 1918).

39. About thirty years after the event, Margaret Duley, suffragist and author, took me, her niece, to the monument when I was a small child. She considered Dickinson, rightly, a model of female heroism who should be remembered by the next generation. I cite this incident to illustrate how strongly her generation of women's rights activists were affected by her memory. Dickinson's aunt was Gertrude (Mrs. Chesley) Ayre. Dickinson was the daughter of Gustavus H. and Selina Dickinson. She studied Domestic Science at McDonald College in Guelph, Ontario.

40. *The Distaff*, 1916, p.11.

41. Nancy M. Forestell, "Women's Paid Labour in St. John's Between the Two World Wars," MA Thesis, Department of History, Memorial University of Newfoundland, August 1987.

42. Minute Books of the Women's Patriotic Association, Sept. 1, 1914, WPA P.8/B/13–#1, Provincial Archives of Newfoundland and Labrador, Colonial Building, St. John's.

43. Remarks of Eleanor T. Macpherson, Honorary Secretary WPA, *Daily News*, December 17, 1914.

44. See for example *Daily News*, October 2, 1914.

45. *Daily News*, March 16, 1917.

46. *Daily News*, June 10, 1916; also *Daily News*, July 8, 1916.

47. *The Letters of Mayo Lind*. With an Introduction by J. Alex Robinson, LL.D., St. John's, Newfoundland: Robinson and Company, 1919, p. 135.

48. "A Pair of Grey Socks," p. 15.

49. WPA Minutes, April 13, 1917.

50. *Daily News*, October 2, 1918; *Distaff*, 1916, pp. 19–20.

51. WPA Minutes, June 1, 1917, Feb. 9, 1917, Oct. 20, 1914; *Newfoundland Quarterly*, XV(1) (July, 1915).

52. WPA Minutes, June 1, 1917.

53. Davidson to Harcourt, Nov. 25, 1914, Governor's Dispatches to the Colonial Office, GN1/1/7; and Harris to Long, May 14, 1918 (Secret) Provincial Archives of Newfoundland and Labrador; also *The Plaindealer*, April 27, 1918.

54. Harris to Colonial Office, Sept. 28, 1918 (Secret).

55. WPA Donations Book, Sept. 1917 to Sept. 1918.

56. WPA Minutes, April 13, 1917.

57. James Baird, Ltd. advertisement, *Daily News*, May 14, 1915.

58. See for instance draft letter of the Methodist College Ladies Aid Society to Lady Harris (1918), Records Methodist College Literary Institute, W.Y. 900/Box 2, United Church of Canada Archives, St. John's, Newfoundland.

59. Governor's Dispatches, Harris to Long, June 14, 1918, June 29, 1918, March 25, 1919, Jan. 31, 1919 and Oct. 2, 1920.

60. *Daily News*, May 12, 1920.

61. M.C.L.I. Debate Woman Suffrage, *Daily News*, January 21, 1921; *Daily Star*, June 23, 1920, *Daily News*, May 19, 1923.

62. [Agnes Ayre], "Current Events Club—Woman Suffrage—Newfoundland Society of Art," *Book of Newfoundland*, Vol. I. p. 200. Though this article is unsigned, internal evidence points to Agnes Ayre as the author.

63. [Agnes Ayre], "Current Events Club," p. 199.

64. "Newfoundland Report" by Fannie McNeil in *Jus Suffragi* (Newspaper of the International Alliance of Women), March 1922, p. 91.

65. Peter Neary and Patrick O'Flaherty suggest the war had made rebels of Newfoundland women, especially those who had gone overseas, and that the suffrage movement was a "testament of youth." In fact it was largely led by their mothers. See Peter Neary and Patrick O'Flaherty, *Part of the Main: An Illustrated History of Newfoundland and Labrador*, St. John's, Newfoundland, Breakwater Books, 1983, p. 144.

66. Biographical sources include interviews with Elizabeth Baird (Mrs. J. Makinson), Joan Roberts (Mrs. Dr. Jim), Kathleen Knowling (Mrs. W.A.), August 2, 1987; the Hon. R.S. Furlong, August 26, 1986; and the late Dorothy Henderson (Mrs. Charles), July 10, 1987; *Evening Telegram*, Christmas Number, 1891; *Newfoundland Quarterly*, XXXVIII, 1 (July 1938), p. 22; *Evening Telegram*, April 30, 1925, January 27, 1927, and January 10, 1929; Obituary, *Evening Telegram*, February 24, 1928 and *Daily News*, February 24, 1928; and Fannie McNeil File, Centre for Newfoundland Studies, Memorial University of Newfoundland.

67. [Agnes Ayre], "Current Events Club," p. 200.

68. [Agnes Ayre], "Current Events Club," p. 200.

69. Biographical sources include *Encyclopedia of Newfoundland and Labrador*, Vol. 2; interview, Agnes O'Dea (friend and relative), August 1986; *Evening Telegram*, January 29, 1927; Cowan Mission records; *Daily News*, April 27, 1925. The words are those of her dying brother, as reported by Agnes O'Dea. Her political philosophy is outlined in a speech at the suffrage victory dinner, *Daily News*, April 27, 1925.

70. Biographical information, *Jus Suffragi*, March, 1925, 90–91; *Evening Telegram*, March 19, 1928; *Daily News*, Dec. 19, 1942. p. 3; *Encyclopedia of Newfoundland and Labrador*, Vol. 1, "D'Alberti Transcript"; Conversations with Ella Hutton (Mrs. Hubert) and Basil Hutton. Anecdotes from Ella Hutton, August 29, 1986.

71. Paul Woodford, *Charles Hutton: Newfoundland's Greatest Musician and Dramatist, 1861–1949*, St. John's, Newfoundland: Creative Printers and Publishers, 1983.

72. See for example *Daily Star*, June 9, 1920, p. 2.

73. D'Alberti Papers. Correspondence, incoming and outgoing, between the Colonial Office and the Governor's Office in Newfoundland, London, 1780–1925. Handwritten transcripts, Provincial Archives of Newfoundland and Labrador.

74. Woodford, p. 19.

75. Anecdotes from Ella Hutton (Mrs. Hubert), July 29, 1986.

76. Biographical information from Magistrate John Pius Mulcahy (nephew); *Daily News*, April 19, 1897, January 30, 1913 and Dec. 3, 1929; *Evening Telegram*, Jan. 26, 1928; *Who's Who*, 1927 and 1952;

Correspondence Sister Madonna Gatherall, Sisters of Mercy Generalate, October 7, 1987.

77. Correspondence Hilda I. White (niece), June 23, 1988; *Jus Suffragi*, October 1921, p. 12; *Daily News*, Dec. 26, 1899, January 20, 1913 and April 12, 1920; interview, Hon. W.J. Browne, June 30, 1987.

78. Biographical sources include the late Elsie Wylie (Mrs. Herbert), interviews December 1985 and December 1986; Honourable R.S. Furlong, July 28, 1986; Ella Hutton (Mrs. Hubert), July 29, 1986; *Newfoundland Quarterly*, XVI(2):13 (Oct. 1916); XVIII(1):19 (July 1918); and XVIII(3):19 (1918); Paul O'Neill, *A Seaport Legacy: The Story of St. John's, Newfoundland*, Erin, Ontario: Press Porcepic, 1976, p. 479; *Report of St. Andrew's Presbyterian Church*, 1916; and *Daily News*, November 8, 1911 and September 18, 1913; lobbying anecdote from [Agnes Ayre], "Current Events Club," pp. 199–200.

79. Information from the Honourable Robert S. Furlong and the late Elsie Wylie and the late Emma Reid; and *Jus Suffragi*, October, 1924, p. 1; *Newfoundland Quarterly*, XVIII(2):14 (Oct. 1918) and XXXI(2):33 (Oct. 1931); *Evening Telegram*, Aug. 11, 1986; Correspondence Miss C. Easterbrook, Senior Reference Librarian, State of Jersey Library Service, March 23, 1988; Jersey Register of Births; St. Helier Census, 1871; Correspondence Miss M.J. De La Haye, Librarian, Société Jersiaise, March 29, 1988. (The first names of Easterbrook and De La Haye are unknown.)

80. Information about musical activities from the late Elsie Wylie. She believed Adeline Browning may have studied music in Germany. Other orchestra members in the 1920s included Sybil Dunfield, Marguerite Mitchell, and Elsie Warren Wylie.

81. Biographical sources include P.K. Devine, *Ye Olde St. John's*, St. John's, 1989, p. 22; Presbyterian Marriage Records; *Jus Suffragi*, October 1921, p. 12; Interviews Sandra Munn (Mrs. Thomas M.) and Margaret Anderson (daughters), July 8, 1987.

82. Biographical information includes Janet Murphy, "Agnes Marion Ayre," *Remarkable Women of Newfoundland and Labrador*, Valhalla Press for the St. John's LCW, 1976; *Encyclopedia of Newfoundland and Labrador*; [Agnes Ayre], "Current Events Club," pp. 199–201; *Jus Suffragi*, October 1921, p.12; Interview, Gertrude Crosbie (niece), July 5, 1987.

83. [Agnes Ayre], "Current Events Club," p. 199.

84. Biographical information includes *Daily News*, June 16, 1920; *Murray Family History* (privately printed, St. John's Newfoundland); interview, Gertrude Crosbie (daughter), July 5, 1987; interview Honourable Robert S. Furlong; WPA Records.

85. *Evening Telegram*, March 16, 1928.

86. Interview with the late Emma Reid, August 1988.

87. *Daily News*, January 13, 1921.

88. *Bay Roberts Guardian*, January 19, 1923.

89. *Legislative Council Proceedings*, May 9, 1921, p. 82.

90. "M," *Daily News*, June 8, 1920.

91. *Daily News*, June 17, 1920.

92. *Daily News*, June 17, 1920.

93. Fannie McNeil, *Daily News*, June 9, 1920, p. 5.

94. "Women's Political Emancipation," *Daily News*, June 8, 1920, p. 8.

95. "M," *Daily News*, May 26, 1920, p. 2.

96. F[rances] Hanham, *Daily News*, January 9, 1920, p. 2.

97. "Suffragist," *Daily News*, May 26, 1920, p. 2.

98. F[rances] Hanham, *Daily News*, June 9, 1920, p. 3; also, "Bethel," "Women's Rights," *Daily News*, July 7, 1920.

99. Fannie McNeil, Newfoundland Report, *International Alliance of Women for Suffrage and Equal Citizenship, Report of the Tenth Congress, Paris, 1926*, London, 1926; and Agnes Ayre, letter to *Daily Star*, June 1920.

100. Gwendolyn M. Cooper (Mrs. L.R.) had been born in England in 1865. She founded the first Brownie Pack in Grand Falls, and was district commissioner of the Girl Guides. She was also an artist and active in the WPA. She was central to the growth of civic and cultural groups in Grand Falls including amateur theatricals, folk singing, sports, and help for the blind. Sources: Girl Guide Records; Personal conversations with Monica Kirby (daughter), Vera Alcock (Mrs. W.D.), Viola Arklie (Mrs. R.G.), and Lillian Locke (Mrs. Harry); *Remarkable Women of Newfoundland and Labrador*, 35–36. The contemporary newspaper report only identified the speaker as "G.M.C." In response to a column by Dorothy Inglis (*Evening Telegram*, August 3, 1991), a number of persons helped me to make this identification.

101. *Daily News*, July 6, 1920.

102. *Daily News*, April 29, 1921. For a detailed study of women's roles in rural communities see Hilda Chaulk Murray, *More Than Fifty Percent: Woman's Life in a Newfoundland Outport, 1900–1950*, St. John's, Newfoundland: Breakwater Books, 1979.

103. *Daily News*, June 9, 1920.

104. See for example article by the Very Reverend Prior McNabb, *Evening Herald*, May 31, 1920, p. 5.

105. *Evening Herald*, June 9, 1920.

106. *Evening Herald*, June 10, 1920.

107. *Daily News*, May 26, 1920.

108. R.A. Squires to A.N. Gosling and others, June 2 1920, Squires Collection, Centre for Newfoundland Studies, Memorial University of Newfoundland.

109. See LeGrow, Small, Vinnicombe, Crosbie and Higgins in House of Assembly Proceedings, May 20, 1920, pp. 447–450.

110. *Daily News*, August 18, 1921.

111. A.N. Gosling and others, "Newfoundland. History of the Woman's Franchise Bill," *Jus Suffragi*, October 1921, p. 12.

112. Rosemary Squires Mersereau (daughter), "Memories of Helena Squires," Verbatim Transcript (June 13, 1990), from Provincial Advisory Council on the Status of Women, Newfoundland and Labrador; also "First Lady elected to Parliament in Newfoundland," *Newfoundland Quarterly*, XXX(1):14–15 (July 1930); and "Lady Helena Squires," *Remarkable Women of Newfoundland and Labrador*, pp. 37–38.

113. Some have challenged the notion that Helena Squires opposed the suffragists. All available evidence points to her opposition. The suffragists certainly believed it to be the case. The *Daily News*, May 20, 1930 claimed she had been an opponent. In the second day of the legislative session when Lady Squires first took her seat, the Leader of the Opposition, Frederick Alderdice, stated "it was ironical to the women of the country who had fought so hard for Women Suffrage to have elected as the first woman, one who had fought so hard against the movement." Though Lady Squires participated in this debate, she did not correct Alderdice or the *Daily News* (see *Daily News*, May 29, 1930, p. 5).

114. See Mersereau's valuable and revealing remarks.

115. Interview in *N.Y. Evening Journal* reprinted in *Evening Telegram*, April 21, 1931.

116. *Daily Star*, June 11, 1920.

117. *Daily Star*, June 23, 1920.

118. *Western Star*, November 10, 1920 and March 23, 1921 (collected by Kathy Drover) "Newsclippings from the 'Western Star' concerning Women's Suffrage, 1920–21;" File, Provincial Advisory Council on the Status of Women. Also, microfilm holdings of *Western Star*, 1920–25, Provincial Archives. Drover's photocopies include some editions of the *Western Star* available at its offices that are not included in the microfilm collection.

119. Speech by the Hon. Mr. Bishop, Legislative Council Proceedings, May 9, 1921, p. 83.

120. Fannie McNeil, Newfoundland Report, January 25, 1922 in *Jus Suffragi*, March 1922, p. 91.

121. A.N. Gosling and others, "Newfoundland. History of the Women's Franchise Bill," *Jus Suffragi*, October 1921, pp. 11–12.

122. *House of Assembly Proceedings*, July 7, 1921, p. 1067.

123. *Jus Suffragi*, March 1922, p. 91.

124. *Jus Suffragi*, March 1922, p. 91.

125. Kate E. Trounson had been chief welfare superintendent for the Aeronautical Inspection Department, Ministry of Munitions, G.B., during World War I. She was also acting secretary of the National Council for the Unmarried Mother, and a lecturer in economics for the London County Council schools. *Jus Suffragi*, April, 1922, p. 98.

126. A hostile Squires "mole" at the meeting reported there were only thirty men present.

127. International Alliance of Women, Report of Paris Congress, London: International Alliance of Women for Suffrage and Equal Citizenship, 1926, p. 256.

128. *Western Star*, March 23, 1921.

129. International Alliance of Women, Report of Rome Congress, London: International Alliance of Women for Suffrage and Equal Citizenship, 1923, p. 43.

130. International Alliance of Women, Proceedings of Rome Congress, May 15 and May 17, 1923.

131. International Alliance of Women, Report of Paris Congress, 1926, p. 16.

132. International Alliance of Women, Report of Paris Congress, 1926, p. 257.

133. [Agnes Ayre], "Current Events Club," p. 200.

134. *Daily News*, April 11, 1923, pp. 4–6.

135. *Daily News*, May 7, 1923.

136. Suffragist, *Daily News*, May 19, 1923.

137. *Daily News*, March 3, 1925, p. 9; also [Agnes Ayre], "Current Events Club," p. 200.

138. [Agnes Ayre], "Current Events Club," p. 200.

139. See Janet S. Chafetz and Anthony G. Dworkin, *Female Revolt: Women's Movements in World and Historical Perspective*, Totowa, New Jersey: Rowman and Allanheld, 1986.

140. *Daily News*, March 15, 1913.

141. Walter Monroe, *House of Assembly Proceedings*, 1925, p. 292; [Agnes Ayre], "Current Events Club," p. 200.

142. See Gaynor Rowe, "The Woman Suffrage Movement in Newfoundland," paper submitted to Professor Matthews, December 1973, Centre for Newfoundland Studies, Memorial University of Newfoundland.

143. *House of Assembly Proceedings* 1925, pp. 292, 299, 304, 322.

144. *Daily News*, February 19, 1925.

145. Prime Minister Monroe, *House of Assembly Proceedings*, March 9, 1925, pp. 291–295.

146. *Daily News*, March 10, 1925.

147. *House of Assembly Proceedings*, March 10, 1925, p. 321.

148. International Alliance of Women, Report of Paris Congress, 1926.

149. *Daily News*, April 27, 1925.

150. Voting statistics calculated by Janice O'Brien, "Woman's Suffrage in Newfoundland: A Determined Goal," p. 10.

151. "Votes for Women," *Daily News*, February 4, 1925.

Chapter 3

*This essay would not be complete without acknowledging the friends and colleagues who offered information and encouragement along the way. Special thanks are due to Linda Kealey, Department of History, Memorial University of Newfoundland, Shelley Smith, government archivist, Provincial Archives of Newfoundland and Labrador, Gail Wallace, librarian, Law Library, Court House, Judge J.A. Woodrow, Provincial Court of Newfoundland and Labrador and Chris Curran, Law Reform Commission. Thanks are also due to Ronald Penney and Sean Cadigan for reading an earlier draft of the manuscript.

1. Nancy Forestell, "Women's Paid Labour in St. John's Between the Two World Wars," MA thesis, Department of History, Memorial University of Newfoundland, 1987, p. 10.

2. Keith Matthews, *Collection and Commentary on the Constitutional Laws of Seventeenth Century Newfoundland*, St. John's: Memorial University of Newfoundland, 1975, p. 7.

3. Alan W. Mewett and Morris Manning, *Criminal Law*, Toronto: Butterworths, 1978, p. 3.

4. Matthew, *Collection*, p. 10.

5. Keith Matthews, *Lectures on the History of Newfoundland*, St. John's: Breakwater Books, 1988, p. 90.

6. Christopher English and Christopher P. Curran, *Silk Robes and Sou'Westers: The Supreme Court, 1791–1991*, St. John's: Jesperson Press., 1991. English and Curran note the companies included the London and Bristol Company and the Western Company of Adventurers in 1634; individuals included Sir Humphrey Gilbert (1578), Lord Baltimore (1610).

7. Matthews, *Collection*, pp. 8–11.

8. William H. Whiteley, "Governor Hugh Palliser and the Newfoundland and Labrador Fishery, 1764–1768," *Canadian Historical Review*, 50(2);141, June 1969. See also Keith Matthews, *Lectures on the*

History of Newfoundland, St.John's: Breakwater Books, 1988 for an excellent discussion of the complexity of the development of law in early Newfoundland.

9. English and Curran, *Silk Robes and Sou'Westers*, p. 5.

10. Matthews, *Lectures*, p. 138.

11. English and Curran, *Silk Robes and Sou'Westers*, p. 8. See also Matthews, *Lectures*, p. 135.

12. English and Curran, *Silk Robes and Sou'Westers*, pp. 8–13.

13. W. Gordon Handcock, *So longe as there comes noe women: Origins of English Settlement in Newfoundland*, St.John's: Breakwater Books, 1989, p. 92.

14. Planters were settlers who owned both fishing premises and boats; byeboatkeepers migrated annually between England and Newfoundland as paying or working passengers on sailing ships. See also Handcock, *So longe*, pp. 25–29, for further description of the classes of workers in the Newfoundland fishery during the 17th century.

15. Handcock, *So longe*, p. 52.

16. Records of the Colonial Office 195/1,41, cited in Handcock, *So longe*, pp. 31–32.

17. Handcock, *So longe*, p. 32.

18. Matthews, *Lectures*, p. 19. The breakdown by sex and age: 804 planters (men), 931 women, 714 children, totalling 2,676 people who were year-round, permanent residents of Newfoundland in 1750.

19. Handcock, *So longe*, pp. 92–95. See also GN 2/1/A, Vol.1–4, 1749–70, Box 1, Colonial Secretary's Office, Outgoing Correspondence, Governor Hugh Palliser, July 2, 1764, Provincial Archives of Newfoundland and Labrador.

20. Handcock, *So longe*, p. 93.

21. English and Curran, *Silk Robes and Sou'Westers*, p. 23. See also Brenda Griffin, "Law and Order in Newfoundland in the Eighteenth Century, 1741–1792," and G. Deir, "A Study of Capital Crimes in Newfoundland, 1750–1800." Both are unpublished essays found in the Maritime History Archives, Memorial University of Newfoundland.

22. Matthews, *Lectures*, p. 138.

23. Matthews, *Lectures*, pp. 135–137.

24. Matthews, *Lectures*, p. 140. See also *Newfoundland Law Reform Commission, Legislative History of the Judicature Act, 1791–1988*, St. John's: Newfoundland Law Reform Commission, 1989.

25. Matthews, *Lectures*, pp. 137–138.

26. Gertrude E. Gunn, *The Political History of Newfoundland, 1832–1864*, Toronto: University of Toronto Press, 1966, p. 3.

27. R.G. Moyles, *"Complaints is many and various, but the odd Divil likes it": Nineteenth Century Views of Newfoundland*, Toronto: Peter Martin Associates, 1975, p. 83.

28. James Hiller, personal communication to Linda Cullum, June 22, 1990.

29. 1 Victoria, c.4, 1837, An Act to extend the Criminal Laws of England to this Colony under Certain Modifications.

30. *Statutes of Newfoundland*, 1837, c.4, s.3.

31. Judge J. A. Woodrow, Provincial Court of Newfoundland and Labrador, personal communication to Linda Cullum, September 19, 1991.

32. Elspeth Tulloch, *We, The Undersigned*, Moncton: New Brunswick Advisory Council on the Status of Women, 1985, p. 77.

33. See *Sentencing Reform, A Canadian Approach, Report of the Canadian Sentencing Commission*, Ottawa: Ministry of Supply and Services, Canada, 1986, p. xxxii.

34. Tulloch, *We*, p. 77.

35. Clara Brett Martin and Marie Gerin Lajoie, "Legal Status of Women in Canada, 1900," quoted in Ramsay Cook and Wendy Mitchinson (eds.), *The Proper Sphere, Women's Place in Canadian Society*, Toronto: Oxford University Press, 1976, p. 94.

36. In *Re CONGDON, An Infant* (1884–96), Newfoundland Law Reports, pp. 572–577.

37. *Evening Herald*, November 12, 1915.

38. Governor's Miscellaneous and Local Correspondence, GN 1/3A, Dispatch #131, Provincial Archives of Newfoundland and Labrador.

39. *Re Sarah Jane Harvey* (1846–1853) Newfoundland Law Reports, pp. 143–144.

40. *Re Sarah Jane Harvey* (1846–1853), Newfoundland Law Reports, p. 144.

41. *Re Harriet Sophia Rutherford* (1854–1864), Newfoundland Law Reports, pp. 589–591.

42. *Re Harriet Sophia Rutherford* (1854–1864), Newfoundland Law Reports, p. 590.

43. R. Gushue and David Day, *Family Law in Newfoundland*, St. John's: Supply and Services, 1973, pp. 51–53.

44. *Vokey v. Vokey*, and *Walsh v. Walsh*, both in (1927–1929) Newfoundland Law Reports, pp. 73–78 and pp. 240–243.

45. 22 George 5, C.12, 1931, The Health and Public Welfare Act.

46. *Revised Statutes of Newfoundland*, 1952, The Judicature Act.

47. Gushue and Day, *Family Law*, p. 54.

48. *Statutes of Newfoundland*, 1964, No.45, The Child Welfare Act.

49. *Statutes of Newfoundland*, 1964, No. 45, The Child Welfare Act, section 47, cited in Gushue and Day, *Family Law*, p. 54.

50. Constance B. Backhouse, "Shifting Patterns in Nineteenth-Century Canadian Custody Awards," in David H. Flaherty (ed.), *Essays in the History of Canadian Law*, Vol. 1, Toronto: University of Toronto Press, 1981, p. 233. The entire chapter (pp. 212–248) is an excellent resource on the development of Canadian custody law. The law is 50 Victoria, c.21, An Act respecting the Guardianship of Minors.

51. Right Reverend G.F. Bartlett, letter "to Mr. L. Crummy," Secretary, Department of Public Health and Welfare, October 15, 1947, GN 13/2/A, Box 51, File #1, "Welfare of Children Amendment Act," Provincial Archives of Newfoundland and Labrador.

52. Linda Silver Dranoff, *Women in Canadian Life: Law*, Toronto: Fitzhenry and Whiteside, 1977, p. 36.

53. Hilda Chaulk Murray, *More Than Fifty Percent: Woman's Life in a Newfoundland Outport, 1900 to 1950*, St. John's: Breakwater Books Ltd., 1979, pp. 33–40. Murray's book chronicles the experiences of women in the Elliston, Bonavista Bay area between 1900 and 1950. The work contains rich detail of the responsibilities, expectations and customs of women in that time and place.

54. Cecilia Benoit, "The Poverty of Mothering: A Case Study of Women in a Newfoundland Community," unpublished M.A. thesis, Department of Sociology, Memorial University of Newfoundland, 1982, p. 65.

55. Martin, *Legal Status*, p. 94.

56. Sean Cadigan, personal communication to Linda Cullum, August 14, 1990. I am grateful to Sean Cadigan for the insight into use of this law.

57. Murray, *More*, p. 40.

58. Benoit, "The Poverty," p. 69.

59. *Evening Herald*, May 28, 1895.

60. Martin in Cook and Mitchinson, *The Proper Sphere*, p. 94.

61. Murray, *More*, p. 39.

62. Paul O'Neill, *A Seaport Legacy*, Erin: Porcepic Press, 1976, pp. 777–778.

63. Frank Graham, *Ahead of Her Time, A Biography of Ellen Carbery*, St. John's: Creative Publishers, 1987, note 4, p. 7.

64. O'Neill, *A Seaport*, p. 777.

65. 6 William 4, 1836, c.13, An Act for the encouragement of Education in this Colony.

66. 7 Victoria, 1844, c.3, An Act to Provide for the Establishment of an Academy at St. John's.

67. O'Neill, *A Seaport*, pp. 784–785.

68. Graham, *Ahead*, 1987, pp. 8–10.

69. Frederick W. Rowe, *The Development of Education in Newfoundland*, Toronto: Ryerson Press, 1964, pp. 55–56.

70. Nancy Forestell, "Women's," footnote 12, p. 72.

71. Dr. Edith Mary Manuel, "From Outport Schools to Bishop Spencer College," in Phillip McCann (ed.), *Blackboards and Briefcases, Personal Stories by Newfoundland Teachers, Educators and Administrators*, St. John's: Jesperson Press, 1982, pp. 193–209.

72. O'Neill, *A Seaport*, p. 785.

73. Manuel, "From Outport Schools," p. 201.

74. Manuel, "From Outport Schools," pp. 201–202.

75. Greta Hussey, *Our Life on Lear's Room, Labrador*, St.John's: Robinson-Blackmore Printing and Publishing, 1981, p. 69.

76. Hussey, *Our Life*, p. 70.

77. Sean Cadigan, personal communication to Linda Cullum, August 14, 1990.

78. Murray, *More*, pp. 56–58.

79. Murray, *More*, p. 56.

80. Bartlett, letter "to Mr. L. Crummy," Secretary, Department of Public Health and Welfare, October 15, 1947, GN 13/2/A, Box 51, File #1, "Welfare of Children Amendment Act," Provincial Archives of Newfoundland and Labrador.

81. *Acts of the Honourable Commission of Government*, 1942, An Act Respecting School Attendance, No. 32.

82. Nancy Forestell, "Women's," footnote 12, p. 72. See also re School Attendance, *Acts of the General Assembly of Newfoundland*, 1980, p. 28; *Acts of the Honourable Commission of Government of Newfoundland*, 1942, pp. 135–144. Re Welfare of Children Act, *Acts of the Honourable Commission of Government of Newfoundland*, 1944, pp. 303–315.

83. *Daily News*, October 7, 1947.

84. 3 Victoria, (2nd Sess.), 1840, c.1., An Act to defray certain charges that have arisen for the support of Aged and Infant Paupers up to the First of February, 1840.

85. O'Neill, *A Seaport*, p. 796.

86. Marcia Bruner, "Medicine in Newfoundland: From Shacks to Grenfell," in *Doctor's Review*, March 1987, Health File, Centre for Newfoundland Studies, Memorial University of Newfoundland, p. 96.

87. George F. Durgin, *Letters from Labrador*, Concord: Rumford Publishing Company, 1908, p. 49.

88. Murray, *More*, p. 40.

89. Dona Lee Davis, *Blood and Nerves, An Ethnographic Focus on Meno-pause*, St. John's: Institute of Social and Economic Research, 1983, p. 57.

90. Forestell, "Women's," footnote 12, p. 72. See also *Acts of the General Assembly of Newfoundland*, 1908, 8 Edward 7, c.6, s.1., 1908, pp. 28–35.

91. Wendy Martin, *Once Upon A Mine: Story of Pre-Confederation Mines On the Island of Newfoundland*, Montreal: Canadian Institute of Mining and Metallurgy, 1983, p. 6.

92. Martin, *Once*, p. 6.

93. Martin, *Once*, especially p. 7 and p. 20.

94. *Evening Telegram*, February 18, 1908, p. 3, *Proceedings of the House of Assembly*, February 4, 1908.

95. *Evening Telegram*, February 18, 1908, p. 3.

96. Constance Backhouse, *Petticoats and Prejudice, Women and Law in Nineteenth-Century Canada*, Toronto: Women's Press, 1991, pp. 289–290.

97. Backhouse, *Petticoats*, p. 289.

98. Angela John, *By the Sweat of Their Brow*, London: Croom Helm, 1984, cited in Backhouse, *Petticoats*, p. 289.

99. *Evening Telegram*, February 18, 1908, p. 3, speech of Right Honourable The Premier.

100. Forestell, "Women's," p. 223.

101. Forestell, "Women's," p. 75.

102. Forestell, "Women's," pp. 67–69.

103. Forestell, "Women's," p. 75.

104. Forestell, "Women's," footnote 55, p. 84.

105. *Consolidated Statues of Newfoundland*, Vol. X, 1892, pp. 620–628, "Trial By Jury," Chapter 56, Section 39.

106. *Brief to Government of Newfoundland and Labrador Regarding Jury Duty*, by Newfoundland Status of Women Council, June 1973.

107. 15 George 5, 1925 c.7, s.2.

108. Eleanor McKim, "A Woman Born too Soon . . . Julia Salter Earle," *Evening Telegram*, October 25, 1965, pp. 5–6.

109. *The Newfoundland Quarterly*, 30(1):15, July, 1929.

110. St. John Telegraph-Journal, quoted in *The Literary Digest*, June 14, 1930, p. 16.

111. Nancy Forestell, "Working Women in St. John's, The 1920's," in *Proceedings of the First Newfoundland Historical Society Conference*, St. John's: Newfoundland Historical Society, 1986, p. 224.

112. Linda Silver Dranoff, *Women*, p. 17.

113. Clara Brett Martin in Cook and Mitchinson (eds.), *The Proper Sphere*, p. 96.

114. Sean Cadigan, personal communication to Linda Cullum, August 14, 1990.

115. Forestell, "Working Women," p. 223.

116. Nancy Forestell, "Women's," p. ii.

117. Forestell, "Women's," p. 83.

118. Forestell, "Women's," p. 76.

119. *Seventh Day Adventist Encyclopedia*, Washington, D.C.: Review and Herald Publishing, 1976, p. 1329. See also Desmond E. Tinkler, *Sixty-five Years of Progress*, Seventh Day Adventist Church in Newfoundland and Labrador, 1960. Thanks to Bernice Morgan, Women and History Group Committee, 1991, St. John's, Newfoundland for this information.

120. Marian A. White (ed.), *A Woman's Almanac: Voices from Newfoundland and Labrador*, St. John's: Breakwater Books, 1990, September, no page number.

121. The Honourable Rupert W. Bartlett, *The Legal Profession in Newfoundland*, St. John's: The Law Society of Newfoundland, 1984, p. 9.

122. *Acts of the General Assembly of Newfoundland*, 1910, c. 16, s. 1., An Act to amend Chapter 54 of the Consolidated Statues (Second Series), entitled "Of the Law Society, Barristers and Solicitors."

123. Bartlett, *Legal Profession*, p. 9.

124. Bartlett, *Legal Profession*, p. 9.

125. *Book of Newfoundland*, Vol. 1, 1937, p. 199.

126. *Newfoundland Quarterly*, 3(1):15, July 1929.

127. White, *Almanac*, no page number; see also *Daily News*, June 15, 1969.

128. *Evening Herald*, August 29, 1895.

129. *Newfoundland Quarterly*, 15(3):17, December 1915.

130. Forestell, "Women's," Table 2–3, p. 64.

131. *Evening Telegram*, April 24, 1895.

132. Forestell, "Women's," Table 2–3, p. 64.

133. Aubrey Tizzard, *On Sloping Ground, Reminiscences of Outport Life in Notre Dame Bay, Newfoundland*, St. John's: Memorial University of Newfoundland Folklore and Language Publications, Community Studies No. 2, 1979, pp. 108–112.

134. Harry Cuff, *A History of the Newfoundland Teacher's Association, 1890–1930*, St. John's: Creative Publishers, 1985, Appendix L.

135. Bernice Morgan, personal communication to Linda Cullum, August 13, 1990.

136. *Evening Herald*, October 30, 1895.

137. Forestell, "Working Women," p. 219.

138. *Evening Herald*, September 4, 1895.

139. *Evening Herald*, May 10, 1890.

140. Forestell, "Working Women," note 22, p. 226.

141. *Evening Herald*, March 8, 1895. See also *Evening Telegram*, September 15, 1930; *Daily News*, October 3, 1938.

142. Dranoff, *Women*, p. 17.

143. Murray, *More*, p. 39.

144. Forestell, "Working Women," p. 220.

145. *Evening Chronicle*, September 21, 1909.

146. *Evening Telegram*, August 8, 1912.

147. *Evening Herald*, August 8, 1890.

148. *Evening Telegram*, March 13, 1895; *Evening Herald*, May 8, 1890; April 4, 1895; August 14, 1895; October 1, 1895.

149. *Evening Herald*, August 22, 1890.

150. *Evening Herald*, May 10, 1895; September 5, 1895.

151. Forestell, "Working Women," pp. 2–3.

152. *Evening Telegram*, June 14, 1921.

153. Forestell, "Working Women," p. 3.

154. James Overton, "Public relief and social unrest in Newfoundland in the 1930's: An evaluation of the ideas of Piven and Cloward." *Canadian Journal of Sociology*, 13(1–2):150, Winter-Spring 1988.

155. Overton, "Public relief," pp. 152–155.

156. Melvin Baker, *History 3120 by Correspondence*, course manual, School of Continuing Studies and Extension, Memorial University of Newfoundland, p. 69.

157. Keith Connolly, "The Social Impact of World War II on St. John's," unpublished paper, Maritime History Archive, Memorial University of Newfoundland, 1982, p. 5.

158. Cecilia Benoit, "The Poverty," pp. 97–98.

159. Mess Hall Worker, born 1916, cited in Benoit, "The Poverty," p. 99.

160. Connolly, "The Social Impact," p. 5.

161. Forestell, "Working Women," p. 4.

162. Forestell, "Women's," p. 64.

163. Forestell, "Women's," p. 128.

164. Forestell, "Women's," p. 144.

165. Forestell, "Women's," pp. 129–132.

166. Forestell, "Women's," p. 130.

167. Forestell, "Women's," p. 139.

168. Forestell, "Women's," p. 140.

169. Forestell, "Women's," p. 140.

170. *Evening Herald*, August 30, 1895.

171. *Evening Herald*, October 27, 1915.

172. *Evening Herald*, April 26, 1890.

173. Forestell, "Women's," p. 136.

174. Forestell, "Women's," p. 136; see also *Evening Telegram*, January 12, 1923; August 18, 1924; April 25, 1931; January 4, 1934.

175. *Statutes of Newfoundland*, 1977, c.52, s.27, s.s. (e), Labour Standards Act.

176. Order-in-Council Number 344-88, Section 81, April 1, 1991. Information courtesy Doug French, Department of Labour, Government of Newfoundland and Labrador. Telephone conversation with Linda Cullum, October 15, 1991.

177. Governor's Miscellaneous and Local Correspondence, GN 3B, October 1, 1757, Provincial Archives of Newfoundland and Labrador. See also G.M. Story, W.J. Kirwin and J.D.A. Widdowson (eds.), *The Dictionary of Newfoundland English*, Toronto: University of Toronto Press, 1982, p. 608, which defines a whirlygig as an instrument of torture (1477–1623); revolving cage in which offenders are placed for punishment.

178. *Evening Herald*, August 18, 1890.

179. *Evening Herald*, October 12, 1895.

180. *Evening Herald*, October 16, 1895.

181. 48 and 49 Victoria, 1885, Part II, Section 13.

182. *The Statutes*, Volume XVI, 1884–1886, 48 and 49 Victoria, 1885, Part II, s.13, s.s.1, pp. 334–335.

183. Constance Backhouse, "Nineteenth Century Canadian Prostitution Law, Reflection of a Discriminatory Society," *Histoire Sociale/Social History*, xviii(36):387–423, (Novembre-November, 1985). See also *Petticoats*,, pp. 228–259.

184. Backhouse, "Nineteenth Century," p. 403.

185. Backhouse, "Nineteenth-Century," pp. 407–408.

186. Harvey J. Graff, "'Pauperism, Misery and Vice': Illiteracy and Criminality in the Nineteenth Century," *Journal of Social History*, 11(2):262 (Winter 1977), cited in Backhouse, "Nineteenth-Century," p. 408.

187. Dranoff, *Women,* pp. 70–74.

188. Dranoff, *Women,* pp. 70–73; Elspeth Tulloch, *We,* pp. 100–107.

189. White, *Almanac,* no page number.

190. Forestell, cited in *A Woman's Almanac,* 1990, December, no page number.

191. Forestell, *Almanac,* no page number.

192. Forestell, "Women's," pp. 90–93.

193. *Acts of the Honourable Commission of Government,* 1936, The Shop Closing Hour Act, 1936, s. 2(a) and (b).

194. The goods sold in the exempt shops include ice cream, confectionery, tobacco and smoking materials, soft drinks, bread, milk, newspapers and magazines. See also *Acts of the Honourable Commission of Government, 1936,* The Shop Closing Hour Act, St. John's, No. 8, 1936.

195. *Acts of the Honourable Commission of Government, 1936,* An Act to Regulate the Closing Hours of Shops and Other Matters in Connection Therewith, No. 8, S.10 and s.13, pp. 21–25.

196. *Acts of the Honourable Commission of Government, 1936,* No. 24, s.1, An Act to Amend the Act No. 8 of 1936 Entitled "An Act to regulate the closing hours of shops and other matters in connection therewith," p. 114.

197. Forestell, "Women's," p. 92.

198. *Revised Statutes of Newfoundland,* 1952, c.267, s.9, The Shops Act.

199. *Revised Statutes of Newfoundland,* 1952, c.267, s.9, The Shops Act.

200. *Acts of the Honourable Commission of Government, 1941,* No. 31, s.2, An Act Further to Amend the Act No. 8 of 1936 Entitled "An Act to regulate the closing hours of shops and other matters in connection therewith," pp. 223–226.

201. *Revised Statutes of Newfoundland,* 1952, c.268, s.6, St. John's Shops Act.

202. *Statutes of Newfoundland,* 1963, no. 69, s.9, Hours of Work Act.

203. Forestell, "Women's," pp. 93–95.

204. *Acts of the Honourable Commission of Government, 1944,* No. 17, An Act to Prohibit the Payment of the Wages of Workmen in Goods or Otherwise Than in Money.

205. Department of Justice files, GN 13/2/A, Box 77, File #31, Labour (Minimum Wage) Act, confidential memo from the Honourable Commissioner for Public Utilities and Supply, October 24, 1946, Provincial Archives of Newfoundland and Labrador.

206. *Acts of the Honourable Commission of Government, 1947,* No. 31, pp. 313–319, Labour (Minimum Wage) Act.

207. *Acts of the Honourable Commission of Government, 1947*, No. 31, s.1, ss.(f), Labour (Minimum Wage) Act.

208. Department of Justice files, GN 13/2/A, communication "from J.S. Neill, Commissioner of Public Utilities," November 18, 1947, Provincial Archives of Newfoundland and Labrador.

209. Department of Justice files, GN 13/2/A, letter "to Honourable Commissioner for Justice and Defence from the Commissioner for Public Works," November 12, 1947, Provincial Archives of Newfoundland and Labrador.

210. See for example the Memorial University (Pensions) Act, *Statutes of Newfoundland, 1950*, no. 19, s.17.

211. *Pension Reform for Women*, Canadian Advisory Council on the Status of Women, Discussion Paper, 1981.

212. Dranoff, *Women*, p. 17.

213. *Statutes of Newfoundland*, 1952, c.160, Solemnization of Marriage Act.

214. Murray, *More*, pp. 80–81.

215. Benoit, "The Poverty," p. 70.

216. 4 William 4, 1834, c.7, section II, An Act to provide for the Maintenance of Bastard Children.

217. 4 William 4, 1834, c.7, section II, An Act to provide for the Maintenance of Bastard Children.

218. 4 William 4, 1834, c.7, section III, An Act to provide for the Maintenance of Bastard Children.

219. Governor's Miscellaneous and Local Correspondence, GN 1/3A, Magistrate's Reports, 1938, #9, Clarenville, June 1, 1938, Provincial Archives of Newfoundland and Labrador.

220. 4 William 4, 1834, c.7, s.4, An Act to provide for the Maintenance of Bastard Children.

221. 12 George 5, 1922, c.18, An Act to provide that a woman who wilfully causes the death of her newly born child may, under certain conditions, be convicted of infanticide.

222. 21 James 1, 1623, c.27, s.2, An Act to prevent the destroying and murdering of Bastard children.

223. Constance Backhouse, "Desperate Women and Compassionate Courts: Infanticide in Nineteenth-Century Canada," *University of Toronto Law Journal*, XXXIV(4):449, Fall 1984.

224. 43 George III, 1803, c.58, s.s. 3, 4, An Act for the further prevention of malicious shooting and attempting to discharge loaded firearms. . . and for repealing "An Act to prevent the destroying and murdering of bastard children."

225. Backhouse, "Desperate Women," p. 453.

226. 9 George 4, 1828, c.31, s.14, Offences Against the Person Act (1828).

227. Backhouse, "Desperate Women," p. 455.

228. Backhouse, "Desperate Women," p. 447. See also the *Queen vs Travers* [1860] Newfoundland Reports 521 (Newfoundland Supreme Court) for one of the earliest cases of infanticide in Newfoundland heard in 1860. A single young woman named Travers was charged with " . . . endeavouring to conceal the birth of the infant child by placing the body of the said child between her bed and the lacing thereof." The charges against the woman were dismissed because there was no proof that she had actually attempted to conceal the child's birth. According to the case report, the young woman had been employed the previous summer by William Walsh as a fishery servant in Labrador.

229. Backhouse, "Desperate Women," pp. 447–448.

230. Backhouse, "Desperate Women," p. 457. She also adds that many were working class and served long hours in isolated conditions for low pay; commonly, these women were the victims of sexual exploitation by their employer and his sons.

231. Backhouse, "Desperate Women," p. 447.

232. *Evening Mercury*, June 8, 1889, p. 1.

233. *Evening Mercury*, June 7, 1889, p. 1.

234. *Evening Mercury*, June 8, 1889, p. 1.

235. See Governor's Miscellaneous and Local Correspondence, GN 1/3A, Dispatch #104, May 29, 1899, and Dispatch #54, February 24, 1900, Provincial Archives of Newfoundland and Labrador.

236. Backhouse, "Desperate Women," p. 469.

237. *Evening Telegram*, May 11, 1900.

238. *Evening Telegram*, February 1, 1900.

239. Backhouse, "Desperate Women," pp. 477–478.

240. *Evening Herald*, October 22, 1895.

241. *Statutes of Canada*, 1953–54, c.51, s.204 and s.208.

242. *Statutes of Canada*, 1953–54, c.51, s.215.

243. *Statutes of Canada*, 1953–54, c.51, s.214.

244. *R. v. Smith* (1976), 24 Newfoundland & Prince Edward Island Reports, 161 (Newfoundland District Court), p. 172.

245. *R. v. Smith* (1976), 24 Newfoundland and Prince Edward Island Reports, 161 (Newfoundland District Court), p. 172.

246. Christine Boyle, *A Feminist Review of Criminal Law*, Ottawa: Supply and Services, 1985, p. 34.

247. 1900 Survey Respondent cited in Gail Hogan, "Female Labour in the Labrador Floater Fishery," unpublished paper, Maritime History Archives, Memorial University of Newfoundland, 1983, p. 7. See also

Colonial Office 194: 247, p. 2302, Provincial Archives of Newfoundland and Labrador.

248. Greta Hussey, *Our Life on Lear's Room, Labrador*, St. John's: Robinson-Blackmore Printing and Publishing, 1981, p. 43.

249. Hogan, "Female Labour," p. 8.

250. Hogan, "Female Labour," p. 8.

251. Hussey, *Our Life*, p. 44.

252. Hogan, "Female Labour," p. 11.

253. Colonial Office 194:247, p. 292 cited in Hogan, "Female Labour," p. 4.

254. Hogan, "Female Labour," p. 7.

255. *Evening Telegram*, November 3, 1899.

256. Colonial Office 194:247, p. 292, "Letter from Sir Henry McCallum to the Honourable Chief Justice," cited in Hogan, "Female Labour," p. 1. See also *Daily News*, November 6, 1899, p. 2.

257. Governor's Miscellaneous and Local Correspondence, GN 1/3A, Dispatch #94, December 8, 1900, p. 2, Provincial Archives of Newfoundland and Labrador.

258. Governor's Miscellaneous and Local Correspondence, GN 1/3A, Dispatch #94, December 8, 1900, pp. 1–2, Provincial Archives of Newfoundland and Labrador.

259. Hogan, "Female Labour," p. 4; see also *Consolidated Statutes of Newfoundland, 1892*, Chapter 115; 45 Victoria, c.10, pp. 878–880.

260. Hogan, "Female Labour," table 3.

261. Hogan, "Female Labour," p. 9.

262. Hogan, "Female Labour," p. 10.

263. Governor's Miscellaneous and Local Correspondence, GN 1/3A, Dispatch #253, December 9, 1909, p. 6, Provincial Archives of Newfoundland and Labrador.

264. Governor's Miscellaneous and Local Correspondence, GN 1/3A, Dispatch #94, "Female Labour on Labrador, Supplementary, Second Report," no page number, Provincial Archives of Newfoundland and Labrador.

265. Keith Matthews Collection, Series 3, Newfoundland fisheries, 1901/03/04, 13.A.M1.069, Maritime History Archives, Memorial University of Newfoundland, letter "to the Governor from T.J. Murphy," March 1, 1901.

266. Keith Matthews Collection, Series 3, Newfoundland fisheries, 1901/03/04, 13.A.M1.069, Maritime History Archives, Memorial University of Newfoundland, letter "to Hon. Chief Justice from Governor Henry McCallum," March 4, 1901, p. 4.

267. Kate Knox, "Kate Knox, St. Brendan's Island," *Decks Awash*, 4(5):35, October 1975.

268. Knox, "Kate Knox," p. 35.

269. Dranoff, *Women*, p. 18.

270. Suzanne P. Boivin, "To Marry or Not to Marry? A Study of the Legal Situation of Common-Law Spouses in Canadian Law," in Elizabeth Stene, (ed.), *Family Law in Canada: New Directions*, Ottawa: Canadian Advisory Council on the Status of Women, 1985, p. 170.

271. 4 William 4, 1834, cap. 7, session 2, An Act to provide for the Maintenance of Bastard Children.

272. Dranoff, *Women*, p. 19.

273. Dranoff, *Women*, p. 19.

274. *Revised Statutes of Newfoundland*, 1970, c. 403, s.2(i), Workmen's Compensation Act.

275. Dranoff, *Women*, p. 23.

276. Sir William Blackstone, quoted in Martin, "Legal Status," in Cook and Mitchinson, (eds.), *The Proper Sphere*, p. 95.

277. Tulloch, *We*, 1985, p. 84.

278. Dranoff, *Women*, p. 23.

279. Alastair Bisset-Johnson and Winifred H. Holland, *Matrimonial Property Law in Canada*, Toronto: Carswell, 1980, p. N-3. See also R. Gushue and David Day, *Family Law in Newfoundland*, St. John's: Supply and Services, 1973, p. 462 and p. 475.

280. Margaret McCaughan, *The Legal Status of Married Women in Canada*, Toronto: Carswell, 1977, p. 5.

281. McCaughan, *The Legal Status*, p. 5.

282. Lee Holcombe, *Wives and Property: Reform of the Married Women's Property Law in Nineteenth-Century England*, Toronto: University of Toronto Press, 1983, pp. 37–47.

283. *Jodrell v. Jodrell* (1845), 50 England Reports, 259, p. 261.

284. Such clauses were referred to as a "restraint on anticipation or alienation" clause. See Gushue and Day, *Family Law*, p. 218.

285. McCaughan, *The Legal Status*, p. 5; See also *Mason, Templier & Co. v. De Vries*, [1909] 2 K.B. 831 (C.A.).

286. A.V. Dicey, *Lectures on the Relation Between Law and Public Opinion in England During the Nineteenth Century*, cited in Holcombe, *Wives and Property*, p. 46.

287. In *RE Estate Thos. and Mary Spracklin* (1880), Newfoundland Reports 210 (Newfoundland Supreme Court), pp. 210–216.

288. In *RE Estate Thos. and Mary Spracklin* (1880), Newfoundland Reports 210 (Newfoundland Supreme Court), pp. 214–215.

289. In *RE Estate of Thos. and Mary Spracklin* (1880), Newfoundland Reports 210 (Newfoundland Supreme Court), p. 216.

290. The *Royal Gazette*, now the *Newfoundland Gazette*, was Newfoundland's first newspaper. It published some local news, shipping news, letters, legal and official notices and advertisements. After the establishment of the Legislature and the Supreme and Circuit courts, the *Royal Gazette* carried the proceedings of these bodies. See also Suzanne Ellison, *Historical Directory of Newfoundland and Labrador Newspapers, 1807–1987*, St. John's: Memorial University of Newfoundland, 1988, p. 154.

291. 39 Victoria, 1876, c.11, An Act to amend the Law relating to the Property of Married Women.

292. *Consolidated Statutes of Newfoundland*, Vol. V, 1892, c.81, Of the Property of Married Women.

293. *Consolidated Statutes of Newfoundland*, Vol. V, 1892, c.81, Of the Property of Married Women, s.1.

294. Joseph Legrandais, Registry of Wills, Volume 4, pp. 305–306, micro A–10–5, Provincial Archives of Newfoundland and Labrador.

295. Elizabeth Goudie, *Woman of Labrador*, Agincourt: The Book Society of Canada Limited, 1983, p. 20.

296. Philip Buckingham, "Policy Influences and the Matrimonial Property Act (1979): An Examination," unpublished paper, Department of Political Science, Memorial University of Newfoundland, April 1986.

297. "No One Likes to Think About Divorce," *Decks Awash*, 4(5):45, October 1975, "Women of Newfoundland,". Irene Murdoch was an Alberta rancher's wife. She worked daily on the farm, contributed money to buy property, ran the farm in her husband's absence. In 1968, Irene and her husband argued and then lived apart for five years. With the divorce in 1973, Irene was denied any share in the family property and goods, despite all her work. The court awarded her only a small maintenance allowance. Helen Rathwell's story is very similar. After 23 years of marriage, farm work in Saskatchewan and contributing to the downpayment to purchase the farm, she was awarded $150 a month maintenance allowance. Her husband had always promised her half the farm if the marriage ended.

298. Justice Mifflin, cited in David Day (ed.), *Social Work and Family Law Volume II, Course No. 4112*, St. John's: Memorial University Printing Services, 1985, p. 7-7. See also *Bu v. Bu*, (1975), Newfoundland Supreme Court (Trial Division).

299. *Report of the Royal Commission on the Status of Women in Canada*, Ottawa: Information Canada, 1970, p. 246. See also Buckingham, "Policy Influences," p. 5.

300. Justice Noel Goodridge, cited in *Evening Telegram*, September 12, 1977, p. 3, "Ex-wife can't claim her share." See also *Cook v. Cook*, 14

Newfoundland and Prince Edward Island Reports and 33 Atlantic Provinces Reports, pp. 318–334, especially p. 333.

301. James Faris, *Cat Harbour, a Newfoundland Fishing Settlement*, St. John's: Institute of Social and Economic Research, 1965, p. 75.

302. McCaughan, *The Legal Status*, 1977, p. 63.

303. Tulloch, *We*, pp. 84–85.

304. Dranoff, *Women*, p. 111.

305. Tulloch, *We*, p. 85.

306. Dranoff, *Women*, p. 30 .

307. Dranoff, *Women*, p. 30.

308. This is an English case. Norman S. Marsh, "The Wife's Interest in the Consortium," in *Law Review Quarterly*, 67:37–41, January 1951. See also [1952] 2 All England Reports, pp. 394–401.

309. Marsh, *The Wife's Interest*, p. 38.

310. McCaughan, *The Legal Status*, p. 64.

311. Marsh, *The Wife's Interest*, p. 41.

312. Dranoff, *Women*, p. 32.

313. *Rose v. Kavanagh* (1941–1946), Newfoundland Law Reports, pp. 428–437.

314. Dranoff, *Women*, p. 96.

315. Dranoff, *Women*, p. 96.

316. Margaret Chang Collection, P6/A/44, "Chinese Come to Newfoundland, 1895–1906," p. 1, unpublished paper, Provincial Archives of Newfoundland and Labrador.

317. Chang, "Chinese," p. 3.

318. Robert Hong, "'To Take Action Without Delay': Newfoundland's Chinese Immigration Act of 1906," unpublished B.A. Honours Thesis, Department of History, Memorial University of Newfoundland, January, 1987.

319. 6 Edward 7, 1906, c.2, An Act respecting the Immigration of Chinese Persons.

320. Chang, "Chinese," p. 3.

321. 6 Edward 7, 1907, c.14, s.1, An Act to amend 6 Edward 7, c.2, entitled An Act respecting the Immigration of Chinese Persons.

322. Chang Collection, Box 1, File "1946–8 Department of Justice, Box 106, file #85," letter to Secretary for Justice from Chief Commissioner of Immigration," July 16, 1947, Provincial Archives of Newfoundland and Labrador.

323. Chang Collection, Box 1, File "1946–48 Department of Justice, Box 106, File #85," letter "Higgins to J.C. Howell," November 26, 1946, Provincial Archives of Newfoundland and Labrador.

324. Chang Collection, Box 1, File "1946–48 Department of Justice, Box 106, File #85.," letter "Howell to Secretary for Justice," November 29, 1946, Provincial Archives of Newfoundland and Labrador.

325. Chang Collection, Box 1, File "1946–48, Department of Justice, Box 106, File #85," letters January 27, 1947; July 16, 1947; see also File "Home Affairs and Education Memos," 1947–48, Provincial Archives of Newfoundland and Labrador.

326. Chang Collection, Box 1, File "Home Affairs and Education Memos," 1947–48, letter from H.L. Pottle, March 29, 1948, Provincial Archives of Newfoundland and Labrador.

327. Chang Collection, Box 1, File "Home Affairs and Education Memos," 1947–48, letter March 29, 1948, Provincial Archives of Newfoundland and Labrador.

328. Dranoff, *Women*, p. 97.

329. Chang Collection, Box 1, File 1900–1932, "Chinese Come to Newfoundland, 1895–1906," p. 24, unpublished paper, Provincial Archives of Newfoundland and Labrador.

330. Dranoff, *Women*, p. 97.

331. Benoit, "The Poverty," p. 72.

332. Benoit, "The Poverty," p. 76.

333. Benoit, "The Poverty," p. 73; *Daily News*, February 7, 10, 11, 14, 19, 20, and March 14, 1902.

334. Benoit, "The Poverty," p. 58.

335. Cecilia Benoit, "Midwives and Healers, the Newfoundland Experience," *Healthsharing*, Winter, 1983, p. 23.

336. Janet E. McNaughton, "The Role of the Newfoundland Midwife in Traditional Health Care, 1900–1970," unpublished Ph.D. thesis, Department of Folklore, Memorial University of Newfoundland, 1989.

337. Midwife, quotes in Benoit, "The Poverty," p. 77.

338. McNaughton, "The Role," p. 55. See also "Child Welfare Report of Community Nurse Rogers," in *Daily News*, September 14, 1918, p. 2.

339. McNaughton, "The Role," pp. 78–86.

340. 11 George 5, 1920, c.18, An Act concerning the Registration of Midwives.

341. Governor's Miscellaneous and Local Correspondence, GN 1/3A, Dispatch #173, 1920, Letter "to Sir R. Squires from Sir Alexander Harris," April 21, 1920, Provincial Archives of Newfoundland and Labrador. See also, McNaughton, "The Role," p. 79, footnote 55.

342. McNaughton, "The Role," p. 83.

343. *Acts of the Honourable Commission of Government, 1936*, No. 22, An Act to Govern the Practice of Midwifery.

344. McNaughton, "The Role," pp. 84–85.

345. McNaughton, "The Role," p. 103.

346. McNaughton, "The Role," pp. 23–30. See also Cecilia Benoit, "Midwives and Healers: The Newfoundland Experience," *Healthsharing*, Winter 1983, pp. 22–26.

347. Dranoff, *Women*, p. 38.

348. Mother of Ten Children, quoted in Benoit, "The Poverty," p. 62.

349. *Acts of the Honourable Commission of Government, 1949*, No. 65, An Act Respecting Mothers' Allowances.

350. Forestell, "Working Women," p. 223.

351. Forestell, "Working Women," p. 223.

352. *Evening Herald*, 16 May 1890, February 21, 1890, August 27, 1890; *Evening Telegram*, April 22, 1895, July 27, 1895; *Evening Herald*, September 27, 1895; *Evening Telegram*, August 23, 1895.

353. Forestell, "Women's," pp. 183–184.

354. "Current Events Club—Woman Suffrage—Newfoundland Art Society," *Book of Newfoundland*, Vol. 1, 1937, p. 199.

355. "Ruby Cabot, West St. Modeste," *Decks Awash*, 4(5):10, October 1975.

356. McCaughan, *The Legal Status*, pp. 10–11.

357. McCaughan, *The Legal Status*, p. 11.

358. *Rankin v. Walsh* (1883), Newfoundland Reports, p. 497 (Newfoundland Supreme Court).

359. McCaughan, *The Legal Status*, p. 57.

360. *Acts of the General Assembly of Newfoundland*, 1876, 39 Victoria, c.11, s.11 and s.12, An Act to amend the Law relating to the Property of Married Women.

361. *Act of the Honourable Commission of Government*, 1947, No. 32, Civil Service Act.

362. *Statutes of Newfoundland*, 1947, no. 32, s.19(2), The Civil Service Act.

363. *Statutes of Newfoundland*, 1964, No.80, s.5, Civil Service Amendment Act.

364. *Statutes of Newfoundland*, 1979, c.39, s.3 (2).

365. *Statutes of Newfoundland*, 1949, c.55, The Memorial University Act.

366. *Statutes of Newfoundland*, 1988, c.39, 2.11.

367. See LeeAnn Montgomery, *Report of A Study Commissioned on the Problems of Working Women in Newfoundland and Labrador 1981–1982*, 1982, no publisher listed.

368. Sir W. Scott, quoted in Dranoff, *Women*, p. 62.

369. The cases are too numerous to mention in full here. A sample of cases through the years would be: *Evening Herald*, June, 1890; *Evening Herald*, March 12, 1895; *Evening Telegram*, July 3, 1906; *Evening Herald*, March 2, 1915; *Bay Roberts Guardian*, February 26, 1926; *Daily News*, March 26, 1926; *Daily News*, November 2, 1929.

370. Backhouse, *Petticoats*, pp. 175–176.

371. *Evening Herald*, April 10, 1890.

372. *Evening Herald*, February 10, 1890.

373. Tulloch, *We*, p. 85.

374. *Evening Herald*, April 26, 1890, "Police Court" column.

375. *Consolidated Statutes of Newfoundland*, 1892, Second Series, Vol. X, Chapter 63, Of the Application of the Criminal Law of England and Certain Local Enactments.

376. *The Laws of England*, Volume IX, Part XI, Offences Against the Person, section 2, s.s.1, number 1236, p. 611, London: Butterworth & Co., 1909.

377. Susan Brownmiller, *Against Our Will, Men, Women and Rape*, New York: Bantam, 1975, p. 21, cited in Dianne Kinnon, *Report on Sexual Assault in Canada*, Ottawa: Canadian Advisory Council on the Status of Women, 1981, p. 38. See also Constance Backhouse, "Nineteenth-Century Canadian Rape Law, 1800–92," in David H. Flaherty (ed.), *Essays in the History of Canadian Law*, Volume II, Toronto: University of Toronto Press, 1983, pp. 234–235.

378. Alan W. Mewett and Morris Manning, *Criminal Law*, Toronto: Butterworths, 1978, p. 5.

379. 55–56 Victoria, 1892, c.29, s.266, *The Criminal Code* cited in Backhouse, "Nineteenth-Century," p. 234.

380. Tulloch, *We*, p. 112.

381. *Statutes of Canada*, 1955, c.51, s.137, The Criminal Code.

382. *Revised Statutes of Canada*, 1970, c.C–34, s.143; *Acts of the General Assembly of Newfoundland*, 1834, c.6; Reenacted 1841, c.7; Repealed 1865, c.6, s.17.

383. Kinnon, *Report*, p. 43. See Bill C–52 introduced in May 1, 1978 by then Justice Minister Ronald Basford. The bill was considered unsatisfactory by a number of women's groups.

384. Backhouse, "Nineteenth-Century," p. 235.

385. Kinnon, *Report*, p. 36.

386. Backhouse, "Nineteenth-Century Canadian Rape Law, 1800–92," p. 201.

387. Kinnon, *Report*, p. 37.

388. *Revised Statutes of Canada*, 1970, c.C–34, s.148.

389. L.J. Applegath, "Sexual Intercourse with a Feeble-Minded Female Person: Problems of Proof." (1964) 7 *Criminal Law Quarterly*, pp. 480–484.

390. Governor's Miscellaneous and Local Correspondence, GN 1/3A, Dispatch #56, April 1907, Provincial Archives of Newfoundland and Labrador.

391. Governor's Miscellaneous and Local Correspondence, GN 1/3A, Dispatch #56, April 1907, letter "from O'Donnell to Honourable Sir E.P. Morris," May 4, 1907, Provincial Archives of Newfoundland and Labrador.

392. Hon. P. T. McGrath, Legislative Council Proceedings, discussion of Amendment to Rape Law, May 28, 1920, p. 91. Courtesy of Margot Duley.

393. Backhouse, *Petticoats*, p. 99.

394. Governor General's Correspondence, GN 1/3A, Dispatch #99, January 1918, Provincial Archives of Newfoundland and Labrador.

395. Governor's Miscellaneous and Local Correspondence, GN 1/3A, Dispatch #99, January 1918, Provincial Archives of Newfoundland and Labrador.

396. Governor's Miscellaneous and Local Correspondence, GN 1/3A, Dispatch #199, August 14, 1900, Provincial Archives of Newfoundland and Labrador.

397. Governor's Miscellaneous and Local Correspondence, GN 1/3A, Dispatch #199, August 14, 1900, Provincial Archives of Newfoundland and Labrador.

398. Governor's Miscellaneous and Local Correspondence, GN 1/3A, Dispatch #199, August 14, 1900, Provincial Archives of Newfoundland and Labrador.

399. Governor's Miscellaneous and Local Correspondence, GN 1/3A, Dispatch #199, August 14, 1900, Provincial Archives of Newfoundland and Labrador.

400. Glanville Williams, quoted in C.C. Savage, "Corroboration in Sexual Cases" [1963–64] 6 *Criminal Law Review*, pp. 283–313.

401. *R. V. Kavanagh* (1960), 128 Newfoundland & Prince Edward Island Reports 191 (Newfoundland Supreme Court), p. 201.

402. *Statutes of Canada*, 1975, The Criminal Law Amendment Act.

403. Kinnon, *Report*, p. 43.

404. Neil Brooks, "Rape and the Laws of Evidence," in *Chitty's Law Journal*, 23(1):5, 1975, cited in Kinnon, *Report*, p. 41.

405. *R. v. O'Brien* (1976), 14 Newfoundland & Prince Edward Island Reports 250 (Newfoundland District Court).

406. *R. v. O'Brien* (1976), 14 Newfoundland & Prince Edward Island Reports 250 (Newfoundland District Court), p. 268.

407. Kinnon, *Report*, p. 42.

408. Kinnon, *Report*, p. 42.

409. In August, 1991, the Supreme Court of Canada struck down the so-called "rape shield" protection for women. The past sexual history of women is once again allowed as a result of this decision. Judges are empowered to decide in each case whether such evidence is permissible.

410. *R. v. Chase* (1984), 40 Criminal Reports (3d) 282 (New Brunswick Court of Appeal).

411. Christine Boyle, *R. v. Chase*, (1984), 40 Criminal Reports (3rd) 282 (New Brunswick Court of Appeal), p. 283.

412. Dranoff, *Women*, p. 26.

413. *Statutes of Newfoundland*, 1834 (2nd session), c.8. Re-enacted 1841, c.7. Repealed 1865, c.6, s.17.

414. *Statutes of Newfoundland*, 1865, c.6.

415. Maeve Baird, Interview with David Day, August 10, 1989.

416. *Evening Herald*, October 29, 1915.

417. *Evening Telegram*, "In the Police Court To-day," April 29, 1895.

418. 22 George 5, 1931, c.12, s.709, Health and Public Welfare Act.

419. 22 George 5, 1931, c.12, s.575, Health and Public Welfare Act.

420. Governor's Miscellaneous and Local Correspondence, GN 1/3A, 1936, Dispatch #705/36, letter "to Malcolm MacDonald, Secretary of State for Dominion Affairs from Humphrey Walwyn, Governor," March 18, 1937, Provincial Archives of Newfoundland and Labrador.

421. *Revised Statues of Newfoundland*, 1952, c.65, The Maintenance Act.

422. Gushue and Day, *Family Law*, p. 94.

423. Gushue and Day, *Family Law*, p. 469.

424. Gushue and Day, *Family Law*, p. 468.

425. *Rideout v. Rideout* (1949), 25 Maritime Provinces Report 11, Newfoundland Supreme Court, App. D., p. 14.

426. *Rideout v. Rideout* (1949), 25 Maritime Provinces Report 11, Newfoundland Supreme Court, p. 21.

427. *Skinner v. Skinner* (1953), 31 Maritime Provinces Report 113, Newfoundland Supreme Court, pp. 113–115.

428. Maeve Baird, Interview with David Day, August 10, 1989.

429. Roberta Buchanan, "Divorce: Newfoundland Style," in *Canadian Dimension,* 10(8):16–17 (1975).

430. Gushue and Day, *Family Law*, pp. 461–462.

431. McCaughan, *The Legal Status,* p. 15.

432. Lord Lyndhurst cited in McCaughan, *The Legal Status*, p. 15.

433. Gushue and Day, *Family Law*, p. 461.

434. Gushue and Day, *Family Law*, p. 476.

435. Gushue and Day, *Family Law*, p. 462.

436. *Hounsell v. Hounsell* (1949), 3 Dominion Law Reports 38, Newfoundland Supreme Court. See also Gushue and Day, *Family Law*, p. 462.

437. *Hounsell v. Hounsell* (1949), 3 Dominion Law Reports 38, Newfoundland Supreme Court, p. 62.

438. Gushue and Day, *Family Law*, p. 485.

439. *Downton v. Royal Trust Co. et al.*, [1973] 2 Supreme Court Report 437.

440. Maeve Baird, Interview with David Day, August 10, 1989.

441. Gushue and Day, *Family Law*, p. 476, footnote 2.

442. Dranoff, *Women*, p. 63.

443. Gushue and Day, *Family Law*, p. 476.

444. Gushue and Day, *Family Law*, p. 479.

445. Gushue and Day, *Family Law*, p. 490.

446. Gushue and Day, *Family Law*, p. 476.

447. Alastair Bissett-Johnson and David Day, *The New Divorce Law*, Toronto: Carswell, 1986, p. 6.

448. Barbara Doran, *Brief to Committee on Constitutional Review from Newfoundland Status of Women Council*, Ottawa, 1980, p. 2. See also Gushue and Day, *Family Law*, pp. 607–608.

449. Bissett-Johnson and Day, *The New Divorce Law*, p. 6.

450. Dranoff, *Women*, p. 67.

451. Bissett-Johnson and Day, *The New Divorce Law*, p. 94.

452. Maeve Baird, Interview with David Day, August 10, 1989.

453. *Sharpe v. Sharpe* (1971), 1 Newfoundland & Prince Edward Island Reports 628, Newfoundland Supreme Court, Trial Division, p. 629.

454. Bissett-Johnson and Day, *The New Divorce Law*, p. 15.

455. Veronica Strong-Boag, *The New Day Recalled, Lives of Girls and Women in English Canada, 1919–1939*, Toronto: Copp Clark Pitman Ltd, 1988, p. 184.

456. Letter to the editor from fisherman, Elliston, *Fishermen's Advocate*, February 1912, cited in "The Patchwork of Women's History: Piecing Together Our Past," workshop kit, presented St. John's and Stephenville, June 1989.

457. 3 Victoria (2nd Session), 1840, c.1.

458. Paul O'Neill, *The Oldest City: The Story of St. John's, Newfoundland*, Erin: Porcepic Press, 1975, p. 296.

459. *Evening Herald*, May 21, 1895.

460. *Evening Herald*, February 27, 1890; *Evening Telegram*, July 15, 1895. See also the Governor's Miscellaneous and Local Correspondence, GN 1/3/A, 1908, Dispatch #77, "Letter from Colonial Secretary to Governor Sir William MacGregor," July 11, 1908, Provincial Archives of Newfoundland and Labrador. The Colonial Secretary describes cases of selling of liquor as "representative of a class that is widespread and affects a number of poor people." The fine in Widow Barnes case, as cited in this correspondence, was fifty dollars.

461. *Evening Herald*, February 27, 1890.

462. Governor's Miscellaneous and Local Correspondence, GN 1/3A, Dispatch #138, July 20, 1905, letter "to Sir William from D.W. Prowse," Provincial Archives of Newfoundland and Labrador.

463. Governor's Miscellaneous and Local Correspondence, GN 1/3A, Dispatch #138, July 20, 1905, letter "to Sir William from D.W. Prowse," Provincial Archives of Newfoundland and Labrador.

464. Governor's Miscellaneous and Local Correspondence, GN 1/3A, Dispatch #138, July 20, 1905, letter "to Sir William from D.W. Prowse," Provincial Archives of Newfoundland and Labrador.

465. Governor's Miscellaneous and Local Correspondence, GN 1/3A, Dispatch #138, July 20, 1905, letter "to Sir William from D.W. Prowse," Provincial Archives of Newfoundland and Labrador.

466. Governor's Miscellaneous and Local Correspondence, GN 1/3A, Dispatch #138, July 20, 1905, letter "Telegram," Provincial Archives of Newfoundland and Labrador.

467. Marilyn Porter, "Mothers and Daughters: Linking Women's Life Histories in Grand Bank, Newfoundland," unpublished paper, Department of Sociology, Memorial University of Newfoundland, 1986, p. 12.

468. Laura Barnes, widow with two small children, quoted in Porter, "Mothers and Daughters," p. 15.

469. Davis, *Blood and Nerves*, p. 71.

470. Stuart Godfrey, *Human Rights and Social Policy in Newfoundland, 1832–1981*, St. John's: Harry Cuff Publications, 1985, p. 34.

471. Nancy Forestell, "Women's," p. 129.

472. Forestell, "Women's," pp. 113–114.

473. Forestell, "Women's," p. 125.

474. Ilka D. Dickman, *Appointment to Newfoundland*, Manhattan, Kansas, 1981, p. 27, cited in Beth Light and Ruth Roach Pierson (eds.), *No Easy Road, Women in Canada 1920s to 1960s*, Toronto: New Hogtown Press, 1990, p. 339.

475. Dranoff, *Women*, p. 111.

476. Sean Cadigan, "The Gender Division of Labour in the Households of the Northeast Coast Fishery of Newfoundland, 1785–1855," unpublished paper, Department of History, Memorial University of Newfoundland, 1990, pp. 8–11.

477. Tulloch, *We*, p. 94.

478. Tulloch, *We*, p. 93.

479. Dranoff, *Women*, p. 59.

480. Dranoff, *Women*, p. 59.

481. Forestell, "Women's," p. 76, note 22.

482. 22 George 5, 1931, c.12, s.575, Health and Public Welfare Act.

483. Governor's Miscellaneous and Local Correspondence, GN 1/3A, Dispatch #865, November-December, 1922, letter "Mrs. Frank Barron to King George V," November 9, 1922, Provincial Archives of Newfoundland and Labrador.

484. Governor's Miscellaneous and Local Correspondence, GN 1/3A, Dispatch #865, letter "Mrs. Frank Barron to King George V," November 9, 1922, Provincial Archives of Newfoundland and Labrador.

485. Davis, *Blood and Nerves*, p. 70.

486. Jane Robinson, *A Widow's Handbook*, St. John's: Newfoundland and Labrador Women's Institutes, 1984, p. 46.

487. *Acts of the Honourable Commission of Government, 1949*, No. 65, Mother's Allowances Act, pp. 449–456.

488. 1 George 5, 1911, c.29, An Act to Provide for the Payment of Old Age Pensions.

489. Forestell, "Women's," note 22, p. 76.

490. *Acts of the Honourable Commission of Government, 1942*, p. 83; *Acts of the Honourable Commission of Government, 1943*, p. 15.

491. Dranoff, *Women*, pp. 82–83.

492. Leah Cohen, *Small Expectations: Society's Betrayal of Older Women*, Toronto: McClelland and Stewart, 1984, p. 129 cited in Light and Pierson (eds.), *No Easy Road*, p. 318.

493. Louise Dulude, *Pension Reform with Women in Mind*, Ottawa: Canadian Advisory Council on the Status of Women, 1981, cited in Carman Cameron, *Women and Aging, Towards Tomorrow*, St. John's: Newfoundland Status of Women Council, 1981, p. 9.

494. Dranoff, *Women*, pp. 82–83.

495. Louise Dulude, in *A Widow's Handbook*, p. 21.

Chapter Four

1. This essay was first written in the summer of 1988 by Sharon Gray Pope, based on research of written materials, interviews with women who were involved in the women's movement, and visits to a number of women's centres in Newfoundland. Jane Burnham revised and updated the document in the fall of 1991 to reflect recent events. While the authors recognize that this is not a complete history of the modern women's movement in the province, we have tried to provide an overview of major events and touch on some of the personalities that helped shape local feminist activities. Our hope is that this short account will inspire others to record their memories, and fill the gaps that remain in our rich and colourful history.

2. Canada's Royal Commission on the Status of Women was established February 16, 1967. Public hearings were held in 14 cities of the 10 provinces. The final report of the Royal Commission was published September 28, 1970. The terms of reference instructed the Royal Commission to "inquire into the status of women in Canada . . . to ensure for women equal opportunity with men in all aspects of Canadian Society." Commission chairperson was Florence Bird and the commissioners were: Jacques Henripin, John P. Humphrey, Lola M. Lange, Jeanne Lapointe, Elsie Gregory MacGill and Doris Ogilvie.

3. Agnes Richard, "A History of the Formation of the Jubilee Guilds/ Women's Institutes of Newfoundland and Labrador," unpublished M. Ed. thesis, Memorial University of Newfoundland, 1987, p. 91. Subsequent to the initial research for this essay, Ms. Richard wrote *Threads of Gold: Newfoundland and Labrador Jubilee Guilds, Women's Institutes*, St. John's, Creative Publishers, 1989.

4. NONIA was started in 1920 to set up home industrial centres around the island and provide financial support for nursing services in small communities.

5. St. John's Local Council of Women, *Remarkable Women of Newfoundland and Labrador*, St. John's, Valhalla Press, 1976.

6. *A Brief on the "Status of Women"* by the St. John's Club of the Canadian Federation of University Women, March 1968, p. 2.

7. *A Brief*, St. John's CFUW, p. 3

8. *Brief Presented to the Royal Commission on the Status of Women*, by Dorothy Wyatt, Sept. 16, 1968.

9. *Brief on the Status of Women, Corner Brook and West Coast of Newfoundland*, by Doris Janes, September, 1968, p. 2.

10. *Brief presented to the Royal Commission on the Status of Women*, by Ella Manuel, July 1968, p. 2.

11. Anne Budgell, videotape of the 15th Anniversary of the St. John's Status of Women Council, 1987.

12. Fran Innes, videotape of the 15th Anniversary of the St. John's Status of Women Council, 1987.

13. *Newsletter of the Women's Place*, published by the Newfoundland Status of Women Council (NSWC), Jan. 16, 1973, page 4. The newsletter of the St. John's-based Council has undergone several name changes throughout the years. The first newsletter of NSWC was published July, 1972 under the name *Newsletter of the Newfoundland Status of Women Council*. In August 1972 a newsletter called *The Woman's Place Newsletter* was published as issue #2. On September 29, 1972 under the title *NSWC Newsletter* another "second issue" was published. In September 1972 *The Woman's Place Newsletter*, issue #3, was published. This was followed by an Oct.–Nov. 1972 issue under the changed name *The Women's Place/NSWC Newsletter*. Subsequent newsletters followed this title until Dec. 1973 when the name settled on *Newsletter, Newfoundland Status of Women Council*. That name was used until July 1984 when, in conjunction with the change of name for the Council, it became *Newsletter, St. John's Status of Women Council*. In September 1985 the Council's newsletter adopted the name *WEB* and was published under that title until the Oct. 1989 issue when the name changed to *Spokes/woman*. The first volume of NSWC newsletters (1972–73) are filed in the Centre for Newfoundland Studies, Memorial University, under the volume title Women's Place; from 1974–1984 they are under the volume titles *Newfoundland Status of Women Council Newsletter*; from 1985–89 under the volume title *WEB*; and subsequently under *Spokes/woman*. A number of issues under the title *St. John's Status of Women Council Newsletters* are also on file. Newsletters from other Status of Women Councils are available only at individual Women's Centres or through the Provincial Advisory Council on the Status of Women.

14. The first edition of *Women and The Law in Newfoundland* was published by the St. John's Women's Bureau in 1972. A second edition, revised by Lillian Bouzanne, was published by NSWC in 1976; both are available at the Centre for Newfoundland Studies, Memorial University.

15. Diane Siegel, videotape of the 15th Anniversary of the St. John's Status of Women Council, 1987.

16. Sally Davis, telephone interview with Jane Burnham, October, 1991.

17. Helen Porter, taped interview with Susan Hart, July 3, 1987.

18. Davis, telephone interview.

19. Published by Woman's Place, St. John's, 1974. Available in the Centre for Newfoundland Studies, Memorial University of Newfoundland Library.

20. *The Woman's Place Newsletter*, issue #2, Aug. 1972.

21. *Newsletter* of Women's Place/NSWC, Oct–Nov., 1972.

22. *Newsletter* of NSWC, IV(2), April–May 1977, text of Pauline Bradbrook's report on 1976 NSWC activities presented at International Women's Day, March 8, 1977.

23. Come-from-away or CFA is a commonly-used expression in Newfoundland to describe those residents not born in the province.

24. Sheilah Mackinnon Drover, telephone interview with Sharon Gray Pope, August 1988.

25. Mackinnon Drover, telephone interview, August 1988.

26. Wendy Williams, telephone interview with Jane Burnham, November 1991.

27. Published by Valhalla Press, 1976. Available in the Centre for Newfoundland Studies, Memorial University of Newfoundland Library.

28. *From this Place*, a selection of writings by women of Newfoundland and Labrador edited by Bernice Morgan, Helen Porter, Geraldine Rubia, St. John's: Jesperson Press, 1977.

29. Susan Moller Okin, *Women in Western Political Thought*, Princeton: Princeton University Press, 1979.

30. Wendy Williams, taped interview with Sharon Gray Pope, June 20, 1988.

31. Lillian Bouzanne, videotape of the 15th Anniversary of the St. John's Status of Women Council, 1987.

32. *Women and Newfoundland Fact Sheet, Series No.2:1*, Women's Policy Office, St. John's: Government of Newfoundland and Labrador, March 1987.

33. Marie Newhook (Corner Brook), telephone interview with Sharon Gray Pope, October 1988.

34. Marie Newhook, taped interview with Cathy Drover, July 1988.

35. *Women's Forum*, Corner Brook Status of Women Council newsletter, December 1985.

36. Press release, Corner Brook Status of Women Council, January 18, 1976.

37. Ann Bell, taped interview with Sharon Gray Pope, July 5, 1988.

38. Marie Newhook, telephone interview with Sharon Gray Pope, September 1988.

39. Ann Bell, taped interview with Sharon Gray Pope, July 15, 1988.

40. Marilee Pittman, *Women Speak*, newsletter of the Provincial Advisory Council on the Status of Women, Winter 1984.

41. Dorothy Robbins, taped interview with Sharon Gray Pope, July 12, 1988.

42. Linda Ann Parsons, "Passing the Time: the Lives of Women in a Northern Industrial Town," unpublished MA Thesis, Department of Sociology, Memorial University of Newfoundland, 1986, p. 209.

43. Liz Batstone, taped interview with Sharon Gray Pope, July 5, 1988.

44. Batstone, interview, July 5, 1988.

45. Gwen Tremblett, telephone interview with Sharon Gray Pope, July 1988.

46. Until December 1992 the St. John's Women's Centre held the distinction of being the longest continuously-running women's centre in the country. At the time of writing, the centre's future was uncertain following a temporary closure. At the fifteenth anniversary celebrations of the NSWC in Oct. 1987, "founding mothers" were honoured with certificates for their early involvement in the NSWC and the St. John's Women's Centre.

47. Dorothy Inglis' report on the day of discussion, May 27, 1978, was carried in the Aug. 1979 issue of the *NSWC Newsletter*.

48. *NSWC Newsletter*, published by the Newfoundland Status of Women Council, May 1980.

49. Frances Ennis, taped interview with Sharon Gray Pope, July 6, 1988.

50. Linda Dale, *Women's Health Education Project 1981--1984: An Evaluation*; prepared for the Atlantic Office of Health Promotion Directorate, Health and Welfare Canada, October 1984.

51. Barb Maidment, telephone interview with Sharon Gray Pope, October 1988.

52. *Newsletter*, Labrador West Status of Women Council, April 1982.

53. *Women's Forum*, Corner Brook Status of Women Council newsletter, May 1982.

54. Dorothy King, telephone interview with Sharon Gray Pope, September 1988.

55. Marie Matheson, taped interview with Sharon Gray Pope, July 20, 1988.

56. Gerry Devereaux, taped interview with Sharon Gray Pope, July 20, 1988.

57. Crystal Eagan, taped interview with Sharon Gray Pope, July 20, 1988.

58. Joyce Hancock, taped interview with Sharon Gray Pope, Oct. 1988.

59. Ella Pilgrim, telephone interview with Sharon Gray Pope, October 1988.

60. Gateway Status of Women Council, from the council's promotional brochure.

61. Melin Foley, taped interview with Sharon Gray Pope, July 22, 1988.

62. Sandra Perry, taped interview with Sharon Gray Pope, July 5, 1988.

63. Ruby Piercey, taped interview with Sharon Gray Pope, July 23, 1988.

64. Linda Hyde, telephone interview with Sharon Gray Pope, September 1988.

65. Judy Vanta, taped interview with Sharon Gray Pope, July 6, 1988.

66. Vanta, taped interview, July 6, 1988.

67. *NTA Bulletin*, Newfoundland Teacher's Association, March 1988.

68. Susan McConnell, "NAC Report" in *Feminist Action*, National Action Committee on the Status of Women, January 1987.

69. Hyra Skoglund, telephone interview with Sharon Gray Pope, September 1988.

70. Wendy Murdoch, taped interview with Sharon Gray Pope, July 11, 1988.

71. *Trinity Bay South Women on the Move, Women working for Women.* MUN Extension and Women's Involvement Committee of Upper Trinity South, 1983.

72. *Brief to the MacDonald Commission on the Economy*, by the WIN Committee, September 20, 1983.

73. Murdoch, taped interview, July 11, 1988.

74. Murdoch, taped interview, July 11, 1988.

75. Bell, taped interview, July 15, 1988.

76. Shirley Goundrey, *A History of the Newfoundland Status of Women Council from April 1972–January 1975*, St. John's: Newfoundland Status of Women Council, 1975, p.3.

77. CARAL originally stood for the Canadian Association for the Repeal of the Abortion Law. The name was later changed to the Canadian Abortion Rights Action League.

78. Marie Matheson, taped interview with Sharon Gray Pope, July 20, 1988.

79. *NSWC Newsletter*, by the Newfoundland Status of Women Council, July 1986.

80. Dorothy Inglis, "Bread and Roses Column," *Evening Telegram*, March 14, 1987.

81. Diane Duggan, taped interview with Sharon Gray Pope, September 28, 1988.

82. *NSWC Newsletter*, by the Newfoundland Status of Women Council, October, 1983.

83. *Brief to the Special Committee on Pornography and Prostitution*, by the Newfoundland Teacher's Association, May 7, 1984.

84. Dorothy Inglis, "Pornography: A Newfoundland Solution," undated offprint, available at the Provincial Advisory Council on the Status of Women.

85. *Growing Up Female: A Study of Adolescent Women in Newfoundland and Labrador.* Committee on Young Women's Issues, 1987.

86. The other female cabinet minister at the time was Hazel Newhook of Gander, Minister of Municipal Affairs.

87. From a one-page statement from the 52% Solution. Available at the Provincial Advisory Council on the Status of Women.

88. Bell, taped interview, July 15, 1988.

89. Doran, taped interview, September 28, 1988.

90. Luanne Leamon, telephone interview with Jane Burnham, November 1991.

91. Leamon, telephone interview, November 1991.

92. Doran, taped interview, September 28, 1988.

93. Doran, taped interview, September 28, 1988.

94. Doran, taped interview, September 28, 1988.

95. Batstone, taped interview, July 5, 1988.

96. *Newsletter*, Labrador West Status of Women Council, January 1982.

97. *NSWC Newsletter*, by the Newfoundland Status of Women Council, February 1982.

98. *Women and the Constitution*, Final Report of a provincial conference to discuss the implications of the new Canadian Constitution and Charter of Rights, November 1984. Privately published, available at the Provincial Advisory Council on the Status of Women.

99. *Report of the Newfoundland and Labrador Second Women's Annual Provincial Lobby*, no author, privately published, March 23, 1987.

100. Doran, taped interview, September 28, 1988.

101. Duggan, taped interview, September 28, 1988.

102. Joanne Dunne Glassman, *Report on Comprehensive Daycare for the Province of Newfoundland,* for the Provincial Advisory Council on the Status of Women, March 1982.

103. *Newsletter* of the Bay St. George Status of Women Council, June 1987.

104. "Victory '90," videotape edited by Peggy Keats for the St. John's Status of Women Council, 1990.

Glossary

Alimony: financial support paid by the husband to wife while
  they live separately (but before they are divorced.)

Appeal: review by a senior court of a decision made by a lower
  court

Articling: the apprenticeship of a law student to a barrister and
  solicitor

Beneficiary: one who is to receive the benefit of a will

Case Law: the rules which come from the accumulation of judges'
  decisions in individual cases

Chancery: division of the high court; developed to deal with
  situations which common law could not handle effectively

Chattel: an article of personal property

Civil Law: legal system derived from Roman Law

Common Law: body of law developed in England; rules developed
  from court decisions, rather than legislative enactment; a
  body of rules which are inflexible and fixed and which
  judges were unable to adjust in the interests of equity

Concealment: of birth; the hiding of the body of a dead child so as
  to conceal it from others; a lesser charge than infanticide,

concealment does not attempt to prove the child died at the hands of its mother

Consortium: the conjugal relation of husband and wife and the right of each person to the affection, companionship and services of the other

Contract: written or oral agreement that is legally binding

Court Order: pronouncement by a judge which binds the parties named in it to obey the order

Custody: physical care and control of a child

Divorce: legal dissolution of the marriage bond

Guardianship: control of a child's property

Infanticide: killing of a child by its mother soon after it is born

Legislation: laws made and enacted by a legislature, either provincial or federal

Maintenance: monetary allowance paid by one spouse to another after divorce

Necessaries: minimal needs according to the family's standard of living

Property: exclusive right to a thing; includes both real estate and personal property such as cars, stocks and bonds, furniture, bank accounts

Rape: sexual intercourse forced by a man upon a woman without her voluntary, informed consent

Separation: a cessation of cohabitation of husband and wife

Statute Laws: acts of parliament establishing rules for the community

Title: evidence of ownership of property

Trust: a right of property held by one party for the benefit of another

Source: Linda Silver Dranoff 1977 *Women in Canadian Law*. Toronto: Fitzhenry and Whiteside.

Index

PRINTED IN CANADA